CW01207014

Poets of the
Chinese Revolution

Poets of the Chinese Revolution

Chen Duxiu
Zheng Chaolin
Chen Yi
Mao Zedong

Edited by Gregor Benton and Feng Chongyi
Translated by Gregor Benton

VERSO
London • New York

First published by Verso 2019
Translation © Gregor Benton 2019
Collection © Gregor Benton and Feng Chongyi 2019

All rights reserved

The moral rights of the authors have been asserted

1 3 5 7 9 10 8 6 4 2

Verso
UK: 6 Meard Street, London W1F 0EG
US: 20 Jay Street, Suite 1010, Brooklyn, NY 11201
versobooks.com

Verso is the imprint of New Left Books

ISBN-13: 978-1-78873-468-4
ISBN-13: 978-1-78873-470-73 (UK EBK)
ISBN-13: 978-1-78873-471-4 (US EBK)

British Library Cataloguing in Publication Data
A catalogue record for this book is available from the British Library

Library of Congress Cataloging-in-Publication Data

Names: Benton, Gregor, editor, translator. I Feng, Chongyi, 1961– editor. I Container of (expression): Chen, Duxiu, 1879–1942. Poems. English. Selections. I Container of (expression): Zheng, Chaolin, 1901– Poems. English. Selections. I Container of (expression): Chen, Yi, 1901–1972. Poems. English. Selections. I Container of (expression): Mao, Zedong, 1893–1976. Poems. English. Selections.
Title: Poets of the Chinese revolution : Chen Duxiu, Zheng Chaolin, Chen Yi, Mao Zedong / edited by Gregor Benton and Feng Chongyi ; translated by Gregor Benton.
Description: London ; Brooklyn, NY : Verso, 2019.
Identifiers: LCCN 2018042175I ISBN 9781788734691 I ISBN 9781788734714 (US Ebook) I ISBN 9781788734707 (UK Ebook)
Subjects: LCSH: Revolutionary poetry, Chinese—Translations into English. I Chinese poetry—20th century—Translations into English.
Classification: LCC PL2658.E3 P65 2019 I DDC 895.1/1520803581—dc23
LC record available at https://lccn.loc.gov/2018042175

Typeset in Sabon and Fang Song by Biblichor Ltd, Edinburgh
Printed and bound by CPI Group (UK) Ltd, Croydon CR0 4YY

Contents

Acknowledgements	xi
Chronology of Dynasties	xii
List of Poets and Emperors Quoted or Mentioned in the Poems	xiii
Note on the Translation	xvii
Note on Transcription	xix
Introduction	1

Chen Duxiu

	Introduction	15
1.	Lament for Wang Xiyan	21
2.	Inscription on a Painting of Saigō Nanshū Hunting	22
3.	Indignation at the Habits of the Day	23
4.	A Poem Written for Wang Huibo on the Occasion of His Journey to the East	25
5.	Lament for He Meishi	26
6.	The Fourth of Ten Poems	27
7.	Before Lingyin Temple	28
8.	A Visit to Taoguang	29
9.	A Visit to Hupao	30
10.	Ode to the Crane	31
11.	Stirred Emotions (First of Twenty Poems)	32
12.	Tears alongside Luxury and Debauchery (Fourteenth of Fifty-Six Poems)	33
13.	Tears alongside Luxury and Debauchery (Fifty-Sixth of Fifty-Six Poems)	34
14.	To Shen Yinmo (Fourth of Four Poems)	35
15.	Recollections of Guangzhou in the Spring	36

Zheng Chaolin

	Introduction	39
1.	Poet in Space	46
2.	Buried Alive	48
3.	Stamps (1)	50
4.	Dr Faust	54
5.	How the Mighty Fall	58
6.	My Native Place	62
7.	Fading Beauty	65
8.	*Quo Vadis?*	68
9.	My Tiny Cell	74
10.	Training Monkeys	75
11.	Commemorating Li Yu	77
12.	Boat Tour	80
13.	Blind Man on a Blind Horse	83
14.	The Earth Turns	86
15.	Dreamtime	88
16.	Suzhou Gardens (1)	91
17.	Suzhou Gardens (2)	93
18.	*Our Grandchildren's Grandchildren*	94
19.	Duckweed	96
20.	The Seasons	98
21.	When *Yin* Attains Its Limit	100
22.	The Host	102
23.	Loneliness	105
24.	Where Is the Warmth?	108
25.	A Revolution without Breaks or Interruptions	109
26.	My Career	112
27.	Meeting Liu Jingzhen	114
28.	Christmas	116
29.	Moonrise	118
30.	To My Wife and Child	121
31.	My Son's Death	123
32.	A Handsome Place	125
33.	Forever Dissident	127

34. Human Bustle	129
35. Magpie Bridge	130
36. Guttering Candles	131
37. The Waxing and the Waning Moon	132
38. Wartime Sojourn in Anhui	133
39. Memorial to Ding	140
40. Two Birthday Poems	144
41. Sending Off the Stove God	148
42. But for His Unyielding Character	154
43. Buddha's Birthday	158
44. Autumn Thoughts	159
45. Autumn Night	161
46. A Poem for New Year's Day	162
47. Qingming	163
48. Intoning History (Three of Six Poems)	164
49. Memories of Deep Autumn (Six of Fourteen Poems)	167
50. Stamps (2)	169

Post-Prison Poems

51. Boat Trip	172
52. A Playful Four-Line Poem Echoing Yang Muzhi	174
53. In Imitation of Yang Muzhi	176
54. Bide Not Your Time	177
55. A New Guest on Deep Lane	179
56. The Firewood Cutter and the Taoyuan Spring	181
57. Gong Zizhen Railed at Wrongs	185
58. The Waking of the Insects	186
59. Requesting Criticism from Comrade Xie Shan	188
60. Reflections on a Tour of the Historic Site of the *Buersaiweike* [Bolshevik] Editorial Department	190
61. An Assemblage of Gong Zizhen's Poetry for Self-Consolation	192
62. Landscape Painting	193
63. A Response to Rong Sun	194
64. Response to Mr Chen Jingxian's Gift of a Poem	195
65. A Reply to Comrade Xie Shan	197

Chen Yi

	Introduction	203
1.	In Mourning for Comrades Ruan Xiaoxian and He Chang	210
2.	Climbing Dayu Mountain	211
3.	Bivouacking	212
4.	Guerrilla Fighting in Gannan	214
5.	On My Thirty-Fifth Birthday	218
6.	Three Stanzas Written at Meiling	219
7.	To Friends	221
8.	Lines Improvised While Coming Down the Mountains on the Occasion of the Second United Front between the Guomindang and the Communists	223
9.	Arriving in Gaochun for the First Time during the Eastern Expedition	225
10.	Ten Years	227
11.	Reunion with Comrades of the Eighth Route Army Sent South, Some of Whom I Have Not Seen for More Than Ten Years	232

Mao Zedong

	Introduction	235
1.	Changsha	242
2.	The Long March	244
3.	Snow	246
4.	The People's Liberation Army Captures Nanjing	249
5.	Reply to Mr Liu Yazi	251
6.	Reply to Mr Liu Yazi	252
7.	Beidaihe	254
8.	Swimming	256
9.	Reply to Li Shuyi	258
10.	Farewell to the God of Plague (1)	260
11.	Farewell to the God of Plague (2)	262
12.	Shaoshan Revisited	264
13.	Climbing Lushan	266

14. Trotsky Visits the Far East (Reflections on
    Reading the Press)   267
15. An Inscription on a Photograph of Militia Women   269
16. Reply to a Friend   270
17. An Inscription on a Picture Taken by Comrade Li Jin
    of the Fairy Cave on Lushan   272
18. Reply to Comrade Guo Moruo   273
19. Ode to the Plum Blossom   275
20. Winter Clouds   277
21. Reply to Comrade Guo Moruo   278
22. On Reading History   281
23. Climbing the Jinggang Mountains Again   283
24. Two Birds: A Dialogue   285
25. The Desire for Action   287
26. Inspection   288
27. Presented to Guo [Moruo] the Elder after Reading
    On Feudalism   290

Acknowledgements

Drinking tea with Marx on the Red Terrace on Copper Coloured Mountain in the Pure Land, in the centenary year of May Fourth and the seventieth year of the Revolution, four poets point their cups earthwards in a celestial salute to Verso for bringing out this book. The true heirs of the poets, and of the May Fourth movement and the Revolution they set going, are the young dissenters now jailed for supporting workers' pickets in the south – the book is dedicated to them and the strikers, as present-day incarnations of the rebel spirit of the Revolution, now old and ailing but here immortalised. We are grateful to Verso for agreeing to print the poems in facing-page English and Chinese with diacriticised Pinyin, accompanied by same-page commentary and annotation – a complex and technically taxing arrangement even in the age of digital typography, kept readable by Verso's skilled compositing. As a result, Chinese speakers and learners can read the original poems and admire their formal and technical properties. Our thanks, therefore, to everyone at Verso, in particular Tariq Ali, Sebastian Budgen, Duncan Ranslem, Lorna Scott Fox, Emilie Bickerton, and Catherine Smiles. Others (apart from Nagahori and Feng) who helped Benton with difficult points in the translation of Zheng Chaolin's poems and in other ways include (in alphabetical order) Rebecca Urai Ayon, Lam Chi Leung, Shen Yuanfang, Vincent Sung, and Xue Feng. Again, many thanks to all these people.

Chronology of dynasties

Spring and Autumn period (771–476 BCE)
Zhou (ca. 1050–256 BCE)
Warring States period (475–221 BCE)
Qin (221–206 BCE)
Han (206 BCE–220 CE)
Three Kingdoms (220–c. 265)
Six Dynasties (220–589)
Sui (581–618)
Tang (618–906)
Five Dynasties (907–960)
Song (960–1279)
Northern Song (960–1127)
Southern Song (1127–1279)
Yuan (1271–1368)
Ming (1368–1644)
Qing (Manchus) (1644–1912)

Republic of China (1912–1949)
People's Republic of China (1949–)

Poets and Emperors Quoted or Mentioned in the Poems

Bai Juyi (772–846), Tang poet and official.
Cen Shen (715–770), Tang poet.
Chen Yuyi (1090–1139), Song poet.
Chen Zhu (1214–1297), Song poet.
Chen Zi'ang (661–702), Tang poet.
Du Fu (712–770), Tang poet.
Du Mu (803–852), Tang poet.
Feng Yanji (born 903), Southern Tang poet and politician.
Gao Guoding (dates unknown), Ming or Qing poet.
Ge Hong (284–364), Eastern Jin Dynasty Daoist scholar and chemist.
Genghis Khan (1162–1227), founder of the Mongol Empire.
Gong Zizhen (1792–1841), Qing poet, calligrapher and intellectual.
Guo Moruo (1892–1978), modern Chinese scholar and poet.
Han Wu (157–87 BCE), an emperor of the Han Dynasty.
Han Yu (768–824), Tang poet and official.
Hong Sheng (1645–1704), Qing poet.
Huang Tingjian (1045–1105), Song poet.
Jia Dao (779–843), Tang poet.
Jiang Kui (1155–1209), Song poet.
Jiang Yan (444–505), Southern and Northern Dynasties poet.
Kangxi (1654–1722), an emperor of the Qing Dynasty.
Li Bai (701–762), Tang poet.
Li He (790–816), Tang poet.
Li Qingzhao (1084–1155), a woman poet.
Li Qunyu (813–860), Tang poet.
Li Shangyin (813–858), Tang poet.

Poets and Emperors Quoted or Mentioned in the Poems

Li Yu (937–978), Southern Tang poet.
Li Yuan (565–635), founder of the Tang Dynasty.
Li Zhiyi (1038–1117), Song poet.
Li Zhongyuan, twelfth-century Song poet.
Linshuan Shanren (dates unknown), a Qing writer.
Liu Bang (256–195 BCE), founder of the Han Dynasty.
Liu Ling (221–300), Daoist poet and famous tippler.
Liu Yixi (772–842), Tang poet.
Liu Yong (987–1053), Song poet.
Lu You (1125–1209), Southern Song poet.
Liu Zongyuan (773–819), Tang scholar and poet.
Qin Guan (1049–1100), Song writer and poet.
Qin Shi Huangdi (259–221 BCE), first emperor of the Qin Dynasty.
Qu Dajun (1630–1696), late-Ming early-Qing scholar and poet.
Qu Yuan (c. 340–278 BCE), poet of Warring States period.
Shen Quanqi (656–729), Tang poet.
Sima Xiangru (179–117 BCE), writer and favourite at the court of Emperor Wu.
Song Taizu (927–976), founding emperor of the Song Dynasty.
Song Yu (c. 298–c. 222 BCE), poet of the Warring States period.
Su Shi (1037–1101), Song writer, poet, pharmacologist and statesman.
Sui Yang (569–618), second emperor of the Sui Dynasty.
Tang Taizong (598–649), second emperor of the Tang Dynasty.
Wang Dingbao (870–941), official and poet of the Southern Han state.
Wang Guan (1035–1100), Song poet.
Wang Wei (699–761), Tang Daoist poet.
Wen Tingyun (c. 812–866), Tang poet.
Wu Qian (1196–1262), Southern Song poet.
Wu Wenying (c. 1200–c. 1260), Southern Song poet.
Xin Qiji (1140–1207), Southern Song poet.
Xu Wei (1521–1593), Ming painter and poet.
Yan Jidao (c. 1030–1106), Song poet.
Yan Shu (991–1055), Song statesman and poet.
Yang Jian (541–604), founder of the Sui Dynasty.
Yang Wanli (1127–1206), Southern Song poet.

Poets and Emperors Quoted or Mentioned in the Poems

Ye Xianzu (1566–1641), Ming poet and playwright.
Zeng Zao (?–1151), Song writer.
Zhuangzi (c. 369–c. 286 BCE), Daoist sage.

Note on the Translation

Our versions broadly conform to the guidelines laid down by Arthur Waley in the 'Method of Translation' with which he prefaced his famous and seminal anthology of Chinese poems. In his words: 'I have aimed at literal translation, not paraphrase ... Above all, considering imagery to be the soul of poetry, I have avoided either adding images of my own or suppressing those of the original.' He went on:

> Any literal translation of Chinese poetry is bound to be to some extent rhythmical, for the rhythm of the original obtrudes itself. Translating literally, without thinking about the metre of the version, one finds that about two lines out of three have a very definite swing, similar to that of the Chinese lines ... In a few instances where the English insisted on being shorter than the Chinese, I have preferred to vary the metre of my version, rather than pad out the line with unnecessary verbiage.

Only on one point, that of rhyme, do we challenge Waley's procedure. Waley advised against rhyming, 'because it is impossible to produce in English rhyme-effects at all similar to those of the original, where the same rhyme sometimes runs through a whole poem. Also, because the restrictions of rhyme necessarily injure either the vigour of one's language or the literalness of one's version.'[1] It is true that the complex rules that govern the rhyme schemes of classical Chinese poetry cannot be reproduced in English, which is why rhyme gradually disappeared from Western translations of Chinese poetry in the course of the twentieth century (in part because of

---

[1] Arthur Waley, trans., *A Hundred and Seventy Chinese Poems*, London: Constable, 1918, pp. 19–20.

Note on the Translation

Waley's precept), and free verse became the norm. However, while it is obvious that no translation can ever rhyme in the same way as the original Chinese and still preserve the meaning, many translators would argue that end rhymes or near-rhymes are acceptable and even welcome where they do not appear forced or unnatural and do not disturb sound, sense or tempo. For rhyming, as long as it does not flout idiomatic sensibility in English, unifies sense and sound, 'sets up pleasing resonances', and helps modulate pace and rhythm.[2]

---

[2] This justification for the use where possible of rhyme draws on Charles Kwong, 'Translating Classical Chinese Poetry into Rhymed English: A Linguistic-Aesthetic View', *TTR: traduction, terminologie, rédaction*, vol. 22, no.1 (2009), pp. 189–220.

Note on Transcription

This book uses Hanyu Pinyin spelling to romanise Chinese, except in the case of historical figures (such as Chiang Kai-shek) and geographical names (such as Hong Kong or the Yangtze River) better known in other transcriptions. Most, but not all, Pinyin letters make approximately the sounds English speakers might expect. Those that depart most radically from their English pronunciation are 'c', 'q', 'x', and 'zh', roughly similar to English 'ts', 'ch', 'sh', and 'j'.

Introduction

This book of Red Chinese poetry in the classical and semi-classical style illustrates the complex relationship between Communist revolution and Chinese cultural traditions. Revolutionaries seeking to break from traditional ways were, at the same time, heir to them, both culturally and politically. To varying extents, they preserved past political traditions and cultural heritages – of peasant rebels, imperial rulers, and the literati, as the poems in this volume show.

The book begins with Chen Duxiu, founder of the Chinese Communist Party (CCP) and leader, together with the philosopher Hu Shi, of the New Culture Movement of the late 1910s, which is generally seen as a prelude to China's revolution; and ends with Mao Zedong, Chinese Communism's most famous political leader and poet. The best Red poet after Mao in the consolidated leadership of the official Party was probably Marshal Chen Yi. Chen Yi was in many ways an odd man out in the Party's leading core, and had a habit of acting and thinking independently. This was perhaps in part because of his anomalous political and military career as leader of the Red guerrillas in the Three-Year War in the South starting in 1934 (when Mao went on the Long March) and of the New Fourth Army born of it in the south in 1938 (when Mao was with the Party's mainstream Eighth Route Army in the north).

Interposed between the sections on Chen Duxiu and Chen Yi, the centrepiece and biggest chapter belongs to Zheng Chaolin, the poet, Communist veteran, and Trotskyist political leader who was persecuted under two Chinese regimes (Nationalist and Communist) and spent more than a third of his long life behind bars. Zheng's courage and human decency would, under a less cruel and repressive regime, have brought him great distinction. Unsurprisingly, however, because of his imprisonment and the eradication of his Trotskyist

Introduction

party, he is the least known of the four. This book was originally conceived as an act of homage to him.

The book therefore presents a relatively rounded picture of some of the best classical Red poetry in China, including the writings of a poet in the early days of the revolution, a poet in power, a poet who spent most of his adult life in jail, and a poet sometimes on the margins, who wrote in forest bivouacs or on the battlefield. The four belonged to a Party in which opposition was wherever possible extinguished and where Mao as the 'Red Sun in the Hearts of the People of the World' eclipsed all other contributions to the revolution, pictured as a monolithic event in which difference was branded as 'splittism' or disruption. But, beyond their differences, the four poets had much in common. All dedicated their lives to revolution, and were connected to one another in various ways. Mao confessed himself to be Chen Duxiu's pupil (though he later opposed him and abandoned his teachings). Zheng Chaolin was Chen Duxiu's loyal lifetime follower, both in the official Party and in the Trotskyist opposition. Zheng Chaolin and Chen Yi both joined the Chinese work-study scheme set up by anarchists in Paris around 1920, from which numerous important leaders of the CCP later emerged; Zheng worked in the Central Committee at the same time as Mao, in the mid 1920s (though Mao later imprisoned him). Mao and Chen Yi fought shoulder to shoulder on the battlefield in the late 1920s and the early 1930s, and Chen Yi helped lead the new regime under Mao after 1949 (though he got into trouble in the 1960s for adopting maverick positions).

Between the late 1930s, when Mao's ascent to unchallenged leadership of the CCP began, and the late 1970s – and even for a couple of years after his death in 1976 – Mao's persona dominated Party politics and its history as written in the Party's history schools. This Maocentric view has been reflected in studies of Chinese communism by non-Chinese historians of the revolution, some of whom for years promoted Mao's role in the events with a diligence little short of that of their Chinese colleagues. Not so much because they were pulled by the same tide, but because the flow of information was systematically censored by Chinese authorities – even many of Mao's works were made available only in heavily edited form. The history of the revolution was distorted to magnify Mao's role in it and to put the contribution of other leaders into deepest shade.

Introduction

Historians subjected Party institutions to the same process of rewriting and concealing as they did individuals. The role of institutions connected with Mao was grossly inflated, while that of institutions in which Mao played little part, whose true history might have contradicted the Mao cult, was neglected or ignored. A case in point, relevant to this book because of Chen Yi's prominence in it, was the Communists' New Fourth Army, the history of which was consistently neglected until after Mao's death, in favour of the Eighth Route Army under Mao.

Work on the dismantling of Maocentrism in Chinese Communist historiography began in China in the late 1970s. It was both anticipated and replicated in non-Chinese scholarship starting in the 1970s and 1980s, for example with the new attention to leaders other than Mao (including Peng Pai, Li Dazhao, and Chen Duxiu), to revolutionary base areas in the 1930s and the 1940s other than the central Jiangxi and Yan'an bases in which Mao operated, and to political traditions like anarchism and Trotskyism that had long been taboo in China. Figures as obscure as Wang Shiwei, the CCP's first literary martyr (arrested in 1942, executed in 1947) and Zheng Chaolin came into view. After Zheng Chaolin's release from prison in 1979, his role in the Party in Paris, Moscow, and Shanghai in the 1920s became a serious object of study, and his memoirs and other writings – including the prison poems at the centre of this book – were published in successive editions.

Was Mao a good poet? Maomania dominated the view of Red poetry in the classical style in China for years, and still largely does, even abroad. But despite the praise that admirers heaped on him, Mao himself was perhaps less confident of the quality of his work. In a letter to his editor in January 1957, when he finally decided to publish his poems at the age of sixty-five, he wrote: 'Until now I never wanted to make these things known in any formal way, because they are in the old style and I was afraid this might encourage a wrong trend and exercise a bad influence on young people. Besides, they are not up to much as poetry, and there is nothing outstanding about them.'[1] In a letter to Chen Yi in July 1965, explaining why he was not

---

1 Mao Zedong, 'Letter to Zang Kejia', 12 January 1957, in Zhonggong zhongyang wenxian yanjiu shi, eds, *Jianguo yilai Mao Zedong wengao* ('Mao Zedong's

Introduction

qualified to revise Chen's poems (which Chen had asked him to do), Mao confessed that he was not familiar with the basic rules of the *wulü* and *qilü* rhyme schemes.[2] Self-deprecation is an accepted part of Chinese face-work, and there is no reason to think that this was Mao's settled view of himself. However, knowledgeable observers have tended to agree that his poetry was middling. For example, the poet and sinologist Arthur Waley declared that 'if poetry were painting, I would say that Mao was better than Hitler but not as good as Churchill.'

Many Chinese Communist leaders wrote classical poetry that was as good as or better than Mao's, but their work has for decades been overlooked and even suppressed. This is because classical poetry was seen as retrograde, hence Mao's proscription of it in 1942 at the Yan'an Forum on Art and Literature – a proscription applicable to everyone but himself, as it transpired. Other Communist leaders (apart from those in this volume) who wrote poems in the classical style included Dong Biwu (1886–1975), Lin Boxu (1886–1960), Xie Juezai (1884–1971), Ye Jianying (1897–1986), and Zhu De (1886–1976), but all were denied the opportunity to publish their work while Mao lived. Like Chen Yi, Ye Jianying and Zhu De earned the title of 'poet generals', fighting men who were good at poetry. They were prolific – Chen left behind 700 poems, Ye 179, and Zhu 550.[3] Lin Boxu, Xie Juezai, and Dong Biwu were pillars of the Huaian Poetry Society established by the CCP in Yan'an in September 1941, a forum for Communist leaders to swap poems.[4] Their poetry typically expressed political aspirations in heroic and solemn language. However, it also

---

Manuscripts since the Establishment of the People's Republic of China'), Beijing: Zhongyang wenxian chuban she, 1992, vol. 6, p. 296.
2   Mao Zedong, 'Letter to Chen Yi', 21 July 1965, in Zhonggong zhongyang wenxian yanjiu shi, eds, *Mao Zedong shuxin xuanji* ('A Collection of Mao Zedong's Letters'), Beijing: Renmin chuban she, 1983, p. 607.
3   Zhonggong zhongyang wenxian yanjiu shi, eds, *Chen Yi shici ji* ('A Collection of Chen Yi's Poems'), Beijing: Zhongyang wenxian chuban she 2001; Zhonggong zhongyang wenxian yanjiu shi, eds, *Ye Jianying shici ji* ('A Collection of Ye Jianying's Poems'), Beijing: Zhongyang wenxian chuban she, 2008; Zhonggong zhongyang wenxian yanjiu shi, eds, *Zhu De shici ji* ('A Collection of Zhu De's Poems'), Beijing: Zhongyang wenxian chuban she, 2007.
4   Yuan Xiaolun, 'Ye Jianying yu Huai'an shishe zhulao' ('Ye Jianying and Elders of the Huai'an Poetry Society'), *Dang shi zonglan* ('Party History in Perspective'), no. 9 (2007).

expressed the authors' innermost feelings, especially before their Communist conversion. Red poetry in the classical style exhibited a multiplicity of themes and forms, so that its eventual fate under Mao was no different from that of radical Chinese politics in general: both were reduced to a set of Maoist stereotypes.

In China, far more than in the West, poetry has always been a communal and collaborative activity, a main thread in the fabric of society and politics, such that the poet Bai Juyi declared China 'poetry's country' (*shiguo*). Educated men, and some women, celebrated events, friends, and heroes (past and present) and commemorated loss in 'exchange poems', invoking someone either remote in time or space or with whom the writer was personally acquainted.[5] In the West, poetry has long been a vehicle of mainly personal expression, abstracted from society, whereas in China – where poetry rather than fiction has been 'the accepted mode of serious reflection'[6] – the link between poetry and social concerns was always strong. In many respects, only poetry and non-fictional prose were considered serious literature, and fiction and drama were regarded with less esteem.[7]

Chinese poetic composition, 'the expression, in rhymed words, of thought impregnated with feeling',[8] has, from the very start, mixed poetry and song – *shige* ('poem-song') is a standard designation for all forms of poetry. China's poetic tradition dates back to the *Shijing* (Book of Songs), the oldest existing collection of Chinese verse from the eleventh to seventh centuries BCE and one of the Five Classics said to have been compiled by Confucius. It begins:

Poetry is for the expression of emotions. An aspiration felt in the heart is, when expressed in words, called poetry. Feelings well up and take shape in words. When language is not enough to convey feelings, we

---

5 In his research, Tom Mazanec maps the literary relations that underlie exchange poetry using social-network analysis.
6 Bonnie S. McDougall and Louie Kam, *The Literature of China in the Twentieth Century*, London: Hurst, 1997, p. 31.
7 Chow Tse-tsung, *The May Fourth Movement: Intellectual Revolution in Modern China*, Cambridge, MA: Harvard University Press, 1960, p. 270.
8 The Scottish sinologist James Legge's definition.

Introduction

voice them in sighs. When sighs are not enough, we resort to song. When song is not enough, unconsciously the hand begins to move and the feet to dance.

This linking of poetry and song in the lyrical and musical expression of thoughts and emotions was described as follows in the *Shangshu* (Book of Documents), another of the Five Classics: 'Poetry expresses purpose, songs intone language, they echo forever, the law of harmony.'

In the dynasties, the manner of classical composition underwent a long process of evolution, until it more or less settled down during the Song Dynasty (960–1279). Up until the Han Dynasty (206 BCE–220 CE), attention was paid mainly to rhyme and the number of characters in each line. Poems in the *Shijing* used lines of four characters with looser rhymes. Six-character lines predominated in the *Chu ci* (Songs of the South) in the Warring States period (475–221 BCE). In the Han, poems consisting of five-character and seven-character lines with strict rhyme schemes started to become the norm.

Some Communist poets, such as Chen Duxiu, Ye Jianying, and Dong Biwu, wrote *gelü*, using strict tonal patterns and rhyme schemes that had started to take shape during the Southern and Northern Dynasties (420–589), when rules about tones and verbal parallelism (the matching of syntactic functions and of the meanings and tones of characters across lines) were first created. During the early Tang Dynasty (618–907), rules about poetic composition were developed and refined. During and after the Tang, poems with a strict tonal pattern and rhyme scheme were known as 'poems of the modern genre', while those that did not follow the new rules were known as 'poems of the ancient genre'.

Other Communist poets, including Mao, preferred *ci*, which are much more complex in terms of tonal patterns, rhyme schemes, and the length of poems and lines. By expanding the tonal patterns and rhyme schemes of the 'modern genre' and borrowing from folk verse set to music, a new and more diverse variety of *ci* evolved during the late Tang Dynasty, the Five Dynasties (907–960), and the Song. A *ci* poem is composed in accordance with a given tune that determines its structure – the number of lines and characters, the

---

9   This is from the *Daxu* ('Long preface') to the *Shijing* (Book of Songs).

Introduction

rhyme scheme, and the tonal pattern. More than 1,600 such tunes are in existence.

Classical Chinese poetry depends to a considerable extent on analogy (*bi*) and association (*xing*), including allusions to and quotations from classical works. To compose a *ci* using strict tonal patterns, rigorous rhyme schemes, verbal parallelism and so on demands not only a grasp of these techniques but a huge vocabulary from which to draw the necessary sounds and meanings. Since the start of the poetry revolution in the late Qing, rules about tonal patterns have no longer been followed in the same way as in the past, since poems were no longer written for singing. The rhetorical techniques of analogy and association have also declined in importance, and are now generally seen as outdated. This tendency to do away with inflexible rules is already evident in most Red poetry, especially since 1949.

As to content, the Chinese lyric tradition is generally no less personal, intimate, and autobiographical than the Western. However, as Eugene Eoyang pointed out in his comparison of Western and Chinese poetry, reading Tang poems

> one doesn't have the feeling one expects from reading a lyric, that one is overhearing a first-person speaking to himself. The poet is addressing another poet, not unlike himself, often identified in the inscription; as readers, we are assuming the role of a contemporary sharing the experience, the contextual reality that gave birth to the poem. Far from 'overhearing' the poem, the reader is asked to engage in the dialectic of the poem, to supply the allusion, to recall the circumstances enshrined in the poem, to respond with his (or her) reactions (often in the form of an 'answering poem').[10]

Under the Confucian system of rule, poetry was usually a preserve of the scholars and literati who helped run the court and staffed the agrarian bureaucracy, and who through their writings, including their poems,

---

10 Eugene Eoyang, 'Polar Paradigms in Poetics', in Cornelia Niekus Moore and Raymond A. Moody, eds, *Comparative Literature East and West: Traditions and Trends*, Honolulu: University of Hawaii Press, 1989, pp. 11–21, pp. 15–16.

informed virtuous rulers of popular needs and opinion. Poetry served a moral as well as a directly political purpose, expressed in the canonical Confucian maxim *shi yan zhi* ('poetry verbalises aspirations'). Poetry played a role in almost every sphere of Chinese governance, including the imperial examination system that recruited new officials, and the ability to write it could make or break a man's career. Among scholars, 'exchange poetry' grew out of the heavily ritualised practice of 'pure talk', in which the exchange of poems established alliances in society and the state and promoted social cohesion and collective identities.[11]

These practices, carried over into the twentieth century, played a role in twentieth-century radical politics. Poetry figured in two main ways in the Chinese Revolution. In most revolutions, poetry serves as a mirror, medium, and venue of revolutionary activity, either overt or covert, for, as Shelley said, 'poets are the unacknowledged legislators of the world.' This happened in the Chinese Revolution too, where poetry in revolution came close on the heels of revolution in poetry, launched by late-nineteenth-century reformers and revolutionaries. The term 'poetic revolution' was coined in 1899 by the leading thinker and recently converted revolutionary leader, Liang Qichao (1873–1929), who introduced European poetry as a potential guide for the new Chinese poetry and called for the injection of fresh terms, concepts, and ideas along with a new mood into Chinese poetry. However, as the leader of the 'poetic revolution', Liang only advocated a half-way version, one that would use modern vocabulary and concepts in the composition of poems in the ancient style.[12] The more radical wing of the 'poetic revolution' took a more iconoclastic stand, casting aside many of the conventions of traditional Chinese poetry and advocating a poetry written not only in an oral or vernacular idiom (rather than in the classical language), but also in a free and modern style.

---

[11] Wendy Swartz, 'Trading Literary Competence: Exchange Poetry in the Eastern Jin', in Paul W. Kroll, ed., *Reading Medieval Chinese Poetry: Text, Context, and Culture*, Leiden: Brill, 2015, pp. 6–35, p. 6.

[12] Liang laid down three principles for the 'poetic revolution': 'First, a new world of perceptions; second, new vocabularies; and third, incorporating the two into the styles of the ancients' (Liang Qichao, 'Xiaweiyi youji' ['Travel Notes on Hawaii'], in Liang Qichao, *Yinbing shi heji* ['Collection from the Ice-Drinkers' Studio'], vol. 7, Beijing: Zhonghua shuju, 1989, p. 190).

Introduction

This revolution in poetry paralleled that in Chinese fiction but was much harder to bring about, for some fiction had been written in the vernacular in China for centuries. Whereas new-style prose writers could build on a rich tradition that included the four great Chinese classical novels – *Romance of the Three Kingdoms*, *Journey to the West*, *Water Margin* and *Dream of the Red Chamber* – new-style poets had little or nothing Chinese to use as models. The vernacular poets of the Chinese Revolution included Guo Moruo (1892–1978), Zhou Zuoren (1885–1969), Lu Xun (1881–1936), Yu Dafu (1896–1945), Xu Zhimo (1896–1931), and many other patriotic intellectuals. Like their Confucian predecessors, they wrote poems that served a social end, but the end was new – to free the common people from feudal bonds and superstition.[13] Their work is sometimes seen as flat and shallow, lacking the depth, originality, anarchic excess and experimental zeal of Soviet poetry in the first decade after 1917. The Chinese Communists' interest in vernacular poetry also led them, in the regions of China they controlled during the Anti-Japanese War, to promote folk songs and 'street poetry', inspired in part by Soviet examples.[14]

Some Chinese Communist poets followed in the footsteps of Liang Qichao by combining revolutionary spirit with old poetic forms, rather than rid themselves entirely of 'the bondage of the past' by adopting a new vernacular style. Chen Duxiu, the leader (together with Hu Shi) of China's 'literary revolution' and champion of the switch to vernacular literature during the May Fourth Period, insisted that spoken language did not suit the mood, sentiments and taste of poetry.[15] The best-known recusant of this sort was Mao Zedong, who, despite insisting to others that literature must serve the masses and be 'popular' in form, wrote poetry in the classical style, both before and after coming to power.

---

13   Lijun Bi, 'Chinese Language Reform and Vernacular Poetry in the Early Twentieth Century', *International Journal of Business and Social Science*, vol. 3, no. 24 (2012), pp. 56–65.
14   Chang-tai Hung, *War and Popular Culture: Resistance in Modern China, 1937–1945*, Berkeley: University of California Press, 1994, p. 254.
15   Pu Qingquan, 'Wo suo zhidao de Chen Duxiu' ('Chen Duxiu as I knew him'), in Wang Shudi, ed., *Chen Duxiu pinglun xuanbian* ('A Collection of Commentaries on Chen Duxiu'), vol. 2, Zhengzhou: Henan renmin chuban she, 1982, p. 363.

Introduction

In his study of Mao Zedong Thought, the Trotskyist leader Wang Fanxi uses Mao's poems to peer into his soul. There he finds not a modern-day revolutionary but an imperious chieftain in the 'great man' style – self-aggrandising, devoid of the compassion displayed by poetry-writing rebels in dynastic times, and moved not by altruism, or the desire to end human suffering and bring about universal enlightenment, but by personal ambition. Wang argues that Mao's poems 'bring to mind antiquity, not modernity; emperors, kings, generals, and ministers, genius and beauty, not the common people,' and that the formal properties of classical poetry encourage this focus. Wang's conclusions are confirmed by an analysis of the tone and themes of Mao's poems. Some are deeply personal in nature, about Mao's relationships and friendships and the loss of them, revealing human vulnerability and intensity of feeling; but even these personal poems are usually openly or implicitly political. Most are impersonal, and shot through with a tone of hubris, triumphalism, absolute self-assurance, and confidence in the inevitable victory of the cause and his own centrality to it. In the opinion of one translator, Ma Wen-yee, they are above all concerned with themes of 'nature, history, the universe, world revolution, and China's destiny'.[17]

The second way in which poetry figured in the Chinese Revolution was through the networks and alliances that poets formed. This activity was usually confined to the intellectual elite. That goes both for the poetry societies set up after the May Fourth Movement, by poets who adopted the vernacular and tried to follow Western or non-traditional models; and for Communist poets who clung to the classical style. The modern-style poetry societies that mushroomed in the 1920s served as sites of political bonding and debate. Only after 1937, during the Anti-Japanese War and the Civil War, when poems in the demotic style were recited in public in the towns and villages to promote patriotism and resistance, were they linked to a

---

16 Wang Fanxi made these comments in his book *Mao Zedong Thought*, soon to appear in English in the Historical Materialism series at Brill, edited, translated, and with an introduction by Gregor Benton (originally published by Xinda chuban she in Hong Kong in 1973 as Shuang Shan [Wang Fanxi], *Mao Zedong sixiang lungao*).

17 For a complete set of Mao's poems in translation, see *Snow Glistens on the Great Wall: The Complete Collection of Mao Tse-tung's Poetry*, trans. Ma Wen-yee, Santa Barbara: Santa Barbara Press, 1987.

Introduction

mass movement.[18] These societies must be distinguished from the elite poetry clubs set up by Communists like Chen Yi, the New Fourth Army commander in Jiangsu in central China, and by his counterparts in Yan'an in the northwest.[19] Through these clubs, Communist poets writing mainly in the classical style used poetic exchange to forge links with prominent local gentry and intellectuals during the wartime multi-class united front (1937–45). Such exchanges followed many of the conventions of 'exchange poetry' as practised in pre-modern China.

Mao Zedong's classical poetry was also drawn into this literary politics. In 1945, the left-wing Nationalist Liu Yazi, himself a poet in the classical style, used Mao's 'Snow', his best-known poem, written in the voice of a self-proclaimed hero, to promote Mao as a hero in Chongqing (then still Chiang Kai-shek's capital), just as Mao was heading there to negotiate a post-war settlement with Chiang Kai-shek. On Mao's arrival, Liu wrote a poem welcoming him as an 'old friend'. He later wrote another poem matching the length and intonation of each line and reusing all the rhyme-words of Mao's 'Snow', in an ancient form of poetic exchange called *chouchang*. The resulting creation accentuated Mao's image as a military hero of great talent and bold vision. Over the next two months, more than thirty further matching poems were published in Chongqing, some supportive but over half of them critical of Mao, whom they compared to a low-born, failed rebel. Even so, the publicity confirmed Mao's status and authority as a 'cultural insider' destined to lead China.[20]

It is true that the Communist revolutionaries and rulers had an equivocal and at times contradictory relationship with classical Chinese poetry. On the one hand, they were radical revolutionaries vowing to break away from

---

18   Michelle Yeh, 'Modern Poetry of China', in Roland Greene and Stephen Cushman, eds, *The Princeton Handbook of World Poetries*, Princeton, NJ: Princeton University Press, 2016, p. 116.
19   On poetry in the New Fourth Army, see Gregor Benton, *New Fourth Army: Communist Resistance Along the Yangtze and the Huai, 1938–1941*, Berkeley, CA: University of California Press, 1999, pp. 199–200. On Yan'an, see Hung Yok-ip, *Intellectuals in Revolutionary China, 1921–1949: Leaders, Heroes and Sophisticates*, Abingdon: RoutledgeCurzon, 2005, pp. 165–6.
20   Zhiyi Yang, 'Classical Poetry in Modern Politics: Liu Yazi's PR Campaign for Mao Zedong', *Asian and African Studies*, vol. 22, no. 2 (2013), pp. 208–26.

Introduction

'feudal traditions', in poetry too. On the other hand, they belonged to a generation that had received a mixed education in traditional Chinese learning and modern Western learning. Classical Chinese poetry had for centuries been regarded as the embodiment of accomplishment, sophistication and cultivation, the epitome of Chinese high literary culture. Some Chinese Communist leaders could not resist the temptation to use this prestigious genre to express their own thoughts and aspirations.

The present volume introduces a narrow but representative selection of Red poetry in the classical style. Each poet has his own personal style and concerns. Deeply emotional, profoundly learned, and well versed in classical skills and language, Chen Duxiu's poems are closest to those of the traditional literatus. Mao's work is skilfully and gracefully executed, vigorous, rich in style, and pregnant with complex imagery and ideas, but it is self-aggrandising and overweening. Zheng Chaolin's is equally skilfully and gracefully executed, yet it can often be tragic, poignant, self-questioning, intimate and complex. Chen Yi is flamboyant, practical and descriptive, commemorating military exploits and celebrating events in revolutionary history; he is less fond than Mao and Zheng of classical allusions and traditional devices. Chen Yi also liked to write free verse in the vernacular. However, the poems of all four share common themes: aspiration for political and national renewal, mourning for the loss of comrades and loved ones, and celebration of the ubiquity and inevitability of change. All were bold, fearless, and prepared for self-sacrifice, and these traits shine through in their poems.

Chen Duxiu

Introduction

Chen Duxiu (1879–1942) is a surpassing presence in modern Chinese thought and politics. At the start of the twentieth century, he helped prepare the ground for the Revolution of 1911 that overthrew the Manchus and brought in the Republic. Between 1915 and 1919, as Professor and Dean of the Faculty of Arts at Beijing University, he led the New Culture (or May Fourth) Movement that electrified Chinese student youth and laid the intellectual foundations for transforming Chinese society. In 1921, he co-founded the CCP; he was elected general secretary at its first five congresses. In 1929 he became a Trotskyist and in 1931 helped found the Chinese Left Opposition, which he then led. In 1932 he was arrested (for the fifth and last time) and jailed on charges of seeking to overthrow the government and replace it with a proletarian dictatorship. Between his release from prison in 1937 and his death on 27 May 1942, he wrote letters and articles in which he distanced himself still further from international Stalinism, and even seemed to disavow some of his former Trotskyist beliefs.[1]

Chen was a seminal and latitudinarian thinker, broad enough to encompass a host of contradictions. Some see in him the Lenin of the Chinese Revolution, though he lacked Lenin's familiarity and proficiency with theory. Others view him as China's Plekhanov, in that he inspired the rise of Communism in his country and served as a bridge between Marx and Mao, just as Plekhanov bridged Marx and Lenin; or as China's Lassalle, on account of his practical bent, his want of ideological polish, and his strong literary engagement. Another judgment, by his American biographer Lee

---

[1] Gregor Benton, ed., *Chen Duxiu's Last Articles and Letters, 1937–1942*, Honolulu: University of Hawaii Press, 1998.

Introduction

Feigon, is that Chen was more the Moses than the Trotsky or Plekhanov of the Chinese Revolution, for after introducing his people to the new doctrines he was left behind by them when they reached the promised land.[2] But Chen's friend Hu Shi, his fellow leader in the New Culture movement, thought of him as 'an oppositionist for life' to any established authority, and it is perhaps this epithet that fits him best.

Chen Duxiu was a person of many talents – a poet, writer, educator and linguist as well as a lifelong revolutionary. He left more than 130 classical-style poems of great quality, displaying skills and feeling of the sort associated with literati in previous ages and embodying the Enlightenment values of modern Europe.[3] As a thinker, he was versatile, independent-minded and audacious. In a letter he wrote to friends in 1937, he declared:

> I have not the slightest compunction about inclining to the left or to the right, I shall always strive to be extreme, I view with contempt the doctrine of the golden mean, I absolutely detest parrotry, I refuse to utter commonplaces that neither hurt nor itch, I want to be absolutely right and absolutely wrong in all my utterances; the last thing I want is never to say anything wrong and at the same time never to say anything right.[4]

This unconventional, pugnacious spirit pervaded all his writings.

Although he was a giant of modern Chinese politics and letters and an instigator of one of the twentieth century's great revolutions, for several decades after his conversion to Trotskyism Chen Duxiu's name was blackened, his achievements were concealed, and his ideas were condemned by former followers and comrades, especially after they took power in 1949. Chen Duxiu was subjected to the same revilement in China as Leon Trotsky was at the hands of Stalin in the Soviet Union. Today, most of the discredit heaped on Chen has been lifted. His

---

2 Lee Feigon, *Chen Duxiu, Founder of the Chinese Communist Party*, Princeton: Princeton University Press, 1983, p. 236.
3 Anqing shi Chen Duxiu xueshu yanjiu hui, eds, *Chen Duxiu shicun* ('A Collection of Chen Duxiu's Poems'), Hefei: Anhui jiaoyu chuban she, 2006.
4 Gregor Benton, ed., *Prophets Unarmed: Chinese Trotskyists in Revolution, War, Jail, and the Return from Limbo*, Leiden: Brill, 2015, p. 710.

Introduction

writings have been published in new editions, and positive accounts of his life and cause have appeared in the press. Yet in the West, even now, his name is barely known outside small circles.

The CCP that Chen Duxiu founded in 1921 was helped into the world by Moscow envoys, and owed much of its early success to Russian aid. But when in 1927 disaster overtook it, it was in large part the Soviets' doing, for Moscow had, for its own reasons, forced the CCP into a calamitous alliance with the bourgeois Guomindang, which subsequently turned against it and killed many thousands of its members and supporters. In July 1927, having made repeated but unsuccessful calls for the Party's withdrawal from the Guomindang, Chen Duxiu resigned as general secretary. The Comintern made him a scapegoat for the failure of policies, including entering the Guomindang, that he had opposed (though never openly). The strategy of Communist immersion in the Guomindang was not the only issue in the 1920s on which Chen Duxiu's ideas differed from the Russians'. Early on in his political career, Chen had fixed on socialism with democracy as the remedy for China's ills. He may have drawn his inspiration for the Party from the Bolsheviks, but his conception of it was distinct.[5] He opposed the creation of a strong Party chief, and welcomed non-Marxists and anarchists. Under his leadership, different points of view vied freely, and although the outcome of the discussion was settled in Moscow, it was several years before the CCP was wholly transformed along Russian lines. By 1920, Chen had emerged as one of the anarchists' sternest left-wing critics, but he continued to share their commitment to radical democracy and internationalism and their opposition to militarism, even in its 'revolutionary' guise.

Before he became a Communist, Chen's project, as formulated by his journal *Xin qingnian* ('New Youth'), was to rescue China by learning from the West. Just as Europe's early Enlighteners had once looked to China for models of the rational society, so China's enlighteners in 1919 sought illumination in Western thought and practice. But they had to absorb these in

---

5 Feng Chongyi, *Zhonggong dangnei de ziyou zhuyi: Cong Cheng Duxiu dao Li Shenzhi* ('Liberalism within the Chinese Communist Party: From Chen Duxiu to Li Shenzhi'), New York: Mirror Books, 2009.

Introduction

an artificially compressed time, whereas the *philosophes* had had a century to refine and disseminate their ideas. Thus democracy itself was somewhat shallowly rooted in Chen's thinking, and no match for the Russian and Chinese 'Bolshevisers'.

After his conversion to Trotskyism, Chen Duxiu focused his political energies on the struggle for an all-powerful National (or Constituent) Assembly elected by universal secret ballot, to bring together China's disparate economic and political struggles, and relegated issues of socialism, proletarian dictatorship, and soviets to the realm of general propaganda. He had consistently opposed calling for the 'dictatorship of the proletariat', and when he eventually did accept it, it was reluctantly, for he believed it to be too radical for the Chinese context.

Chen Duxiu was a creative and independent-minded thinker, not the sort of man to toe the Party line, but a sceptic and an innovator. He had come to Marxism after a breathless rush through the telescoped -isms of centuries of European thought. Though his revolutionary commitment was total, his grasp of Marxism was quite shaky, and took the form (according to Wang Fanxi) of 'a rough superstructure of foreign style' built on a 'solid Confucian foundation'.[6]

Unlike some of his Trotskyist comrades, Chen was not afraid to challenge accepted beliefs, even those that bore Trotsky's imprimatur. The Chinese and the Russian admired each other; Trotsky even wanted to learn Chinese so as to be able to read Chen's writings. Whereas for most Trotskyists in China, Trotsky was a fount of pure wisdom, for Chen Duxiu – who was Trotsky's age and a veteran revolutionary in his own right – he was an equal. Chen believed that the essence of the greatness of revolutionaries like Lenin was their refusal to be bound by formulae. He was never prepared to accept uncritically the word of foreign Communists, especially after Moscow unfairly blamed him for the defeat of 1927, and he took an even poorer view of Chinese 'red compradors' who 'kowtowed to foreign comrades'.[7]

---

6 Wang Fan-hsi, *Memoirs of a Chinese Revolutionary, 1919–1949*, trans. Gregor Benton, 2nd revised edition, New York: Columbia University Press, 1991, p. 269.
7 Ibid.

Introduction

His Trotskyist comrade and disciple Wang Fanxi described him as follows in his preface to the English translation of Chen's last articles and letters:

> His essential nature [was] to be directed by intuition, to speak straight from the heart, to avoid parroting the views of others, to refuse to strike sentimental poses, and to think and act independently. In that respect, his attitude was the same as that of Marx, illustrated in the preface to *Das Kapital* by a line from Dante: *Segui il tuo corso, e lascia dir le genti!* (Follow your course and let people talk).[8]

Between 1936 and 1938, and again in late 1939 or early 1940, Chen Duxiu and his Trotskyist comrades held vigorous discussions on the issue of democracy. The Moscow show trials and Stalin's pact with Hitler caused Chen to rethink still more deeply many of the critiques of democracy advanced by Lenin and also Trotsky. Chen concluded that Lenin's rejection of democracy was, in part, responsible for Stalin's bureaucratic crimes and that dictatorship of any sort, revolutionary or counterrevolutionary, was unacceptable. After 1938, it seemed to his comrades that he had reverted in his declining years to 'pure' democracy, his intellectual 'first love'. However, he rejected proletarian dictatorship not in favour of capitalism but in the name of Marxism. On the whole, his final views were not irreconcilable with Marxism as Karl Kautsky and others understood it.

In the 1980s, new writings on Chen Duxiu and the Trotskyists began to be available in China, and attracted much attention. This is not surprising, for the official leadership that had slandered the Trotskyists in the 1930s and jailed them in 1952 had been thoroughly discredited in the public eye, and the crisis of faith in Stalinism and Maoism was deep and general. At the same time, many younger historians were taking seriously the regime's call for truthful, factual scholarship. Today, even Chen's Trotskyism is no longer wholly taboo. In 1981, the veteran Communist General Xiao Ke proposed a positive assessment of Chen's leadership of

---

8   Wang Fanxi, 'Foreword', in Benton, *Chen Duxiu's Last Articles and Letters*, p. x.

Introduction

the Party, suggesting that his Trotskyist period, too, deserved an honest appraisal.[9]

Chen's rehabilitation extended to his bones. In 1982, the authorities repatriated his remains to his birthplace in Anqing, Anhui province, for reburial, and his tomb was later designated 'a major tourist resource and site imbued with human and cultural meaning'. By 1995, Chenmania was sweeping Anqing, and the authorities enclosed Chen's tomb in a park of the sort once built for dead emperors or national heroes; or, in recent times, for Party martyrs. Chen was joined in his new mausoleum by his two martyred sons, Qiaonian and Yannian.

The students who occupied Tian'anmen Square in 1989 drew their inspiration directly and explicitly from the May Fourth Movement of 1919, which Chen Duxiu had led. They repeated Chen's famous slogan calling for science and democracy and echoed – consciously or unconsciously – many of his later anti-Stalinist proposals. 'My biography of Chen Duxiu, founder of the CCP, seemed especially relevant to the events of 1989', wrote Lee Feigon, in his analysis of the background to the Tian'anmen Square massacre.[10]

As an 'oppositionist for life', Chen Duxiu stood up against the Manchu regime, the Guomindang regime, and the Party in its middle years, after it had begun to assume more fully Stalinist features. His poems provide an authentic record of the complex political career and spiritual world of a revolutionary. In 1903, when he first started publishing his poems, he was a radical youth devoted to republican revolution. In 1941, when he wrote his last poem before his death, he was frustrated as a revolutionary but still cherished hopes for a democratic and socialist China. By that time he was no longer affiliated to any political organisation, but he retained close ties to Wang Fanxi and other Trotskyists, and after his release from prison continued to correspond with Trotsky himself and to identify with some of Trotsky's ideas.

---

9 Benton, *Prophets Unarmed*, pp. 691–3.
10 Feigon, *Chen Duxiu*, p. ix.

1.

Lament for Wang Xiyan

A *qijue*   *1903*

Chen Duxiu's life as a revolutionary began in 1902 when, as a student at the Kobun Institute in Japan, he joined several anti-Manchu revolutionary organisations. Wang Xiyan (1873–1902) was Chen's close friend from Anhui. He shared Chen's determination to acquire Western learning in order to overthrow the Qing Dynasty and establish a republic. He died of illness in 1902, while studying at the Jiangnan Military School.

> Crying, I read the dreadful news,
> stricken by this early loss.
> Nothing can pain a hero more
> than not to die in battle for one's land.

哭汪希颜   Kū Wāng Xīyán

凶耗传来忍泪看，   Xiōnghào chuán lái rěn lèi kàn,
恸君薄命责君难。   tòng jūn bómìng zé jūn nán.
英雄第一伤心事，   Yīngxióng dì yī shāngxīn shì,
不赴沙场为国亡。   bù fù shāchǎng wèi guó wáng.

A *qijue*: A form of verse with four lines each comprising seven characters.

2.

Inscription on a Painting of Saigō Nanshū Hunting

A *qilü*   *1903*

Chen Duxiu measures himself against a Japanese hero, Saigō Takamori (Takanaga) (1828–1877), a samurai active in Japan's Meiji Restoration (1868–1912), which overthrew the shogunate and brought Japan into the modern age. A poet who has been called 'the last true samurai', he is said to have committed suicide after being wounded in a rebellion. He wrote poetry under the literary name Saigō Nanshū.

> Injustice always summons forth bold deeds,
> whether rushing troops to save the throne or rising in revolt.
> In life there should be nothing to regret –
> why subject freedom to the pointless goal of getting to old age?
> The common herd of goats and swine
> will hesitate to tread on thorn-strewn land.
> A man relies upon his sword to build up his career,
> without a thought for victory or defeat.

题西乡南洲游猎图

勤王革命皆形迹，
有逆吾心罔不鸣。
直尺不遗身后恨，
枉寻徒屈自由身。
驰驱甘入棘荆地，
顾盼莫非羊豕群。
男子立身唯一剑，
不知事败与功成。

Tí Xīxiāng Nánzhōu yóu liè tú

Qínwáng gémìng jiē xíngjì,
yǒu nì wú xīn wǎng bù míng.
Zhí chǐ bù yí shēnhòu hèn,
wǎng xún tú qū zìyóu shēn.
Chíqū gān rù jí jīng dì,
gùpàn mòfēi yáng shǐ qún.
Nánzǐ lìshēn wéi yī jiàn,
bù zhī shì bài yǔ gōng chéng.

A *qilü*: A form of verse with eight lines each comprising seven characters.

3.

Indignation at the Habits of the Day

To the tune of 'Intoxication in Jiangdong' *1904*

This poem appeared in the inaugural issue of *Anhui suhua bao* ('Anhui plain speech journal'), which Chen founded in Tokyo in 1904, using the vernacular, so that the general public could understand it. The paper closed down in 1905, after coming under political pressure. It aimed to spread information through the medium of vernacular Chinese, promote revolutionary ideas, and overcome Chinese people's excessive attachment to the family, to the detriment of the state. In this poem, Chen strives to write in the traditional style while using an approximation to the vernacular.

My motherland of several thousand years is soon to fall,
leaving four hundred million Chinese entrapped.
Those without conscience will not care,
but people capable of feeling pain will start to think.   4
The powers are out to split the Yangtze like a melon.
What is the point of those who cherish money above life but talk
about protecting China,
currying favour and employing   8
base tricks for private gain,
unconscionable
in public life?
So what if foreigners flaunt their strength?   12
What matters more is family demons injuring the family god,
playing godfather to the foreign troops,
courting their favours,
slavishly fawning.   16

Line 1: Echoing a line by Du Fu (for the dates of Du Fu and other classical poets, see 'Poets and Emperors Quoted or Mentioned in the Poems' in this volume.
Line 5: The simile 'cutting up China like a melon' was widely used at the time to describe imperialist predations.

Indignation at the Habits of the Day

醉江东·愤时俗也

眼见得几千年故国将亡,
四万万同胞坐困。
乐的是自了汉,
苦的是有心人。
好长江各国要瓜分,
怎耐你保国休谈,
惜钱如命。
拍马屁,
手段高,
办公事,
天良尽。
怕不怕他们洋人逞洋势,
恨只恨我们家鬼害家神。
安排着洋兵到,
干爹奉承,
奴才本性。

Zuì jiāngdōng: fèn shísú yě

Yǎnjiàndé jǐ qiān nián gùguó jiāng wáng,
sì wànwàn tóngbāo zuòkùn。
Lè de shì zìliǎohàn,
kǔ de shì yǒuxīnrén。
Hǎo chángjiāng gè guó yào guāfēn,
zěn nài nǐ bǎo guó xiū tán,
xīqián-rúmìng。
Pāimǎpì,
shǒuduàn gāo,
bàn gōngshì,
tiānliáng jìn。
Pà bùpà tāmen yángrén chěng yángshì,
hèn zhǐ hèn wǒmen jiāguǐ hài jiāshén。
Ānpái zhe yángbīng dào,
gāndiē fèngchéng,
núcái běnxìng。

4.

A Poem Written for Wang Huibo on the Occasion of His Journey to the East

A *qilü*   1904

Chen Duxiu wrote this poem at the age of twenty-six, as an expression of his wish to be a hero, combining courage and tenderness, and to salute Wang Huibo, who worked with him as a journalist and an anti-Manchu revolutionary activist.

> I hear you are about to board the ferry to Japan.
> Our friendship sees another year go by.
> On my precious sword I shed no tears,
> at all times and in all places women worry to excess.
> The sea-trip to the East reminds me of my former dream.
> However, I am still a prisoner in the south.
> Close by or far away, parting is akin to separation,
> and my heart is smitten by irrational emotion.

赠王徽伯东游

闻君将发扶桑渡,
已识相逢又一秋。
宝剑莫弹知己泪,
诸天终古美人愁。
东航触我追前梦,
南国依然困楚囚。
近别远离同一散,
我心恻恻没来由。

Zèng Wáng Huībó dōng yóu

Wén jūn jiāng fā fúsāng dù,
yǐ shí xiàngféng yòu yī qiū.
Bǎojiàn mò tán zhījǐ lèi,
zhū tiān zhōnggǔ měirén chóu.
Dōngháng chù wǒ zhuī qián mèng,
nánguó yīrán kùn chǔqiú.
Jìnbié yuǎnlí tóngyī sàn,
wǒ xīn cècè méiláiyóu.

Line 6:   Chen, listed as wanted by the Manchu government, wrote this poem in Wuhu, Anhui Province.

5.

Lament for He Meishi

A *wulü*   1904

He Meishi (?–1904) was a colleague of Chen at *Guomin riribao* (China National Gazette) in Shanghai. He died of illness in Tokyo.

> Since parting in Shanghai
> we have gone through many ups and downs.
> Flowers will forever fade,
> and the footsteps of old friends are made as if in water.
> In the starry firmament of dust
> my life is but a finger-snap.
> If Qiqing is still alive,
> I'm sure she will be of one mind with me on this.

哭何梅士

海上一为别，
沧桑已万重。
落花浮世劫，
流水故人踪。
星界微尘里，
吾生弹指中。
棋卿今尚在，
能否此心同。

Kū Hé Méishì

Hǎishàng yī wéi bié,
cāngsāng yǐ wàn ihòng.
Luòhuā fúshì jié,
liúshuǐ gùrén zōng.
Xīngjiè wéi chénlǐ,
wúshēng tánzhǐ zhōng.
Qíqīng jīn shàng zài,
néng fǒu cǐ xīn tóng.

A *wulü*: A form of verse with eight lines, each of five characters.
Line 7: Shen Qiqing was He Meishi's lover, but their relationship was ended by her family. She was brought back to Zhejiang from Shanghai, and was never allowed to meet He again.

6.

The Fourth of Ten Poems

1909

This poem was written in reply to one by Su Manshu (1884–1918), a monk and poet and a close friend of Chen. One might assume that Dandun in line one refers to the French revolutionary hero Georges Danton (1759–1794), who, like Byron, died young (two 'slender threads'). However, Chen says in a note that he means the Italian poet Dante (1265–1321) (whose name is normally rendered differently in Chinese). This would also make sense. Dante supported the vernacularisation of the Bible, a venture fraught with danger in Italy in the late Middle Ages. As language reformers and innovators, Chen and his colleague Hu Shi can therefore count as China's Dantes. Byron too was interested in the reform of Greek literature and language.

My teachers are Dante and Lord Byron,
their lives as slender threads that ride the air above the genial sea.
I continue to pluck the red strings even though my soulmate is now gone,
with whom can I share my loneliness and concern?

本事诗 (之四)

丹顿裴伦是我师，
才如江海命如丝。
朱弦休为佳人绝，
孤愤酸情欲语谁。

Běnshì shī (zhī sì)

Dāndùn Péilún shì wǒ shī,
cái rú jiānghǎi mìng rú sī.
Zhūxián xiū wèi jiārén jué,
gūfèn suānqíng yù yǔ shéi.

Line 3: This line is adapted from a poem by Huang Tingjian. 'Plucking the red strings' denotes profound friendship or love.

7.

Before Lingyin Temple

A *qijue*   1910

The years leading up to the 1911 Revolution were a period of relative calm for Chen Duxiu, who enjoyed the rare luxury of leisure, exchanging poems with friends and delighting in new love. This poem conveys his exuberant spirits at the time.

The village paths are thickly perfumed by the catkins flying off the trees,
with tavern-streamers flapping in the warm wind of my wild youth,
a piebald standing daily tethered to the bridge.
How sad and listless Lady Xiao Jiu seems.

灵隐寺前

垂柳飞花村路香，
酒旗风暖少年狂。
桥头日系青骢马，
惆怅当年萧九娘。

Língyǐnsì qián

Chuíliǔ fēihuā cūnlù xiāng,
jiǔqí fēngnuǎn shàonián kuáng.
Qiáotóu rìxì qīngcōngmǎ,
chóuchàng dāngnián Xiāo Jiǔniáng.

Title: The Lingyin Temple is in a valley northwest of Hangzhou's West Lake.
Line 3: A line associated with the Tang poet Wan Chu, according to whom piebald horses symbolised wealth and power.
Line 4: Lady Xiao Jiu is a character in a Hangzhou drama who used her beauty to seduce a monk, but was rejected by him.

8.

A Visit to Taoguang

A *qilü* 1910

The poem captures Chen Duxiu's placid and carefree mood and feelings of transcendence.

> Three hundred stone steps climb up through the wood,
> winding tier by tier along a narrow mountain path.
> On all sides, bamboo clumps obscure the sky,
> while pure springs pulse out from the rocks along the way.
> I can see the whiteness of the lake amid the hills,
> and hear the bells ring on the evening mist.
> As the distant moon departs the jasper sky,
> dust settles cold and still upon the scarlet decks.

游韬光

石级穿林三百层，
层层仄径绕山行。
碍云密竹两旁立，
裂地清泉一路鸣。
山意不遮湖水白，
钟声疏与暮云平。
月明远别碧天去，
尘向丹台寂寞生。

Yóu Tāoguāng

Shíjí chuānlín sānbǎi céng,
céngcéng zèjìng ràoshān xíng.
Àiyún mìzhú liǎngpáng lì,
lièdì qīngquán yīlù míng.
Shānyì bù zhē húshuǐ bái,
zhōngshēng shūyǔ mùyún píng.
Yuè míng yuǎnbié bìtiān qù,
chén xiàng dāntái jìmò shēng.

Title: The Taoguang Temple is in the same area as the Lingyin Temple.
Line 8: The place where Daoist immortals manufacture the pills of immortality.

9.

A Visit to Hupao

A *qilü*   1910

The poet reflects on the peaceful and secluded surroundings of a temple deep in the mountains in late summer.

> The tiger gods evade the human eye,
> while water from the pure spring flows across the land.
> The monks are poor, and loath to entertain their guests.
> The distant hills prepare to greet the fall.
> The bamboo dons a new green coat,
> while the valley shuts the twilight in.
> After fetching water for a pot of tea,
> I sit back in this quiet, secluded place.

游 虎 跑

神虎避人去,
清泉满地流。
僧贫慵款客,
山邃欲迎秋。
竹沼滋新碧,
山堂锁暮愁。
烹茶自汲水,
何事不清幽。

Yóu Hǔpǎo

Shénhǔ bì rén qù,
qīngquán mǎndì liú.
Sēng pín yōng kuǎn kè,
shān suì yù yíng qiū.
Zhúzhǎo zī xīnbì,
shāntáng suǒ mùchóu.
Pēngchá zì jíshuǐ,
héshì bù qīngyōu.

Title: The Hupao Temple is on Mount Daci to the south of Hangzhou's West Lake.
Line 2:   According to legend, the Hupao spring was created in the Tang Dynasty by two tigers sent down by immortals.

10.

Ode to the Crane

A *wulü*   1910

Chen wrote this poem after visiting the Crane Breeding Pavilion on Gushan, a tiny island in Hangzhou's West Lake. Working at the time as a teacher of history and geography at Hangzhou Military School, he had not abandoned his revolutionary aspirations, which he expressed in the poem by means of an allusion to the immortal crane, a symbol of high ambition.

> You aspire to soar among the clouds
> and dance above the lakes and seas.
> First you rest briefly on the city walls,
> then you climb back into the sky.
> Your cold, thin, lonely shadow wings its way unseen,
> your only company a solitary cloud.
> Sooner or later Daoist adepts like Prince Jin
> will climb the three holy mountains.

咏 鹤   Yǒng hè

本有冲天志，   Běn yǒu chōngtiān zhì,
飘摇湖海间。   piāoyáo húhǎi jiān.
偶然憩城郭，   Ǒurán qì chéngguō,
犹自绝追攀。   yóuzì jué zhuīpān.
寒影背人瘦，   Hányǐng bèi rén shòu,
孤云共往还。   gūyún gòng wǎng huán.
道逢王子晋，   Dào féng wángzǐ Jìn,
早晚向三山。   zǎowǎn xiàng sānshān.

Line 7: Prince Jin (565 BCE–?) of the Zhou Dynasty was said to have no interest in power and devoted himself instead to music and Daoism. According to legend, a crane took him up into the sky, where he became an immortal.
Line 8: According to legend, three mountains (Fenglai, Yingzhou and Fangzhang) host the immortals.

11.

Stirred Emotions (First of Twenty Poems)

A *wulü*   1910

The first of twenty poems that explore Chen's difficulty in reconciling his mood of detachment from the world of politics and power with his inability to stop thinking about China and its fate, while leading a quiet life in Hangzhou between revolutionary storms.

> This beauty lives along a winding lane,
> more lovely than a peach or plum.
> Pearls would add nothing to her charm,
> which matches that of an orchid and an iris.
> If not for infinite commitment,
> she would be disinclined to talk of love.
> She shuts the door and listens to the plucking of red strings,
> but mindful still of world affairs.

感怀二十首 （之一）　　　　　Gǎnhuái èrshí shǒu (zhī yī)

委巷有佳人，　　　　　　　　Wěixiàng yǒu jiārén,
颜色艳桃李。　　　　　　　　yánsè yàn táolǐ.
珠翠不增妍，　　　　　　　　Zhūcuì bù zēng yán,
所佩兰与芷。　　　　　　　　suǒ pèi lán yǔ zhǐ.
相遇非深恩，　　　　　　　　Xiāngyù fēi shēn ēn,
羞为发皓齿。　　　　　　　　xiū wèi fā hàochǐ.
闭户弄朱弦，　　　　　　　　Bìhù nòng zhūxián,
江湖万余里。　　　　　　　　jiānghú wàn yú lǐ.

Line 1: Starting in the Warring States period with Qu Yuan, if not earlier, Chinese literati used the image of a beautiful woman and of fragrant grass to indicate their own virtue and purity.

12.

Tears alongside Luxury and Debauchery
(Fourteenth of Fifty-Six Poems)

A *qijue*   *1934*

This poem is from a cycle of fifty-six that Chen Duxiu wrote while in prison in Nanjing under Chiang Kai-shek in the 1930s. The poems satirise the corruption, debauchery and tyranny of the Chiang regime, its capitulation to Japan and the suffering of the Chinese under it. The title of the series, *Jinfen lei*, denotes Nanjing, the capital of Chiang's Republic, a city historically notorious for luxury and dissipation. *Jinfen* also means 'gold' and 'women', representing corruption and debauchery.

    Schooling and civil rights are the root of evil –
    to put an end to them would nip that evil in the bud.
    The Ying clan sought to keep the throne in perpetuity
    by bamboozling the common folk.

金粉泪 (之十四)   Jīnfěn lèi (zhī shísì)

民智民权是祸胎，   Mínzhì mínquán shì huòtāi,
防微只有倒车开。   fáng wēi zhǐyǒu dàochē kāi.
赢家万世为皇帝，   Yíng jiā wànshì wéi huángdì,
全仗愚民二字来。   quán zhàng yúmín èr zì lái.

Line 3: Ying was the family name of the rulers of the brutal Qin Dynasty (BCE 259–210). *Yingjia* ('Ying clan') can also mean winner.

13.

Tears alongside Luxury and Debauchery
(Fifty-Sixth of Fifty-Six Poems)

A *qijue*   1934

    The fall of states results from evil acts –
    the rise and fall of dynasties is proof of that.
    Luckily, suffering steels the bones, so I retain
    my bookish ways, even as an old man with white hair.

金粉泪(之五十六)   Jīnfěn lèi (zhī wǔshíliù)

自来亡国多妖孽，   Zì lái wángguó duō yāoniè,
一世兴衰照眼明。   yīshì xīngshuāi zhào yǎn míng.
幸有艰难能炼骨，   Xìng yǒu jiānnán néng liàn gǔ,
依然白发老书生。   yīrán báifà lǎo shūshēng.

14.

To Shen Yinmo (Fourth of Four Poems)

A *qijue*   *1939*

Chen insists on the relationship between the trend of the times and the spirit and character of poetry. He is also talking about his own life and affairs. Although a hero, he was, by 1939 – after his release from years in jail – an ailing man without connections to any political force, and therefore powerless to deal with the increasingly harsh reality of Chinese politics. He sighs in recognition of the fact that world affairs are shaped by broad structural forces rather than by the efforts of conscientious individuals.

    Poetry reached its zenith in the Tianbao reign,
    but sadly withered in late Tang.
    Arts fall and rise depending on events,
    not on the talents of a Su Shi or a Huang Tingjian.

寄沈尹默绝句四首(之四)   Jì Chén Yǐnmò juéjù sì shǒu (zhī sì)

论诗气韵推天宝,   Lùn shī qìyùn tuī Tiānbǎo,
无那心情属晚唐。   wú nà xīnqíng shǔ wǎn Táng.
百艺穷通偕事变,   Bǎi yì qióng tōng xié shìbiàn,
非因才力薄苏黄。   fēi yīn cái lì báo Sū Huáng.

Title: Shen Yinmo (1883–1971), a close friend of Chen Duxiu, was a poet, calligrapher, and educator.

15.

Recollections of Guangzhou in the Spring

A *qijue*   1941

Chen wrote this poem in March 1941, around a year before his death in internal exile in Jiangjin, a town near Chongqing in Sichuan. The poem was written in response to a letter from Chen Zhongfan, his former student and director of Jinling University's Literature Department, informing him of his appointment to a post at Sun Yat-sen University in Guangzhou.

> Gazing at the distant swan that flies across the southern sky,
> I dimly discern Mount Luofu as if over seas.
> I still recall the autumn water, clear and vast,
> and the pretty flowers round Lichi Bay.

春日忆广州

江南目尽飞鸿远，
隐约罗浮海外山。
曾记盈盈秋水阔，
好花开满荔枝湾。

Chūnrì yì Guǎngzhōu

Jiāngnán mù jìn fēihóng yuǎn,
yǐnyuē luófú hǎiwài shān.
Céng jì yíngyíng qiūshuǐ kuò,
hǎohuā kāimǎn lìzhī wān.

Line 2: Mount Luofu is near the Dongjiang River in Guangdong.
Line 4: Lichi Bay is to the west of Guangzhou.

Zheng Chaolin

Introduction

The Chinese Trotskyist leader Zheng Chaolin was born in Zhangping, Fujian, in 1901, into a declining old-style landlord family. He died in 1998, making his life almost exactly coterminous with the twentieth century. A dramatic embodiment of the century's main passions and vicissitudes in China, he spent most of his adult life either fomenting revolution or in jail.

As a child, he read novels about heroic exploits and became dissatisfied with reality. Outwardly, however, he remained a quiet, obedient boy, ready to play the role his father and grandfather expected of him. He would probably have ended up like them – a member of the lower gentry who stayed all his life in Zhangping, a minor county capital in what was, at the time, a remote part of China – but for political developments on a national scale. He was saved from a doubtless dull, parochial existence by May Fourth, the movement for cultural renewal and political revolution that broke out in Beijing in May 1919, as the culmination of the New Cultural Movement that had begun in 1915. This movement inspired the governor of Fujian, Commander Chen Jiongming (an 'anarchist warlord', improbably) to order each county magistrate under his control to nominate two or three youngsters to go to Paris, where two of his anarchist comrades had set up a beancurd factory that sustained a work-study scheme. The programme was designed to provide young Chinese with a livelihood while at the same time training them in radical and scientific thinking, so that on their return to China they might act as a revolutionary political yeast. Zheng was among more than thirty young Fujianese chosen to go to France in 1919.

In France, the Marxist Cai Hesen founded a Communist movement among the Chinese work-students. Zheng became a member, and in 1923 went to Moscow to enrol in a Party school. He now spoke good French (the first of his several foreign languages), and steeped himself in Marxist and

Introduction

other political and philosophical writings. Like many Chinese thinkers who discovered Communism in France, he had a broader mind and was a freer, more bohemian spirit than Communist leaders such as Peng Shuzhi (who reached Russia in 1921 and later, in China, became a Trotskyist) or Wang Ming (an arch-Stalinist who rose to power over the Chinese in Russia in 1927). Both Peng and Wang had gone straight to Moscow, without first serving a revolutionary apprenticeship in China.

Zheng stayed for more than a year in Moscow, where (by his own account) he learned no theory and spent most of his time performing 'individual criticism' by 'exposing' other comrades' petty-bourgeois or anarchist faults in meetings and having his own failings picked out (he was the main butt of criticism). This constant fault-finding and the system of 'command and submission' that obtained in Moscow was Zheng's most abiding memory of his time in the Soviet capital. However, the experience did not discourage him, it only made him more stubborn. The two criticisms that he was least willing to accept were that he 'read too much' (rather than take part in 'training' sessions) and that he was friends with a questionable character, the Esperantist Bao Pu, who hobnobbed with Esperantists of other nationalities in Moscow and was thought 'dangerous'. Zheng was also criticised for wanting to learn Russian: according to Peng Shuzhi, who already had some Russian, it was unnecessary, Chinese was enough. Thus friction arose between Zheng's broad, questing mind and Peng's narrow, carping one. This incompatibility survived the passage of both men into the Chinese Trotskyist Opposition in 1931, and lasted until their death.

Back in China in 1924, Zheng was appointed to work as an aide in the Central Committee, where he specialised in editing Party journals and writing for them. After his expulsion from the Party as a Trotskyist in 1929, he became a leader of the Left Opposition and, later, of its offshoots. However, like most Chinese Trotskyists under Chiang Kai-shek, he spent more time in jail than out of it, save during the eight years of Japanese wartime occupation. Then, in 1952, three years into Mao's Communist revolution, he was arrested by his erstwhile comrades and locked up for the next twenty-seven years.

He spent a total of thirty-four years in prison, first under the Nationalists (as a revolutionary – his jailers saw no difference between him and the Communists) and then, under the Communists, as a counterrevolutionary.

Introduction

No doubt there are political prisoners in history, and perhaps even some today, who have spent longer in jail, but there cannot be many. In revolutionary lore, Auguste Blanqui (1805–1881) has always counted as the record-holder for political imprisonment, having spent thirty-three years behind bars for his beliefs, for which he was nicknamed *'l'enfermé'* ('the imprisoned one'). Zheng had beaten Blanqui's record by a year when he finally stepped into conditional freedom in China in 1979, aged seventy-eight, nearly three years after Mao's death.

Many Chinese Trotskyist leaders were writers, and several were poets; had they been made of rougher, more soldierly stuff, they might have followed a different path after the defeat of the revolution in 1927, when Mao and his comrades took to the hills and most Trotskyists stayed in the towns. Zheng's Trotskyist comrade Wang Fanxi often said that had Zheng been born in another age, he would have shone as a poet or philosopher. In fact, Zheng's years in prison and his forced abstention from revolutionary activity gave him the leisure he had previously lacked to compose the poetry he loved. Jail could stop him making revolution, but it could not stop him making poems. In prison, he also wrote other works, including books on 'cadreism' (*ganbu zhuyi*), Mao Zedong Thought, and Stalinism, during a brief period of political relaxation starting in 1964. The books were confiscated and reportedly destroyed when the prison came under military control during the Cultural Revolution,[1] but the poems could not be so easily blotted out. Zheng had a phenomenal memory and retained hundreds of poems in his head, starting with prison poems he had composed in the early 1930s and extending through the entire period of his incarceration. This retention was made easier by the strict rhyme schemes and regular metres of the classical Chinese poetry Zheng espoused. (The Communist literary dissident Hu Feng [1906–1985] also memorised hundreds of poems while in prison, and likewise retrieved them from memory after his release.) Perhaps the poems that Zheng had committed to memory were further refined in the process of their retrieval during the 1980s.

---

[1] Perhaps one day they will resurface, like his memoirs, a manuscript of which miraculously survived pulping by Red Guards in the Cultural Revolution and was later distributed in mimeograph as 'reference material' for Party historians. It was officially published in 1986 in an expurgated version. (I restored the expurgated material to my English translation, published in 1997.)

Introduction

In the mid 1970s, together with Zheng's exiled fellow Trotskyist Wang Fanxi, by then in Leeds, I campaigned for Zheng's release, publishing articles in the international socialist press and in the *Guardian*, *Le Monde*, and the *Washington Post* and persuading Amnesty International to make him their Prisoner of the Month. In the articles, I pointed out that Zheng had studied in France in the early 1920s alongside Deng Xiaoping (1904–1997), who at the time of my writing was China's newly rehabilitated paramount leader. When we ran the campaign, we did not know whether Zheng was alive or dead. I was astonished and delighted when Wang told me, in June 1979, that the Old Man was not only alive but had been freed.

Sadly, four months and ten days later, his beloved wife Liu Jingzhen, who for twenty-seven years had stood loyally by him awaiting his release, died, 'seemingly having completed her appointed task'.[2]

We were under no illusion that our campaign had obtained Zheng's release, but it might have accelerated it, by jogging Deng Xiaoping's memory and pricking his conscience at a time when he was freeing political prisoners anyway. (Deng's daughter later visited Zheng for an interview while she was researching her book on her father, whom Zheng had known in France when Deng was just sixteen.) I secretly met Zheng Chaolin twice in Shanghai in the mid 1980s, once on my own and once in the company of my friend, the Danish Trotskyist Finn Jensen. Finn and I took him a bottle of French cognac (his favourite tipple) and a long tape-recorded message from Wang, which he answered in our presence, also on tape.

My first impression of Zheng at the door of his flat in Shanghai was much like that of the science-fiction writer and biographer Ye Yonglie, who visited him at around the same time: an old man, tiny and bent double, 'wearing a thick brown ski shirt, a blue woollen cap, and a pair of clamshell cotton-padded shoes'. The two men discussed poetry. In my introduction to his memoirs, I called Zheng 'modest, frank, argus-eyed, compassionate, broad-minded, humorous, playful, stubborn, inquisitive, inventive, creative, loyal, free from all vanity and pretensions, and with the memory of an elephant', and described a photograph taken on the eve of his release, showing him and his wife Liu 'smiling serenely and beatifically'. The Communist

---

2 Lou Shiyi, quoted in Benton, *Prophets Unarmed*, p. 1066.

Introduction

poet Lou Shiyi, who was at the same prison as Zheng in Nanjing in the 1930s and liked him despite his Trotskyism, said that after his release he was 'already an old man, but even so, he was warmly hospitable, tirelessly talkative, and overflowing with high spirits, as if he had sustained not the slightest damage from his trials and tribulations ... He reads, he writes, and he receives and instructs an endless flow of comrades researching special issues in the history of the Chinese Communist Party.' Even his Trotskyist critic Peng Shuzhi, looking back, drew an affectionate picture of him in the 1920s:

> Zheng Chaolin was a strapping young fellow with a broad forehead, always smiling and extremely kind-hearted. There is no denying that he was something of a pedant. He had a stammer. And politically, he was rather uninventive. But in his way, he was a linguistic genius, in the very special sense that he could learn at high speed to decipher, read, and render into decent Chinese any language whatsoever, provided that it was at the level of political discourse and provided, above all, that he was never expected to articulate a single sentence or to understand it orally. For example, it only took him a few months in Moscow to disentangle Russian, just as it had taken him only a few months in France to familiarise himself – also at the level of political discourse – with French. To the knowledge – political and bookish – of these two languages he soon added English, German, Italian, and Esperanto.[3]

Like Mao, Zheng Chaolin combined a belief in radical revolution with a love for poetry in the classical style. In a letter to Lou Shiyi, he explained his aversion to poetry in the modern idiom:

> For prose, the literary reform of May Fourth worked. Today no one writes in classical Chinese any more. But for poetry, it failed. The first generation of literary reformers like Chen Duxiu and Lu Xun all wrote poetry in the old style. Poetry needs rules and forms. This is true of poetry (excluding free verse) in all the Western languages. I know of no

---

3 Benton, *Prophets Unarmed*, pp. 1064–7.

Introduction

new-style poetry in Chinese that is broadly read, like Lu Xun's old-style poems. So I take a very serious attitude to old-style poetry and would never stoop to writing doggerel.

Zheng was part of the same poetic discourse as Mao. Although he composed his poems in prison, he usually shared his imprisonment and poems with other political inmates, including some poets. Even during his years in solitary confinement he often engaged poetically with absent, dead or imagined interlocutors, modelling his work on classical archetypes in the form of matching poems and taking part whenever possible in poetic exchanges (as, for example, on one memorable occasion with his cellmate Yu Shouyi, to rebut Yu's proposal that Zheng capitulate to the Maoists). After his release in 1979, most of his poems (including some translated in this volume) were part of such exchanges.

Zheng's poetry has the same technical and formal properties and belongs to the same poetic world as Mao's, but it inhabits a quite different spiritual and affective world. It has none of Mao's brash self-regard and grandiloquence, his sense of personal uniqueness and superiority. An unkind view might be that Zheng's political project was in ruins after 1949 and he had ended up not in power, like Mao, but back in jail, where he spent most of the rest of his life, meaning that he had nothing to boast about. But the truth is that Zheng was by nature a more modest and compassionate man than Mao, and his poetry reflects this difference as well as his defeat and calvary. He never wrote on martial themes, naturally, since he lacked Mao's experience of warfare. In any case he doubted the wisdom and long-term efficacy of the military road to power. Instead, his poems dwell – far more than Mao's do – on personal loss and disappointment. Where he did tackle political topics, he cloaked critical or dissident opinions in cryptic language to fool the censor, using classical allusions to hint at the inevitability of great changes ahead (when seas yield to mulberry fields and vice versa – a metaphor that Mao also used). His poems are often bleak and tragic, but he can also make fun of himself and the world.

Most of Zheng's poems are *ci*, a lyric form that started in the Tang Dynasty (618–907) and reached its full flowering in the Song (960–1279). *Ci* are written in strict, pre-defined rhythmic and tonal patterns with a set

Introduction

number of lines that vary in length, each comprising a set number of characters (monosyllabic words or morphemes). The classical precedents on which *ci* are modelled are songs or cadences, and can be sung. Several hundred *ci* models are available for copying, each determining the shape of the poems derived from it. Conventionally, poets attach the title, or *cipai*, of the model to each *ci*, to show its metre and rhyme scheme. This title is a technical indication of rhyme and tone, a label that does not necessarily say anything about the content of the *ci*. Most of Zheng's poems are titled according to their *cipai* labels and listed by them in the contents page of the book here translated, in which most of the poems first appeared. In a few cases, two poems share the same *cipai*, although they are on different themes. On rare occasions, Zheng added his own title to explain a poem's contents. Where he did not, I have added content titles immediately above the *cipai* title. These titles are mine, except where they are in inverted commas, in which case they are Zheng's.

Zheng's choice of *ci* patterns was constrained by the books available to him in prison. His main source was an anthology of poetry from the Tang and Song dynasties. Another book to which he had access was *Jihai zashi zhu* ('Jihai miscellaneous poems')[4] by Gong Zizhen (1792–1841), a reform-minded official whose ideas influenced the early generation of Chinese revolutionaries and reformers in the late Qing. Zheng wrote several poems modelled on work by Gong. He also knew a huge number of poems by heart.

---

4 Gong Zizhen, *Jihai zashi zhu*, Beijing: Zhonghua shuju, 1978.

1.

Poet in Space

Zheng flees prison after lights out and shoots off into outer space, tumbling and barrelling around the galaxies and planets, while pitying the embattled world below. In the fifth line from the end, the poem incorporates a reference to a comment by Huizi, a philosopher in the Warring States period in the fourth century BCE and a friendly rival of Zhuangzi, the Daoist sage. Huizi told a king who was contemplating going to war with his neighbour: 'On the snail's left horn is a kingdom called provocation; on the right, one called stupidity. These two kingdoms seem forever to have been locked in fighting over territory. The ground is covered with their dead. One army may win victory today, but in two weeks' time the other will rebound.'

To the tune of 'Ecstasy Reaching to the Sky'

The prison gates slam shut,
but gates can't stop me climbing in my dream
into the clouds to streak across the bright night sky.
Old Moon beams tenderly, the myriad stars
wink, calling me to join their game.
Passing clouds zip in and out of sight,
while strong winds grip my armpits,
to lift me ever higher into space.
As waves whip up on every side,
I dart freely among the moon and stars, like a fish.

Poet in Space

Glancing backwards down to earth,
I see it start to blur,
separating into brown and blue.
The Yangtze and the Himalayas
shrink into a belt and pillow,
whole territories and countries dwindle and fade.
I laugh at humankind, and its pointless struggles to the death.
Looking down
on rivers of a thousand leagues of blood,
I hurtle onwards into outer space,
bouncing between galaxies still lovelier.

齐 天 乐   Qí tiān lè

重门不锁凌霄梦，   Chóngmén bù suǒ líng xiāo mèng,
清宵独游天际。   qīngxiāo dú yóu tiānjì.
一月含情，   Yī yuè hánqíng,
众星眨眼，   zhòng xīng zhǎyǎn,
唤我同来游戏。   huàn wǒ tóng lái yóuxì.
浮云远避，   Fúyún yuǎn bì,
觉两腋风生，   jué liǎng yè fēng shēng,
四围浪起。   sìwéi làng qǐ.
恣意翱翔，   Zìyì áoxiáng,
穿梭星月似魴鲤。   chuānsuō xīng yuè sì fáng lǐ.

时时回顾大地，   Shíshí huígù dàdì,
但朦胧一片，   dàn ménglóng yīpiàn,
陵陆沧水。   líng lù cāng shuǐ.
扬子长江，   Yángzǐ chángjiāng,
希麻拉雅，   Xīmálāyǎ,
衣带枕函而已。   yīdài zhěnhán éryǐ.
他州类是，   Tā zhōu lèi shì,
笑蛮触相争，   xiào mán chù xiāng zhēng,
血流千里。   xuè liú qiānlǐ.
接续高飞，   Jiēxù gāo fēi,
远方星更美。   yuǎnfāng xīng gèng měi.

2.

Buried Alive

In the past, some Chinese constructed *shengkuang* or 'living tombs' for themselves or their relatives while they were still alive. For Zheng, life in prison is like being buried alive, in a coffin pit that he has dug for himself. In this bleak poem, which Zheng wrote at the age of around sixty, he reflects on his long years in jail and the mental scars caused by the severing of his relationships with family and friends. The mountain rock stands for the callousness of China's political regime and of prison life. Kiyama Hideo explains that mountain rocks represent lack of feeling, in contrast to Zheng's excess of feeling, and ties the notion that mountains have no sense of time to the Zen saying, 'In the mountains there are no calendars.'

To the tune of 'Spring in the Crimson City'

My career?
It's like the coffin pit you dig before your death,
to potter in while still alive.
As long as I have breath,
I'll doubtless quench my thirst and still my hunger behind bars
– but how to live, when kept apart from family and friends?
These limbs display a thousand rends
cut by the sword that slashes through my ties.
My feelings turn to envy
of the mountain rock that never counts the years.

Buried Alive

Pale and haggard,
emaciated and white-haired,
luckily I can still think straight,
can still tell wrong from right.
Both ears still work,   15
and through the prison wall I hear an opera.
Though lonely, I stroll within the garden of my mind,
plucking flowers of sorrow and regret.
This poem is written for an autumn grave,
but who will do the weeping?   20

绛都春   Jiàngdōu chūn

生涯何似?   Shēngyá hé sì?
似生圹砌就,   Sì shēng kuàng qì jiù,
盘旋圹里。   pánxuán kuàng lǐ.
一息尚存,   Yī xī shàng cún,
渴饮饥餐离人世。   kě yǐn jī cān lí rénshì.
此身本有千丝系,   Cǐ shēn běn yǒu qiānsī xì,
剑斩断血淋心碎。   jiàn zhǎn duàn xiě lín xīn suì.
有情翻羡,   Yǒuqíng fān xiàn,
山中块石,   shānzhōng kuài shí,
不知年岁。   bù zhī niánsuì.

憔悴,   Qiáocuì,
鬓皤腰瘦。   bìn pó yāo shòu.
幸方寸未乱,   Xìng fāngcùn wèi luàn,
是非能理。   shìfēi néng lǐ.
两耳尚堪,   Liǎng ěr shàng kān,
透过重墙闻歌戏。   tòuguò chóngqiáng wén gē xì.
寂寥尚有心园憩,   Jìliáo shàng yǒu xīnyuán qì,
任采撷愁花恨蕊。   rèn cǎixié chóuhuā hènruǐ.
词成付与秋坟,   Cí chéng fùyǔ qiū fén,
赚谁落泪!   zhuàn shéi luòlèi!

Line 16:   Chinese folk opera, staged in villages.
Line 19–20:   These last two lines are a variation on the last two lines of Poem 40, 'Self-Congratulations on My Sixtieth Birthday'.

49

3.

Stamps (1)

In the early 1960s, Zheng's wife Liu Jingzhen sent him a letter franked with eight Yellow Mountain postage stamps, to relieve the monotony of prison life by injecting a few square inches of colour into it.[1] Anhui's Yellow Mountains are said to be the loveliest of China's five best-known mountain ranges. Zheng stroked and fondled the stamps like a child, as thoughts of the past, and of his youth, crowded in. In the early part of the Sino-Japanese War he had lived near the Yellow Mountains, during three years of rural exile to escape the war and recover his health and spirits after nearly seven years in jail, before eventually returning from Anhui to build his party among the workers in Shanghai. He did not personally climb the mountains at that time, for they were out of bounds to civilian visitors. In jail in the 1960s, by then an old man, he regrets his missed chance, realising that it would never be repeated. He thinks back on the high-spirited days of his youth, when he had looked forward to visiting Mount Tai to see the sunrise, Mount Lu to see the waterfalls, and the Yellow Mountains to see the pines – but now he can only dream of such a journey. The poem's third and fourth lines are heavy with classical images hinting at the possibility of radical change in China – Zheng still hoped for a realisation of his political ideals, although he hid his thoughts in literary and religious metaphors. For example, Mount Sumeru is a sacred five-peaked summit in Hindu, Jain, and Buddhist cosmology and the centre of all physical, metaphysical, and spiritual universes. The phrase 'Mount Meru hides mustard seed, mustard seed contains Mount Meru', taken from the Vimalakirti-Nirdesa Sutra, suggests that even something tiny can harbour limitless possibilities within, including the promise of colossal upheaval. Similarly, the phrase 'peaks and valleys' is associated with the idea of perpetual change ('mountains and

---

[1] For Wang Fanxi's obituary of Liu Jingzhen, see Benton, *Prophets Unarmed*, pp. 1170–2 (Wang uses her other name, Wu Jingru).

Stamps (1)

valleys change') and cataclysmic change ('from seas into mulberry fields and from mulberry fields into seas'). The Yellow Mountain stamps, issued in 1963 (this helps us date the poem), were the work of the famous stamp designer Sun Chuanzhe, and a favourite among the Chinese public.[2] The set of sixteen stamps depicts the Yellow Mountains' sixteen famous attractions. In those days people like Liu Jingzhen were too poor to spend money even on small luxuries, so the eight stamps she stuck on to the envelope were probably the set's low-value denominations.

To the tune of 'King of Blue Peak'

Forsaken in my prison cell
I fondle eight green postage stamps
displaying Yellow Mountain scenes.
Inside a mustard seedMount Meru hides,
while in a heartbeat vales turn into peaks   5
and jagged summits from which pine trees jut,
like flags of war.
Visitors on the overhanging cliffs
press up against the safety rail and gawp
down at the billowing clouds that wash the rocks.   10

I've never seen these sights with my own eyes,
but I know them well from books and scrolls.
I lived for three years at the mountains' feet, but at a time
when war flames lit the sky, sirens blared forth from forts, and men
patrolled the slopes with dogs.   15

---

2 Regarding the stamps on Zheng's letter, see Liu Hongyuan's blog at: blog.sina.com.cn/s/blog.
Line 7: Huangshan (Yellow Mountain) pines are a unique tree species (*pinus hwangshanensis*) that grows on peaks high above sea level, clinging improbably to steep cliffs and mountain peaks, where they can live for more than 100 years. They are a symbol of vitality and, for Zheng, of perseverance against all odds.
Line 15: A month after the outbreak of the Sino-Japanese War, in August 1937, Zheng was released from his second spell of imprisonment under the Guomindang. Chen Duxiu arranged through contacts for Zheng and his wife to live in Jixi in Anhui at the foot of the Yellow Mountains. They lived there until March 1940, when they left for Shanghai (see Zheng Chaolin, 'Chen Duxiu and the Trotskyists', in Gregor Benton, *China's Urban Revolutionaries: Explorations in the History of Chinese Trotskyism, 1921–1952*, Atlantic Highlands, NJ: Humanities Press, 1996, pp. 124–202, at pp. 182–5).

Stamps (1)

Now old and jailed,
death nipping at my heels,
I sigh for the chance,
then so near to hand, that I let slip.
As a wild youth,
I longed to see the sunrise on Mount Tai and the Kuanglu waterfalls.
Today I can view them only from my pillow, at dead of night,
in fitful dreams.

兰 陵 王　　　　　　　　　Lánlíng wáng

慰幽独，　　　　　　　　　Wèi yōu dú,
邮票青红八幅。　　　　　　yóupiào qīng hóng bā fú.
黄山景，　　　　　　　　　Huángshān jǐng,
芥子须弥，　　　　　　　　jièzǐ xū mí,
方寸之间见陵谷。　　　　　fāngcùn zhī jiān jiàn líng gǔ.
嵖岈石峰矗，　　　　　　　Chá yá shífēng chù,
如纛，　　　　　　　　　　rú dào,
峰头松木。　　　　　　　　fēng tóu sōngmù.
危崖上，　　　　　　　　　Wēiyá shàng,
有客凭栏，　　　　　　　　yǒu kè pínglán,
俯瞰云涛荡峰腹。　　　　　fǔkàn yúntāo dàng fēng fù.

奇观未经目，　　　　　　　Qíguān wèi jīng mù,
但屡览篇章，　　　　　　　dàn lǚ lǎn piānzhāng,
颇展图轴。　　　　　　　　pō zhǎn tú zhóu.
也曾三载居山麓，　　　　　Yě céng sān zài jū shānlù,
值天际传燧，　　　　　　　zhí tiānjì chuán suì,
戍楼鸣角，　　　　　　　　shù lóu míng jiǎo,
深山险处遍设伏，　　　　　shēnshān xiǎnchù biàn shèfú,
驻军禁游躅。　　　　　　　zhùjūn jìn yóu zhú.

Line 21: Mount Tai, in Shandong, has been a sacred place for 3,000 years. Mount Lu or Lushan, known formerly as Kuanglu, is a famous mountain in northern Jiangxi province, known for its waterfalls.

Stamps (1)

囚狱,
风前烛。
叹交臂名山,
失去难赎。
少年狂态真堪掬,
要泰岱观日,
匡庐瞻瀑。
如今惟有,
向枕上,
梦断续。

Qiú yù,
fēng qián zhú.
Tàn jiāobì míngshān,
shīqù nán shú.
Shàonián kuáng tài zhēn kān jū,
yào Tàidài guān rì,
Kuānglú zhān pù.
Rújīn wéi yǒu,
xiàng zhěn shàng,
mèng duàn xù.

4.

Dr Faust

In this poem, Zheng laments his prison loneliness, growing old, and his longing for his wife. Zheng was no prude. He relished alcohol, and liked to talk about his comrades' love affairs. (See the chapter 'Love and Politics' in his memoir *An Oppositionist for Life*.)[1] Revolutionaries and other political leaders in China, especially in the 1910s, including the Communist Chen Duxiu (Zheng's mentor and inspiration), made no secret of their womanising and brothel-going. Here Zheng pictures himself as Faust, peering into the magic mirror and spying a ruined man, perhaps his alter ego, with echoes of Oscar Wilde's *Dorian Gray*. If Zheng is Faust, who is Mephistopheles? The Communist Party, which portrayed itself as 'steeped in learning', 'loftily striving' and committed to China's rejuvenation, but was in fact a corrupt caricature of a Communist party, creating not a paradise but a hell on earth, to whose lowest circle it consigned the prisoner Zheng. The 'potion' Mephistopheles gives Faust in Zheng's version of the Faustian pact is the offer of surrender – which in real life Zheng turned down, choosing instead the likelihood of death. (In any case, he knew that the Communists would renege on their offer of 'leniency' in exchange for surrender once that surrender had taken place – see poem 33, 'Forever Dissident'.) After his release from prison, Zheng wrote this about the poem in a letter to Xie Shan,[2] with whom he exchanged poems in his later years:

> This poem was written seven years after my arrest, at the time of a struggle waged in the depths of my innermost being. In prison, you had to use hidden language that others would not understand. At the time,

---

1 The chapter 'Love and Politics' was excised from the edition of Zheng's memoir published by the political authorities in Beijing, for limited distribution within the nomenklatura, but was restored in the English translation.
2 Xie Shan (1922–1996) was a Chinese Trotskyist jailed for five years in 1952.

Dr Faust

there were only two roads ahead: death or surrender. I chose the former, I'd rather die than surrender … [In the poem,] old age and feebleness symbolised my having lost my freedom, the return to my youth symbolised the restoration of my freedom, Mephistopheles' 'potion' symbolised surrender. It would have been good to have my freedom restored, but not at the cost of surrender. Even if I had regained my freedom (Mephistopheles' 'potion'), the entire [Trotskyist] organisation was in ruins – under those circumstances freedom would have meant nothing. And I would have been in no end of trouble wherever I went, so it would be better to die – 'is not an old man better off in bed alone?'[3]

To the tune of 'The Flower of the Magnolia is Slow'

An aged Dr Fu
peers into the mirror
and spies sorrow:
back bent,   4
bleached brow,
bleak mien, shades
of dead friends and lovers crowding in.
Borne back to the springtime of his life   8
he leaps into the Pingkang brothel
off the back of a galloping white horse
whipped on by gold-helved whips.
How the girls make eyes at him!   12

---

3 Zheng's letter is reproduced in Hu Luoqing, ed., *Xie Shan yiyao: 'Kukou shici ji'* ('Xie Shan's Legacy: "Bitter Poems"'), expanded edition, Hong Kong: Tiandi, 2016, pp. 156–7.
Line 1: Fu is Faust.
Line 2: In versions of the Faust story, including Goethe's play, Faust looks in a magic mirror and sees Helen of Troy.
Line 11: The phrase 'golden whips and white horses' is from a poem by the Tang Dynasty lyricist Wen Tingyun. Pingkang was the red-light district in Chang'an, China's capital in Tang times. Zheng, who read German and had translated Thomas Mann's *Buddenbrooks* during his second spell in jail in the 1930s (Benton, *Prophets Unarmed*, p. 1065), probably knew that in Mann's *Doktor Faustus*, a retelling of the Faust legend through the life of the composer Adrian Leverkühn, Leverkühn is taken to a brothel where he gets VD. There may also be echoes here of Chen Duxiu's poem 'Before the Lingyin Temple [in Hangzhou]', which has the line 'tavern-streamers flapping in the warm wind of my wild youth.'
Line 12: A line associated with Song Yu, who wrote about beautiful women captivating men.

Dr Faust

16 Unbridled,
Dear Old Mi,
steeped in learning,
loftily striving,
cries: 'Grieve not, for I have
the elixir of youth.'
Fu thinks:
20 elation wanes,
the potion fails,
the spell breaks,
the gloom resumes –
24 is not an old man
better off in bed alone?

木兰花慢

老年浮博士,
又临镜,
自悲伤。
见背脊如弓,
须眉似雪,
神气颓唐。
茫茫,
旧情入梦:
记金鞭白马跃平康。
正值青春年少,
几多窥宋东墙。

Mùlán huā màn

Lǎonián Fú bóshì,
yòu lín jìng,
zì bēishāng.
Jiàn bèijǐ rú gōng,
xūméi sì xuě,
shénqì tuítáng.
Mángmáng,
jiùqíng rù mèng:
Jì jīnbiān báimǎ yuè Píngkāng.
Zhèng zhí qīngchūn niánshào,
jǐ duō kuīsòng-dōngqiáng.

Line 14:   Mi is Mephistopheles.
Line 18:   Goethe's Faust is intrigued by the notion of the immortal soul. Mephistopheles introduces Faust to a witch who concocts a magic elixir to return him to his youth.

56

疏狂,	Shūkuáng,
故友糜郎,	gùyǒu Mí láng,
学深邃,	xué shēnsuì,
求高强。	qiú gāoqiáng.
道:'莫谩伤悲,	Dào: 'Mò mán shāngbēi,
还童返老,	huántóng-fǎnlǎo,
自有仙方。'	zì yǒu xiānfāng.'
思量:	Sīliang:
欢场散尽,	Huānchǎng sàn jǐn,
纵仙方有验亦凄凉。	zòng xiānfāng yǒu yàn yì qīliáng.
况复横生烦恼,	Kuàng fù héngshēng fánnǎo,
不如甘老空床。	bù rú gān lǎo kōng Chuáng.

5.

How the Mighty Fall

In this poem, Zheng in his cell whispers loudly: see how the mighty fall. The poem begins by reminding readers of the rapid collapse of the Qin and the Sui, the shortest-lived of China's main dynasties and the most authoritarian. Ying Zheng, the birth name of Qin Shi Huangdi, founder of the Qin Dynasty (221–206 BCE) and the first emperor of a unified China, and Emperor Yang of the Sui Dynasty (581–618) both behaved like tyrants. The Sui is often likened to the Qin. Mao Zedong explicitly modelled himself, in part, on the first emperor of the Qin, Qin Shi Huangdi, who burned books and buried scholars alive. In a speech in 1958, he said that Qin Shi Huangdi 'buried alive 460 scholars, while we buried 46,000. In suppressing the counterrevolutionaries, did we not kill some counterrevolutionary intellectuals? I once debated with the democrats: You accuse us of acting like Qin Shi Huangdi, but you are wrong; we surpass him one hundred times. You berate us for imitating his dictatorship. We admit it.' While Mao lay dying in 1976, students demonstrating in Tian'anmen Square in Beijing raised the call to 'overthrow Qin Shi Huangdi', meaning Mao and his supporters in the 'Gang of Four'. Zheng composed this poem to the same tune as, and was inspired by, Mao's hubristic 'Snow', written in 1936 and very well known in China after 1949 – Zheng must have read it in prison. ('Snow' is on p. 24 of this volume.)

Zheng's poem repeats a theme, illustrated with terms and phrases drawn from Buddhist and Daoist dialectics and classical writings, that is a constant in his poetry: political power is transient, strength can turn quickly into weakness and weakness into strength. It can be read as a hidden warning to the overweening Mao.

How the Mighty Fall

To the tune of 'Garden in Spring'

In antiquity Ying Qin,
in middle antiquity Yang Sui –
here today, gone tomorrow.
Think of the quelling of the six states, 4
the repelling of the Hu, the drive against the Yue;
the merging of north and south,
the opening of the borderlands.
Earthshaking and all-powerful, 8
they lash the planet –
who dares stand up to them?
But in the twinkling of an eye
war smoke billows 12
from the collapsing beams and pillars.

(continued on next page)

Line 4: The Qin waged wars of unification in the late third century BCE against the other six main states – Han, Zhao, Yan, Wei, Chu, and Qi – within what thus became China.
Line 5: The Yue were non-Han inhabitants of southeastern and southern China, and the Hu of northern China, in ancient times.

Sewing the wedding robes for others,
I hear them talk for hours,
praising the Han and Tang.
I watch the Ying clan build its nest,
the Liu clan take up residence;
Yang planting trees outside the door,
the Li tribe lazing in the shade.
Consider the West,
where Alexander
failed to secure the realm.
Look closer then to now,
where Emperor Na and Kaiser Xi
attest to life's highs and lows
as the sea yields
to mulberry fields
and the trees to seas.

Line 14: This is a famous line that has entered the Chinese language, from the classic poem 'Poor Woman', by the late-ninth-century Tang Dynasty poet Qin Taoyu: Living under a thatch roof, never wearing fragrant silk, / she longs to arrange a marriage, but how could she dare? / Who would know her simple face the loveliest of them all / when we choose for worldliness, not for worth? / Her fingers embroider beyond compare, / but she cannot vie with painted brows; / and year after year she has sewn gold thread / on bridal robes for other girls. The sewing image was often used by ambitious but thwarted officials forced to work for their successful contemporaries, so that *pinnü* (poor woman, as in the poem's title) became practically interchangeable with *pinshi* (impoverished scholar). It is not clear why Zheng quotes the line here, beyond expressing the idea of failure and frustration.
Line 15: The Ying clan is Qin Shi Huangdi's clan, in the Qin Dynasty.
Line 16: Liu Bang founded the Han Dynasty.
Line 17: Yang Jian founded the Sui Dynasty.
Line 18: Li Yuan founded the Tang Dynasty.
Line 22: Zheng says that Alexander the Great 'schemed in vain to set up an imperial group'. Perhaps he means that Alexander, never more than a king by title, failed to prevent the dissolution of the Persian Empire at the hands of his followers after his death in 323 BCE, aged thirty-three, without having designated a successor.
Line 24: Na is the character Zheng uses to transcribe Napoleon, Xi to transcribe Hitler.
Line 28: The source of this metaphor about seas and mulberry fields, an established phrase in Chinese, *cangsang*, was a work titled *Shenxian zhuan* ('Tales of Immortals') by the Eastern Jin Dynasty Daoist scholar and chemist Ge Hong.

沁园春

上古嬴秦,
中古杨隋,
骤兴骤亡。
念削平六国,
拒胡征粤;
混同南北,
辟土开疆。
叱咤风云,
鞭笞寰宇,
并世无人堪比强。
不旋踵,
便烟尘四起,
折柱摧梁。

为人作嫁衣裳。
听国祚绵延歌汉唐。
看嬴氏营巢,
刘家占住;
杨门种树,
李族乘凉。
更看西方,
亚历山大,
枉费心机成帝邦。
殷鉴近,
有拿皇希帝,
说尽沧桑。

Qìnyuán chūn

Shànggǔ Yíng Qín,
zhōnggǔ Yáng Suí,
zhòu xīng zhòu wáng.
Niàn xuēpíng liù guó,
jù Hú zhēng Yuè;
hùntóng nánběi,
pì tǔ kāi jiāng.
Chìzhà fēngyún,
biānchī huányǔ,
bìng shì wúrén kān bǐ qiáng.
Bù xuánzhǒng,
biàn yānchén sìqǐ,
zhé zhù cuī liáng.

Wéi rén zuò jiàyīshang.
Tīng guózuò miányán gē Hàn Táng.
Kàn Yíng shì yíng cháo,
Liú jiā zhàn zhù;
Yáng mén zhòng shù,
Lǐ zú chéngliáng.
Gèng kàn xīfāng,
Yàlìshāndà,
wǎngfèi xīnjī chéng dìbāng.
Yīnjiàn jìn,
yǒu Ná huáng Xī dì,
shuō jìn cāngsāng.

6.

My Native Place

This poem is about Zheng's longing, from his prison on the plains, for his native place in the mountains of southern Fujian. He plays with two images, the chrysanthemum and the crane. The former symbolises the Double Ninth (9 September), which is when Zheng was writing, as well as nobility and strong life; the latter symbolises purity and longevity. On the ninth day of the ninth lunar month, a traditional holiday in China, people eat cake, drink chrysanthemum wine, climb mountains, and appreciate chrysanthemums – late-season bloomers that count as one of the 'four gentlemen' of Chinese art and verse, alongside plum blossom, orchids, and bamboo, and are known as the flower of immortality.

The poem incorporates a phrase associated with the Daoist hero Ding Lingwei, a county magistrate in the Jin Dynasty (266–420) who loved cranes. As an official, Ding was honest and compassionate, opening the state grain barns without permission during a famine, for which he was sentenced to be beheaded. A crane saved him from execution and carried him off into the mountains, where he lived for hundreds of years and himself became a crane. Centuries later, he flew back home, but everything had changed. Back in his village, he perched on a marble column. An archer tried to shoot him, but he flew off singing: 'So many strangers in old places, where are the familiar faces?' Ding Lingwei's story is doubly resonant – with Zheng's plight as an enforced exile and with that of China in the early 1960s, which seems to be when Zheng wrote this poem.

Like Ding after his rescue, Zheng too lived a world away from his birthplace, Zhangping in Fujian. However, as an old man he was invited back there, as a local luminary and honoured guest. He wrote 'A Self-Description at the Age of Ninety' (reproduced in *Prophets Unarmed*, pp. 1108–15) for the town elders, where he declares that Trotsky was right and that there is nothing in his life of which he needs to be ashamed. As for China in the early 1960s, it was in the throes of its worst-ever modern

My Native Place

famine; but the grain barns stayed closed for too long, until officials finally recognized the scale of the crisis.

To the tune of 'Dear Niannu'

West Wind is up, it's Double Ninth,
childhood thoughts come crowding in,
to sadden and delight.
Grass wilts, chrysanthemums crackle into flower.
Respectfully, I take Dad's friends   5
up to the Ming shrine.
How many times
has the temple gate atop the western hills
battled the fierce winds
as the chill streams   10
gush down through the serried peaks?

I left home forty years ago
to live down on the plain,
without a slope in sight.
Do the crysanthemum hedges and the mountain pines still stand?   15
They say the temple wall burned down.
Whistling and swaggering in the mist,
reluctant to forgo
the poetry and wine –
who in the future will preserve our ways?   20
Perched on a millenial stone plinth,
the lonely crane, whose eyes
well up with tears.

Title: Title of a *ci* by Su Shi.
Line 6: This part of the poem is made up of three separate phrases taken from poems by Yang Wanli.
Line 12: Another edition has 'thirty', but forty seems more likely, given the years of Zheng's imprisonment.
Line 13: Zheng swapped the mountains of Fujian for Jiangnan and Shanghai, flatter than a sanded board.
Line 17 A line from a poem by the Qing Dynasty female poet Xue Qiong (dates unknown).
Line 21: The phrase 'thousand-year marble column' is associated with the recalcitrant Daoist Ding Lingwei.

My Native Place

念奴娇

西风重九,
记童年往事,
悲欢交集。
青草枯萎黄菊绽,
杖屦曾陪父执。
明寺门廊,
西山绝顶,
几度当风立。
众峰罗列,
一川寒水流急。

卅载抛撇家门,
平原作客,
无处寻山级。
篱菊山松无恙否?
闻说寺余焦壁。
啸傲烟霞,
流连诗酒,
后辈何人习?
千年华表,
行看孤鹤临泣。

Niànnú jiāo

Xīfēng chóngjiǔ,
jì tóngnián wǎngshì,
bēi huān jiāojí.
Qīngcǎo kūwěi huángjú zhàn,
zhàng jù céng péi fùzhí.
Míngsì ménláng,
xīshān juédǐng,
jǐdù dāng fēng lì.
Zhòng fēng luóliè,
yī chuān hánshuǐ liújí.

Sà zài pāo piē jiāmén,
píngyuán zuòkè,
wú chù xún shān jí.
Líjú shānsōng wúyàng fǒu?
Wén shuō sì yú jiāobì.
Xiào'ào yānxiá,
liúlián shī jiǔ,
hòubèi hérén xí?
Qiānnián huábiǎo,
xíng kàn gūhè línqì.

7.

Fading Beauty

Using the image of a singer's fading beauty and fall from favour, the poet reflects vicariously on his own passage into old age and his political defeat. But the last line, about the Plum Flower Song, suggests that purity has not lost its power, and gives voice to Zheng's integrity and pure heart. This poem, like others in this book, has elements of a *ji* or assemblage, whereby Zheng takes lines or phrases from poems by other poets to express his own feelings. Zheng himself, in his notes from 1996, wrote as follows about the poem:

> In Tang times, [the poet] Xue Feng studied when young to become a *jinshi* and was appointed as an official. However, as an old man, his life was desolate and bleak; one day he was wandering down the road in Chang'an, just as a new *jinshi*[1] was out walking. A street cleaner, seeing this old man walking down the middle of the road, shouted at him: 'Get out of the way, let the new *jinshi* pass.' Xue Feng said: 'Stop nagging. When my grandma was fifteen, she also used to scribble.' In Chang'an slang at the time, that meant 'Good-for-nothing, when my grandmother was young, she too was a dolled-up whore.' Literati who were disappointed in old age often used to compare themselves to prostitutes, it was a fashion at the time, the [Tang poet] Bai Juyi's *Pipa xing* ('Pipa Tune') [written in 816] was a case in point. At first, 'rich young men were competing for her attention, and innumerable rolls of silk were used for just one stage appearance', but now 'ever fewer carriages stopped at her door, and she ended up marrying a merchant.' But the fashion has now passed. After reading *Tang cai zi zhuan* ('Biographies of Talented People in the Tang Dynasty'), I became interested in Xue Feng, so I wrote this *ci*, to give expression to the mood conveyed by local slang in those days.'

---

[1] A successful candidate in the highest imperial examination.

Fading Beauty

To the tune of 'Calling Men of Worth to Service'

At fifteen, languidly
she paints and draws, admiring
her new clothes in the glass,
and her snow-white bust.
5 Eyebrows like young moons,
silk stockings and a filmy gown,
as she sings her graceful song.
In tribute, gifts cascade onto the stage,
to wave after wave of cheers and clapping.

10 My heavy heart!
Where is the fragrance now?
See the white hair, the goatish skin.
I sigh, for now dust raised by the carriages and horses' hooves
no longer chokes the air before her gate –
15 who plucks the pipa now?
Spitefully, the neighbour's daughter mocks her fall from grace –
a youthful beauty,
proud of her looks, a cruel sneer on her face.
I listen to the clear notes of the Plum Flower song.

'To the tune of': The name of a type of *ci*, developed by Jiang Kui.
Line 2: Zheng draws heavily in this poem on Bai Juyi's 'Pipa Tune'. He also quotes lines from a poem by Wang Dingbao.
Line 16: Zheng imagines the jeering of his political rivals and of those out to curry favour with the powerful.
Line 19: The name of a song of the Qiang people, used in a poem by Li Bai, in slightly reconfigured form. The plum tree blossoms in late winter or early spring, and is associated by Li Bai, in exile after the failure of a political rebellion, with coldness and desolation. The plum is also used in traditional poetry to indicate integrity and probity.

征 招

阿婆三五年轻日,
也曾东涂西抹.
莺镜对新装,
露胸肌如雪.
蛾眉弯似月,
试新样缕衣罗袜。
一曲清歌,
缠头无数,
彩声争发.

愁绝!
年芳逝,
到如今空惊麂皮鹤发。
马足与车尘,
叹门前久歇。
琵琶何处拨?
是贫相邻娃调舌。
正妍媚,
且谩骄人,
听《落梅》吹彻。

Zhēng zhāo

Āpó sānwǔ niánqīng rì,
yě céng dōngtú-xīmǒ.
Yīng jìng duì xīnzhuāng,
lù xiōngjī rú xuě.
Éméi wān shì yuè,
sì xīnyàng lǚyī luōwà.
Yī qū qīnggē,
chán tóu wúshù,
cǎi shēng zhēng fā.

Chóu jué!
Nián fāng shì,
dào rújīn kōng jīng jǐpí-hèfà.
Mǎ zú yǔ chē chén,
tàn mén qián jiǔ xiē.
Pípá héchù bō?
Shì pínxiāng lín wá tiào shé.
Zhèng yán mèi,
qiě mán jiāo rén,
tīng 'Luòméi' chuī chè.

8.
Quo Vadis?

The poet populates his poem with characters from the novel *Quo Vadis* by Henryk Sienkiewicz (1846–1926), first published in Polish in 1895.[1] The novel is set in first-century Rome, at the time of Nero, the persecution of Christians and the Great Fire. In it Sienkiewicz, citing the apocryphal Acts of Peter, tell how Peter, fleeing Rome, meets Jesus outside the city:

> The sun appeared over the line of hills; but at once a wonderful vision struck the Apostle's eyes. It seemed to him that the golden circle, instead of rising in the sky, moved down from the heights and was advancing on the road. Peter stopped, and asked,
> 'Seest thou that brightness approaching us?'
> 'I see nothing', replied Nazarius.
> But Peter shaded his eyes with his hand, and said after a while, 'Some figure is coming in the gleam of the sun.' But not the slightest sound of steps reached their ears. It was perfectly still all around.
> Nazarius saw only that the trees were quivering in the distance, as if someone were shaking them, and the light was spreading more broadly over the plain. He looked with wonder at the Apostle.
> 'Rabbi! what ails thee?' cried he, with alarm.
> The pilgrim's staff fell from Peter's hands to the earth; his eyes were looking forward, motionless; his mouth was open; on his face were depicted astonishment, delight, rapture.
> Then he threw himself on his knees, his arms stretched forward; and this cry left his lips,

---

[1] The first Chinese translation, by Xu Xusheng and Qiao Zengqu, inspired by Lu Xun's praise of Sienkiewicz's work in Japanese translation, appeared in 1922. At least forty-one editions have appeared in Chinese or Japanese, including sixteen in China since 2000. (See Marta Tomczak and Krzysztof Iwanek, 'A Polish Classic in Asia', *The Diplomat*, [31 October 2016]). Sienkiewicz won the Nobel Prize for literature in 1905.

Quo Vadis?

'O Christ! O Christ!'

He fell with his face to the earth, as if kissing someone's feet.

The silence continued long; then were heard the words of the aged man, broken by sobs,

'*Quo vadis, Domine?*'

Nazarius did not hear the answer; but to Peter's ears came a sad and sweet voice, which said,

'If thou desert my people, I am going to Rome to be crucified a second time.'

The Apostle lay on the ground, his face in the dust, without motion or speech. It seemed to Nazarius that he had fainted or was dead; but he rose at last, seized the staff with trembling hands, and turned without a word toward the seven hills of the city.

The boy, seeing this, repeated as an echo,

'*Quo vadis, Domine?*'

'To Rome', said the Apostle, in a low voice.[2]

What did *Quo Vadis* mean for Zheng? The cruelty and dissipation of Nero's court and Nero's dictatorship had many obvious parallels with the regime that was oppressing the Chinese people and keeping Zheng in jail, but the metaphor also had a personal meaning for Zheng. When the Chinese Trotskyists finally realised, sometime in 1948, that the Communists were on the brink of victory, Zheng and his Trotskyist party resolved to stay in China to fight for their beliefs, and to send Wang Fanxi alone to Hong Kong, to coordinate their activities from a supposedly 'safe' place. (Their rivals in the other Chinese Trotskyist organisation, under Peng Shuzhi, opted to leave China.) On more than one occasion, Wang used religious imagery to describe Zheng's years in prison, and others have described both Wang and Zheng as saintly. Wang compared Zheng's attitude while awaiting a probable death sentence under Chiang Kai-shek in 1931 to that of 'a Buddhist monk who had attained the Way, and who knew beforehand the date of his achievement of nirvana'. When, in 1949, Zheng accepted his comrades' decision that he stay in China rather than go abroad, Wang likened him to St Peter:

---

2   Henryk Sienkiewicz, *Quo Vadis*, Booklassic, 2016, no pagination.

Quo Vadis?

Even if we leave aside Zheng Chaolin's other strengths, his Peter-like spirit of martyrdom alone will ensure him a lasting place in the history of the Revolution. Our dilemma was similar in many ways to that of the early Christians under Nero – should we stay in the capital or flee to a safe place? Some approached the question from the point of view of their own fate, others from the point of view of the future of the organization as a whole; but Zheng Chaolin did not wait for a voice from the heavens to ask '*Quo vadis?*': his mind was made up from the very outset.[3]

Wang himself, being 'no deserter', admitted that he too 'was moved by the spirit of St Peter', and retreated to his 'safe place' only with extreme reluctance. But Wang was deported almost immediately to Macau. There, he was isolated and unable to carry out the mission with which his party had entrusted him. Zheng, in prison, was not in contact with Wang in 1957, so either the two men adopted the St Peter metaphor of self-sacrifice for the cause independently of one another, or they had already talked about it before Wang's departure for Hong Kong in 1949.

---

3 Benton, *Prophets Unarmed*, pp. 572–3.

On Reading [Henryk] Sienkiewicz's *Quo Vadis* (third of six poems)

To the tune of 'Plucking Mulberry Leaves'

Martial youth captured by beauty so great
that it topples the state – it's love at first sight.
Again and again love's dream comes under siege,
but neither plots nor violence bear fruit.　　　　　　　　　　4

The fair young girl, a follower of Christ,
meets spite with kindness,
guides the headstrong back onto the righteous path,
and in the end achieves reunion and eternal life.　　　　　　8

*

A tyrant's evil deeds reap endless infamy –
matricide, parricide,
and shameless dissipation,
under a courtly veneer of singing, dancing, and fine writing.　　12

Seeking poetic inspiration, Nero beholds Rome burn.
A pusillanimous and craven man,
he shifts the blame
for the innocents' slaughter onto others.　　　　　　　　　　16

*

Line 2 ('state'):　In this line, Zheng borrows a phrase from Chapter 67 of the biographies section of the *Book of Han*, where the historian Ban Gu (32–92) tells how Yannian, the brother of Consort Li, concubine to Emperor Wu of Han, had sung of his sister: 'There is a beauty in the north who stands out among the generations. One look will topple the city's men, another the country's men. Cities and countries toppled because of such a beautiful woman may never happen again!'
Line 2 ('sight'):　*Quo Vadis* tells the story of the love between a young Christian woman, Lycia, and Marcus Vinicius, a Roman patrician and military commander.
Line 3:　A line from a *cai sangzi* by Yan Shu.
Line 6:　A line that draws on a passage in Confucius's *Analects* that counsels 'meeting injury with justice and kindness with kindness'.
Line 16:　Nero blames the Christians.

On Reading [Henryk] Sienkiewicz's Quo Vadis

Peter escapes the closing net.
White-haired, dishevelled, off he slips
into the badlands – where the Lord
20   steps from a jade-green cloud.

Apostle, awestruck, bowing low: '*Quo vadis?*'
Jesus: 'Flee the nest of perils,
tend to yourself, my child,
24   and point the way towards a new and better life.'

采桑子（六首存三）   Cǎi sāngzi: dú Xiǎnkèwēizhī
                             (Liù shǒu cún sān)

读显克微支《你往何处去？》   'Nǐ wǎng héchù qù?'

少年英武逢倾国，   Shàonián yīngwǔ féng qīngguó,
一见钟情，   yījiàn-zhōngqíng,
好梦频惊，   hǎomèng pín jīng,
暴力阴谋两不成。   bàolì yīnmóu liǎng bùchéng.

佳人笃信耶稣教，   Jiārén dǔxìn Yēsū jiào,
德报侵凌，   dé bào qīnlíng,
感化顽冥，   gǎnhuà wán míng,
终得团圆向永生。   zhōng dé tuányuán xiàng yǒngshēng.

                   *   *

Line 18:   A line from a *cai sangzi* by Chen Yuyi.
Line 20:   The image and vocabulary correspond closely to a verse by Ye Xianzu.

On Reading [Henryk] Sienkiewicz's Quo Vadis

暴君恶迹传千古，
弑母屠亲，
无耻荒淫，
解舞能歌复擅文。

为寻诗思烧罗马，
怯懦心魂，
嫁祸他人，
残杀无辜亦殒身。

*

使徒仓卒逃罗网，
白发飘萧，
来至荒郊，
忽见人神降碧霄。

恭身下拜询'何处？'
云：'去危巢，
自牧儿曹，
拼送新生命一条。'

Bàojūn èjī chuán qiāngǔ,
shì mǔ tú qīn,
wúchǐ huāngyín,
jiě wǔ néng gē fù shàn wén.

Wei xún shīsī shāo Luómǎ,
qiènuò xīnhún,
jià huò tārén,
cánshā wúgū yì yǔn shēn.

*

Shǐtú cāngcù táo luówǎng,
báifà piāo xiāo,
lái zhì huāngjiāo,
hū jiàn rén shén jiàng bìxiāo.

Gong shēn xià bài xún 'Héchù?'
Yún:'Qù wēi cháo,
zì mù ercáo,
pīn sòng xīn shēngmìng yī tiáo.'

9.

My Tiny Cell

Zheng was born with the century, so this poem was written at the start of the 1960s, when China was starving and on its knees after the failure of the Great Leap Forward. Zheng must have realised the irony of his access to food and warmth. In this poem, he puts a brave face on his situation.

To the tune of 'Thinking of an Aristocrat'

I pace around my tiny cell, alert, bright-eyed,
my books, though few, enough to keep me occupied.
I've rice to fill my belly, clothes to keep me warm, a pen to scribble with,
thoughts stretching endlessly.
What more could an ailing, waning man of sixty want?

忆王孙

盘旋斗室炯双眸，
书报无多足解愁，
饭饱衣温弄笔头。
思悠悠，
六十衰翁何所求。

Yì wángsūn

Pánxuán dǒushì jiǒng shuāngmóu,
shūbào wú duō zú jiěchóu,
fàn bǎo yī wēn nòng bǐtóu.
Sī yōuyōu,
liùshí shuāiwēng hé suǒ qiú.

'To the tune of':   The name of a *ci* by Li Zhongyuan.

10.
Training Monkeys

Here, the poet has fun at the expense of his jailers in the Communist leadership and also at his own expense. He gives the background to his poem in a footnote: 'Zhuangzi [a Daoist sage in the late Warring States period (476–221 BCE)] said, "The Master lives in the mountain forest and eats chestnuts." He also said, "The monkey trainer gives [the monkeys] chestnuts."' Zhuangzi himself explained his point as follows:

> To exhaust one's spiritual intelligence by seeking to unify things without knowing they are identical is called 'three in the morning'. Why so? A monkey keeper gave the monkeys chestnuts. He said: 'I'll give you three in the morning and four at night.' The monkeys were angry. The trainer said: 'Alright, I'll give you four in the morning and three at night.' The monkeys were now happy. Without changing either the name or the reality of the amount, he accommodated the monkeys' feelings. He reconciled right and wrong, and stood still at the centre of the celestial wheel. This is called going in both directions at once.

In Zheng's poem, the monkey trainer is Bolshevism (in its Stalinist garb, which Zheng personally witnessed during his time in Moscow in the early to mid 1920s and about which he wrote extensively) and Maoism: first Stalin, and then Mao, fooled the people by juggling and fabricating statistics and telling outright lies. But Zheng is also reproaching himself for swallowing and helping to spread those lies after his return to China from Moscow in 1924, right up to his Trotskyist conversion in 1928. The poet 'hides his status' both as a Trotskyist and as Zheng Chaolin, the man who, as an early leader of the CCP, knew its dirty secrets, like the immortal in the poem who had lived through all the dynasties.

Training Monkeys

To the tune of 'Dreaming of Jiangnan'

As a young man and would-be star,
originally I aimed to storm the sky.
First I learned the art of training monkeys.
Then I assuaged their monkey feelings
with four chestnuts at first light and three at night.

Hiding my status,
I love to hum this well-turned phrase:
'Most of those mentioned in these annals were my friends,
but only half the facts are true.'
With whom to share this saw?

梦 江 南	Mèng Jiāngnán
年少日，	Niánshào rì,
豪气欲凌云。	háoqì yù língyún.
曾学狙公驯养术，	Céng xué jūgōng xúnyǎng shù,
亦曾随众作狙群，	yì céng suí zhòng zuò jūqún,
芧果四三分。	xù guǒ sìsān fēn.
身名隐，	Shēn míng yǐn,
佳名爱沉吟：	jiāmíng ài chényín:
'青史古人多故友，	'Qīngshǐ gǔrén duō gùyǒu,
传中事实半非真。'	chuán zhōng shìshí bàn fēizhēn.'
此意共谁论！	Cǐ yì gòng shéi lùn!

'To the tune of': A *ci* by Qu Dajun.
Line 9: [Note by Zheng:] 'These lines are from a poem by Qu Yuan [an alias of Yu Yue, a prominent late-Qing official and an expert in philology and textual studies, 1821–1907]. The poem describes an immortal who attained the Way and lived through the Tang, Song, Yuan, and Ming Dynasties. Half of the great ministers of those times were the immortal's friends. He came to realise that many of the facts as reported in the annals did not accord with his own experience. Yu Yue said in his novel *Seven Heroes and Five Gallants* that the novel is not the same as historical fact. "The achievements of the dynasties are always new, the Tang, Song, Yuan, and Ming all have their own experiences. Most of those mentioned in the annals were my friends, but only half the facts are true." His aim was to alert his reader to to the true nature of facts.' Zheng has the same aim, to alert readers to the true facts about the Chinese Communist Party, through whose history he had lived.

11.

Commemorating Li Yu

This poem is written to the tune of a *ci* by Li Yu (937–978), the last ruler of the Southern Tang Kingdom during the Five Dynasties and Ten Kingdoms period, who is also the poem's subject. After years of trying to appease the stronger Song Dynasty, Li Yu had been captured in 976 by Song armies that annexed his kingdom. He lived under the Song as a prisoner, and was eventually poisoned. An accomplished scholar and poet, he was known as the 'first true master' of the *ci*. Zheng laments Li Yu's tragic fate – his birth into a royal family, where even his great learning and poetic genius could not prevent his eventual murder at the hands of his political enemies. Like Li, Zheng was a political prisoner in Jiangnan as well as a poet and a scholar. At the time of writing this *ci,* no one would have ruled out his ending up in the same way as Li.

The second verse is harder to interpret. Perhaps Zheng imagined himself, on reaching prison in Jiangnan, wandering in a temple dedicated to Li Yu and anxiously tiptoeing away, in order not to pile new troubles onto the sleeping Li Yu. In 1996 he wrote as follows about this poem:

> According to a literary sketch, after [Emperor Taizu of Song, whose personal name was] Zhao Kuangyin, destroyed the Southern Tang he said: 'I destroyed the Southern Tang and seized Li Yu not because the Southern Tang had committed any offence but because I didn't want others putting up beds in my bedroom and disturbing my sleep with their snores.' Zhao was a soldier without airs and graces and spoke the truth; a calculating Emperor, good at propaganda, wouldn't have said that but would instead have set out the Southern Tang and its ruler's 'Ten Great Crimes'[1] and explained that he therefore had good cause to

---

[1] This is the sort of thing the Maoists did. For example, in 1967 their Cultural Revolutionary Group exposed the 'Ten Great Crimes of the Counter-Revolutionary Revisionist Bo Yibo'.

go to war, and that he had destroyed this separatist regime in the interests of the people of the entire nation. When I read Li Yu's *ci* in prison, I thought it surpassed Northern Song poetry, and when I read the note, I wrote this *ci* to the tune of Li Yu's 'Lady Yu.'

To the tune of 'Lady Yu'

Commemorating Li Chongguang

Silent and alone, up at the sickle moon I stare –
how to repair a broken heart?
Daily tears record the passing years,
trapped as I am within the royal court.

Jiangnan – how I recall the dangerous city's fall,
the country innocent and free from blame.
Shedding tears, out through the palace wall I slip,
to let the sleeping king sleep on in a united realm.

'To the tune of': Lady Yu was a royal concubine.
Title: Li Yu's courtesy name.
Line 1: This line is modeled in part on the first line of one of Li Yu's best-known *ci*, 'Alone up the Western Tower', written after his capture. As translated by Chan Hong-mo, the line runs: 'Alone to silence, up the western tower, I myself bestow. Like silver curtain hook, so does the moon glow.'
Line 4: Zheng pities Li Yu.
Line 5: Perhaps a reference to the fall to the Song Dynasty of Li Yu's capital, Nanjing.

Commemorating Li Chongguang

虞 美 人•哀李重光

无言独对如钩月,
争解离肠结!
泪珠日夕洗年华,
应恨托身偏在帝王家.

江南忆昔危城坠,
故国原无罪,
仓皇辞庙最凄然,
只为妨他一统碍他眠。

Yú měirén: Āi Lǐ Chóngguāng

Wúyán dúduì rúgōu yuè,
zhēng jiě lícháng jié!
Lèizhū rìxī xǐ niánhuá,
yīng hèn tuōshēn piānzài dìwáng jiā.

Jiāngnán yìxī wēichéng zhuì,
gùguó yuán wúzuì,
cānghuáng címiào zuì qīrán,
zhǐ wèi fáng tā yītǒng ài tā mián.

12.

Boat Tour

Zheng was arrested for the first time in 1929 and jailed for forty days. Here, he describes his journey to prison for the second time under Chiang Kai-shek, in 1931. He recalls his boat 'tour' along the Grand Canal, on his way through an exquisite waterscape to possible execution in the 'twin heavens' of Suzhou and Hangzhou. Another prisoner-poet on such a journey might have quaked before the tests and terrors ahead, or struck heroic poses, or made grandly optimistic or pessimistic pronouncements about the future of humanity; but Zheng lazily and sensuously delights in the beautiful scenes of Jiangnan's 'land of rice and fish', distracted only by thoughts of food and the prospect of a future proper tour, after the water shield has come into season and the soup is ready. His thoughts turn not to modern-day revolution but to an exiled fourth-century writer and epicure serving as an official in the north, so attached to water-shield soup and the other delicacies for which his birthplace is renowned that he abandons his career to hurry back south. Zheng's nonchalance in the face of death mirrors that of his hero and mentor Chen Duxiu, photographed grinning cheekily and arrogantly alongside his dazed and worried-looking comrade Peng Shuzhi, while the two were on their way to their trial in Nanjing in 1932, not long after Zheng's prison journey.[1]

To the tune of 'Catching Fish in Your Hands'

Even if I come
back to the Earth in ages hence,
Jiangnan will still be beautiful.

---

1   Gregor Benton, 'Zhang's Hat on Li's Head: A Chronic Case of Quid Pro Quo in the History Books', *China Quarterly* (1991), pp. 364–6.
'To the tune of':   A *ci* by Xin Qiji.
Line 3:   The region south of the Yangtze River, known as *yumi zhi xiang*, 'the land of fish and rice.'

Boat Tour

When young, I marvelled at Suzhou and Hangzhou,
and likened them to Heaven.
On my way to jail,
in clanking chains,
I sailed between these cities.
The Grand Canal was matchless.
I recall
we were escorted by a gunboat,
prisoners in thrall,
as our vessel glided through Lake Tai.

At the Songling Road,
I see the long bridge span
the flow, shimmering among the hills,
and remember how Zhang Han
came suddenly to think
at the rising of the autumn wind
of the taste of water shield.
Water shield blooms in May and June,
but now it is still spring
so to my great regret
I will miss its tasty coils below the water's face.
But I will imagine in my dreams
an autumn boat tour to this place,

to drink its soup, flavoured with salt and soybean sauce.

Line 4: Suzhou and Hangzhou, in Jiangnan, are among China's most beautiful cities. Hence the saying 'Above is Heaven, below are Suzhou and Hangzhou.'
Line 20: Water shield is an edible aquatic plant that makes a nutritious soup. It grows from the end of April to the beginning of September, and flourishes in the lakes, rivers, and canals of Suzhou's Wujiang district, the 'water paradise' that the Grand Canal once crossed. Zhang Han, a man of letters in the Western Jin Dynasty (265–316) and a native of the south, longed for water-shield soup while serving as an official in Luoyang in the north of China, to the point where he resigned his post and returned home. According to the *Shishuo xinyu* ('A New Account of Tales of the World'), a book of anecdotes and character sketches of several hundred writers, musicians and painters compiled by Liu Yiqing in the Liu Song Dynasty (420–479), Zhang Han was reminded of the soup by the sudden rising of the autumn wind, which would have signaled the passing of its season.
Line 21: Second month of spring.

Boat Tour

摸鱼儿

纵多回人间换世,
江南依旧佳丽。
少时羡慕苏杭好,
说与天堂相似。
曾系寄,
带铁索锒铛,
共步苏杭市。
运河景美,
忆炮艇护航,
囚徒押解,
船过太湖外。

松陵路,
亲见长桥横水,
波光山影明翠。
追思张翰秋风兴,
顿忆蓴羹滋味。
生此地,
惜时值中春,
未见琼丝缀。
相思梦里,
愿一舸秋遊,
豉盐拌菜,
数箸且尝试。

Mō yú'er

Zòng duōhuí rénjiān huànshì,
Jiāngnán yījiù jiālì.
Shàoshí xiànmù Sū Háng hǎo,
shuō yǔ tiāntáng xiāngsì.
Céng xì jì,
dài tiěsuǒ lángdāng,
gòng bù Sū Háng shì.
Yùnhé jǐng měi,
yì pàotǐng hùháng,
qiútú yājiè,
chuán guò Tàihú wài.

Sōnglíng lù,
qīn jiàn cháng qiáo héng shuǐ,
bōguāng shānyǐng míng cuì.
Zhuīsī Zhāng Hàn qiūfēng xìng,
dùn yì chúngēng zīwèi.
Shēng cǐ dì,
xī shí zhí zhōngchūn,
wèijiàn qióngsī zhuì.
Xiāngsī mènglǐ,
yuàn yīgě qiūyóu,
shìyán bàn cài,
shù zhù qiě chángshì.

13.

Blind Man on a Blind Horse

According to Zheng's 1996 notes, this poem was written in October 1962, at the time of the Cuban crisis. Zheng wrote:

> I read *Liberation Daily* every day. The news became daily more frightening. War would be catastrophic. Could the USSR stand firm? If not, it would lose face. Later, Mao mocked Khrushchev for backing down, but Khrushchev's loss of face was a small thing compared with the need to avoid nuclear war. At the time, I was expecting to be taken out at any moment and shot, so I didn't want to seem panic-stricken and even less to appear to be begging for mercy. During the Incident, I understood more clearly than ever that an individual's living or dying is a trivial thing. I decided to write a poem: 'Prepare to be shocked: / dark clouds collect, / mountains and plains / slide into the sea!' Afterwards, the crisis was resolved and people no longer remembered what I had been talking about.

At another level, the poem can be read as Zheng's attack from behind prison bars on Mao's criminal mismanagement of the Chinese economy in the late 1950s and early 1960s. In a footnote to the poem explaining the language game Huan, Yin and Gu played in the fourth or fifth century, Zheng mentions that the players hid references to their own names in the epigrams they invented. This suggests that Zheng's use in the poem of the character for Mao, in its original meaning of 'hair' ('it scarcely sets his hair on end'), was perhaps no coincidence but a case in point. The footnote said:

> Facing great danger without realising it. From Liu Yiqing's *Shishuo xinyu*, Book XXV, *Paidiao* ('A New Account of the Tales of the World: Taunting and Teasing') [Liu Yiqing (403–444) was a writer of the Liu Song Dynasty (420–479) during the Southern and Northern Dynasties

Blind Man on a Blind Horse

period]. According to Part 61 of *Paidiao* ... Gu Kaizhi [a celebrated painter in Nanjing, 344–406] said: 'The plains have been burned to a cinder.' Huan Xuan [a Jin Dynasty warlord, 369–404] said: 'White cloth is wrapped around the coffin and streamers have been attached.' Yin Zhongkan [a military man, ?-399] said: 'Fish belong in the deep, birds in the sky.' ... Huan said: 'Washing rice at the point of a spear, boiling rice at the point of a sword.' Yin said: 'A hundred-year-old man climbing dead branches.' Gu said: 'Laying the baby on the well-pulley.' One of Yin's generals present at the meeting said: 'A blind man riding a blind horse, a deep pool.' Yin said: 'How terrifying', for he was blind in one eye. Huan, Yin, and Gu were playing a game of witticisms about dangerous situations. Each composed a sentence containing a hidden reference to his own name, or a homophone or synonym of it.

To the tune of 'Eight Beats of a Ganzhou Song'

What is the greatest wonder of the world?
Breadth of mind, so people say.
Consider: 'A blind man leaps without a moment's thought
onto the back of a blind horse
5   and plunges in the black of night
into a deep pool.'
That is surely dangerous?
But it scarcely set his hair on end.
The man drowns and the horse drowns too –
10   but he remains alone in the dark, aloof.

'To the tune of': By Wu Wenying.
Line 8:   Mao ('hair') retains his composure while everything around him is collapsing.
Line 9:   The state and the people are overwhelmed.
Line 10: Can this be understood as a reference to Mao's seeming indifference to the catastrophe of the Great Leap Forward? The reader is reminded of Mao's later self-description, in an interview with Edgar Snow in 1970, as 'a lonely monk walking the world with a leaky umbrella'.

A runaway train
and a drunken driver –
expect havoc!
Or a ship in a storm at sea
and a demented helmsman. 15
Think of the thousand passengers –
should they not also have their say?
Prepare for a shock:
dark clouds gather,
the Divine Land 20
will slide into the sea.

八声甘州   Bā shēng gānzhōu

问世间何事最堪惊?   Wèn shìjiān héshì zuì kān jīng?
名言记胸襟。   Míngyán jì xiōngjīn.
道:'盲人乘兴   Dào: 'Mángrén chéngxìng,
驰驱瞎马,   chíqū xiāmǎ,
夜半临深.'   yèbàn lín shēn.'
此境诚然凶险,   Cǐ jìng chéngrán xiōngxiǎn,
未令骨毛森。   wèi lìng gǔ máo sēn.
人马池中死,   Rén mǎ chí zhōng sǐ,
犹是孤身。   yóu shì gūshēn.

何似列车疾驶,   Hé sì lièchē jíshǐ,
值司机沉醉,   zhí sījī chénzuì,
风雨交侵?   fēngyǔ jiāo qīn?
更海船冲浪,   Gèng hǎichuán chōnglàng,
舵手发狂心?   duòshǒu fākuáng xīn?
念数千车船乘客,   Niàn shù qiān chēchuán chéngkè,
又不如黎庶费沉吟。   yòu bùrú líshù fèi chényín.
惊心是: Jīng xīn shì:
黑云密布,   Hēiyún mìbù,
陵陆将沉!   línglù jiāng chén!

Line 20: This line is modelled on one from Liu Yiqing's *Shishuo xinyu*: 'Causing the Divine Land to plunge into ruin for a century.'

14.

The Earth Turns

In the depths of winter, the poet gets a glimpse of spring, and dreams of love.

> To the tune of 'Young Master An'
>
> The Earth turns,
> the ice melts at the corner of the vacant lot.
> A loose tooth stops me chewing –
> 4   I need to see a nurse.
> Winter has come, time now to hibernate. What can I do but sigh?
> My cellmates – all old men,
> eyes gone to pot, limbs maimed and shot,
> 8   bent-backed, grieved.
>
> The clinic's packed.
> In the dispensary all at once I spot
> a group of juvenile offenders,
> 12   laughing, larking about,
> as if on an outing.
> Pencilled brows and slender waists
> flash before my eyes,
> 16   Du Liniang's ailing heart
> heightened her tender charm.
> Touched by a spring breeze,
> my pure heart warms.

'To the tune of':   A *ci* by Liu Yong.
Line 16: Du Liniang is the heroine of *The Peony Pavilion*, a play by Tang Xianzu (1550–1616). Du meets a dream lover while asleep. She wastes away and dies, but is brought back to life.

安公子

大地生机转,
坚冰融化空场畔。
一齿动摇妨咀嚼,
赴狱中医院。
一冬来蛰处心悽惋,
结芳邻只有高年伴。
更剩目残肢,
曲背弯腰愁惨。

候诊厅堂满,
众中忽见少年犯。
两两三三相戏谑,
似书场宾馆。
又瞥见捧心颦黛纤腰软,
杜丽娘病态添娇艳。
觉一颗冰心,
宛被春风吹暖。

Ān gōngzǐ

Dàdì shēngjī zhuǎn,
jiānbīng rónghuà kōngchǎng pàn.
Yī chǐ dòngyáo fáng jǔjué,
fù yùzhōng yīyuàn.
Yī dōng lái zhéchǔ xīn qīwǎn,
jié fānglín zhǐyǒu gāo nián bàn.
Gèng shèngmù cánzhī,
qūbèi wānyāo chóucǎn.

Hòuzhěn tīngtáng mǎn,
zhòng zhōng hū jiàn shàoniánfàn.
Liǎngliǎng sānsān xiàng xìxuè,
shì shūchǎng bīnguǎn.
Yòu piējiàn pěngxīn-píndài xiānyāo ruǎn,
Dù Lìniáng bìngtài tiān jiāoyàn.
Jué yīkē bīngxīn,
wǎn bèi chūnfēng chuīnuǎn.

15.

Dreamtime

This poem draws on the *Da zhao* ('The Great Summons'), a poem from the *Chu ci* (translated by David Hawkes as *The Songs of the South*) attributed to Qu Yuan (c. 340–278 BCE) and Jing Cuo (late Warring States period). In the notes to his translation of the *Da zhao*,[1] Hawkes shows how its evocation of mythical beasts symbolises the dangers threatening the souls of the dead, while the promise of sensuous delights is meant to tempt the dead soul back to life, as part of shamanic rites. Zheng mentions dangers and hints at sensual pleasures in the poem, which resonates with shamanic practice and intimates Zheng's own spiritual death in prison and his faint hope of resurrection.

Zheng explained in notes written in 1996 the circumstances in which the poem was written in 1965, the year before the start of the Cultural Revolution, and how they shaped its structure. Zheng was in solitary confinement at the time and excluded from joining study sessions, though he was not exempted from manual labour. He had previously been assigned to the Trotskyist manual-labour team, but since his banning from its study sessions, the other Trotskyists were afraid to talk with him. They treated him as an enemy – and some really did see him as one, because of his refusal to admit guilt and to join in the denunciations of the Trotskyists and Chen Duxiu, while others only pretended. The experience depressed him, but sympathy came from an unexpected quarter – that of some non-Trotskyists, whose generosity and open-mindedness surprised and deeply moved him, an episode in his prison life that he described as dreamtime, because it was so precious and remarkable. He could no longer remember at the time of writing his explanation why he had been sent to do manual labour with a group of non-Trotskyist prisoners, but he recalled

---

[1] David Hawkes, *The Songs of the South: An Ancient Chinese Anthology of Poems by Qu Yuan and Other Poets*, Harmondsworth: Penguin Books, 1985.

Dreamtime

that they surprised him by asking questions. He was also surprised to find that none treated him as an enemy. 'Naturally, I couldn't use the opportunity to make propaganda for Trotskyism among them,' he said in 1996, 'but it did a lot for my morale.'

However, the episode was short-lived, and within days he was transferred back to the Trotskyists. That is when he composed this poem. He explained that in it, 'waketime' was the time he spent with the uncommunicative Trotskyist prisoners, 'dreamtime' his brief experience with the other group. In the poem, waketime and dreamtime alternate almost line by line. Lines 1, 3, 6, 8 and 10 are waketime and lines 2, 4–5, 7 and 9 are dreamtime. In lines 6 and 7, white jade (a symbol of innocence) represents Zheng's refusal to join other Trotskyists in admitting guilt, and Zheng hints at their blaming and ostracising him. Zheng's comment that 'If I didn't explain the facts that led me to make this poem, no one would be able to understand its real meaning' was no exaggeration. The final line, where he awakes from dreamtime back into waketime, expresses his unswerving determination to stand by his cause, despite his comrades' real or feigned desertion of it.

To the tune of 'Crushing the Enemy Positions'

1. Waketime among the bare hills and wild streams,
2. dreamtime among the willows and bright blooms of early spring.
3. Brambles as far as the eye can see choke off the ancient path;
4. I hear the bright notes of a bamboo flute,
5. the light steps of heavenly women dancing.

(continued on the next page)

'To the tune of':   A *ci* by Xin Qiji.
Line 2:   The first two lines draw on a poem by Lu You.
Line 3:   Old principles and methods.

Dreamtime

6. Faults on white jade are difficult to miss –
7. sympathy is always hard to buy.
8. The *hui* and the spurting turtle dwell within pure land;
9. beautiful women with bright eyes and white teeth, born of an illusion.
10. Waking, I resume my lonely stand.

破阵子　　　　　　　　　Pò zhènzǐ

醒日山穷水恶，　　　　　Xǐng rì shānqióng-shuǐ'è,
梦时柳暗花明。　　　　　mèng shí liǔ'àn-huāmíng.
触目荆榛迷古道；　　　　Chùmù-jīngzhēn mí gǔdào;
入耳笙箫伴曲声，　　　　rù'ěr shēngxiāo bàn qǔshēng,
天仙舞态轻。　　　　　　tiānxiān wǔ tài qīng.

白璧易招谤诽，　　　　　Báibì yì zhāo bàngfěi,
千金难买同情。　　　　　qiānjīn-nánmǎi tóngqíng.
雄虺短狐真境出　　　　　Xiónghuī duǎnhú zhēnjìng chū;
皓齿明眸幻界生。　　　　hàochǐ-míngmóu huànjiè shēng.
觉来仍独行。　　　　　　Juélái réng dúxíng.

Line 8: These animals are mentioned in the *Da zhao*. The *hui* is a mythical snake, while the animal called a 'short fox' in the *Chu ci* is defined in different ways by different Chinese and non-Chinese commentators. Our translation draws on commentary by David Hawkes and the Scottish sinologist James Legge (1815–1897). According to Hawkes, *The Songs of the South* tell of the shamanic resurrection of a seemingly dead soul beset by dangers and tempted to return to life by the promise of sensual pleasures (Hawkes, *Songs of the South,* pp. 219–22). Legge, citing the *Shuo wen*, a second-century Chinese dictionary, defines the *hui*, otherwise known as a mythological poisonous snake, as a member of the 'short fox' family, as too is the *gui* or archer turtle, which sends jets of sand over people or water over their shadows, killing them. (These animals are mentioned in Wolfram Eberhard, *The Local Cultures of South and East China,* Leiden: Brill, 1968, p. 194.) The pure land is the land of the Daoist immortals.

Line 9: A classical phrase from the poem *Ai jiangtou* ('Grieving by the river') by Du Fu.

16.

Suzhou Gardens (1)

This and the next poem form a pair that can be read together. They exemplify Zheng's high artistic sensibility, and can be read literally, even though they have an ulterior meaning. Did Zheng visit the Suzhou gardens, or is he imagining it? Perhaps he visited Suzhou while in Shanghai, where he lived for several years in unconnected periods in the 1920s, 1930s and 1940s.

To the tune of 'Numerous Small Mountains'

I vividly recall past outings,
dreaming an infinitude of incarnations
amid the plants and flowers of Suzhou's gardens.
I was a prisoner –
bright of eye with gleaming teeth,
but now no longer so.

My hair now white and sparse,
I follow the crowds around the ancient yards
and climb the hills.
I remember best a screech of gulls
and, gracefully erect,
the pagoda's shadow, rippling on the lake.

'To the tune of': A *ci* by Jiang Kui.
Line 2: A line from a poem by Gong Zizhen.
Line 6: This line draws on lines by Du Fu and Xin Qiji. Its exact meaning is unclear. The phrase 'bright of eye with gleaming teeth' usually refers to beautiful women, but here the sentence seems to suggest that it is a reference to his own younger self in Suzhou. Alternatively, it may mean that he was a prisoner without female company.
Line 12: Figuring life's impermanence and ups and downs – a constant image in Zheng's poetry.

Suzhou Gardens (1)

小重山令

历历从头数昔游。
三生花草梦,
在苏州。
当年曾此作羁囚。
明眸远,
皓齿去悠悠。

重至鬓霜稠。
从群游旧苑,
上高丘。
就中最忆一盟鸥,
亭亭立,
塔影共沉浮。

Xiǎo chóngshān lìng

Lìlì cóngtóu shù xī yóu.
Sānshēng huācǎo mèng,
zài Sūzhōu.
Dāngnián céng cǐ zuò jīqiú.
Míngmóu yuǎn,
hàochǐ qù yōuyōu.

Chóng zhì bìn shuāng chóu.
Cóng qún yóu jiùyuàn,
shàng gāoqiū.
Jiù zhōng zuì yì yī méngōu,
tíngtíng lì,
tǎyǐng gòng chénfú.

17.

Suzhou Gardens (2)

Zheng was behind bars in Suzhou in the 1930s, but as the introduction to the previous poem suggests, it seems possible that at some point he visited the gardens. Here he uses the Taoyuan or Peach Orchard as an ironic contrast to his Suzhou prison.

To the tune of 'Remembering Times Past in the Peach Orchard'

Spring has arrived, it's less cold now.
But frosts still fall and winds from the north still sough,
killing the young spring breeze, flattening
the grass that struggles to awake.

Today, I think back on past things and happenings
as winter starts to lose its chill.
How I long to climb the Tiger Hill,
where the Yunyan Tower casts its shade.

桃源忆故　　　　　　　Táoyuán yì gù

立春日后无多冷，　　　Lìchūn rìhòu wú duō lěng,
西北霜飙犹劲，　　　　xīběi shuāng biāo yóu jìng,
欺压春风初阵，　　　　qīyā chūnfēng chū zhèn,
草梦微微醒。　　　　　cǎo mèng wéiwéi xǐng.

多年旧事今重省，　　　Duōnián jiùshì jīn chóng xǐng,
犹记残寒岁尽，　　　　yóu jì cánhán suì jǐn,
忽动虎丘游兴，　　　　hū dòng Hǔqiū yóuxìng,
宝塔亭亭影。　　　　　Bǎotǎ tíngtíng yǐng.

'To the tune of':　The title of a *ci* by Qin Guan.
Line 5:　Echoing parts of a line of a *ci* by Liu Yong.
Line 7:　In Suzhou.
Line 8:　A line from a *ci* by Gao Guoding.

18.

Our Grandchildren's Grandchildren

Zheng Chaolin is entertained by a view of life on Earth in 2107 as imagined by two Soviet science-fiction writers in 1959. Perhaps he was asked to review the novel with an eye to possible translation. Some Soviet literary and theoretical works were made available in China from 1960 to 1964, to facilitate ideological debate between the two countries.

To the tune of 'The Melody of Tranquillity'

On Reading the Soviet Novel
Our Grandchildren's Grandchildren

Hypnotism is a mighty force
beamed down to Earth from outer space.
Stronger than wine that makes the drinker
'drunk for a thousand days and nights', it floors you for a hundred years or more.

Waking, you find the world transformed,
and people too (though hills and rivers not):
white temple-hair gone back to black,
world crises ended once for all.

'To the tune of':   A *ci* by Yan Jidao.
Title: Yuriy Pavlovich Safronov and Svetlana Aleksandrovna Safronova, *Vnuki nashikh vnukov*, Moscow: Molodaya gvardiya, 1959.
Line 7:   A variation on a line by Li Qingzhao: 'Things stay the same but people change.' She was one of Mao Zedong's favourite poets.
Line 8:   'Black temple-hair', hair at the temples, an idiom signifying youth.

Our Grandchildren's Grandchildren

清平乐

催眠力伟,
辐射来天外。
绝胜人间'千日醉',
百五十年沉睡。

醒来世换时移,
山川虽是人非。
白发重成青鬓,
世间销尽危机。

Qīng píng yuè

Cuīmián lì wěi,
fúshè lái tiānwài.
Jué shèng rénjiān 'qiān rì zuì',
bǎi wǔshí nián chénshuì.

Xǐnglái shìhuàn-shíyí,
shānchuān suī shì rén fēi.
Báifà chóng chéng qīngbìn,
shìjiān xiāojǐn wéijī.

19.

Duckweed

Duckweed often features in Chinese poetry, as the symbol of an uncertain life. Zheng evokes the rootless plant as it drifts around in the wind, massing and dispersing on or just below the surface of still or slow-moving water, and accepts it as an image of his own helplessness, loneliness and isolation. In 1996 he described the circumstances in which this poem was written, and revealed its special meaning as an expression of delight in human contact after nine years alone in his cell, when by chance he was momentarily reconnected with other people:

> Once I was arrested, I was segregated from the other prisoners in Detention Centre No. 1. Not only could I not see the other prisoners arrested in the same [Trotskyist] case – I could see no prisoners at all. The guards did everything – sent food, sent drinking water, cut my hair, gave me washing water. In 1956 I was escorted to Detention Centre No. 2, and attended to by penal-servitude prisoners. I could see prisoners from other groups, but I was still kept in solitary confinement. In 1961, the third of the 'three years of natural disasters' [after the Great Leap Forward], I was undernourished and found it hard to walk. Without my requesting it, higher authorities sent me to Tilanqiao Prison's No. 8 block, for a check-up by the prison doctors. During my time there, they forgot to tell the new prison that I had to be kept in solitary confinement, so I was put in a common cell, with two and later three others. The cell was crowded, but for someone who had spent nine years [in solitary], it was great to be able to talk with people. The other prisoners – one middle-aged, one young – were intellectuals, while the third was a middle-aged rough and ready chap. When the two intellectuals saw that I too was an intellectual, they were rather welcoming, even more so when they saw that I had a book of Tang and Song poems with me. The young man borrowed it to read. To test me, he took a poem at random ('The

Duckweed

Divination Song') and asked me to recite it from memory, which I did without a moment's hesitation. We all had a great time. The two intellectuals had read some poems, but they were no poets. After we'd been together for a few days, the middle-aged one asked me to write a *ci* for us to remember each other by. The young man asked for it to be set to the tune of the 'Divination Song.' So I wrote this *ci*, and not long afterwards I was transferred back to the Second Detention Centre.

To the tune of 'The Divination Song'

Spring breezes crease the surface of the pond,
which glasses over into deep green jade.
Duckweed galore, on every side,
enough to fill no end of dippers.

Bobbing along, the mats of duckweed frond
thicken and run riot on the sunlit pond.
I delight in the occasional encounter,
which in a trice becomes mere memory.

卜算子	Bǔ suànzǐ
池水皱春风， 池面凝新碧。 数点浮萍水上瓢， 随处留踪迹。	Chíshuǐ zhòu chūnfēng, chímiàn níng xīnbì. Shù diǎn fúpíng shuǐshàng piáo, suíchù liú zōngjī.
风动叶沉浮， 日照根疏密。 偶尔相逢且尽欢， 散后空相忆。	Fēngdòng yè chénfú, rìzhào gēn shūmì. Ǒu'ěr xiāngféng qiě jìnhuān, sàn hòu kōng xiāngyì.

'To the tune of': A *ci* by Li Zhiyi.
Line 1: Rewritten from a line by Feng Yanji (born 903), a poet and politician of the Southern Tang state during the Five Dynasties and Ten Kingdoms period.
Line 2: Rewritten from a line by Wu Qian.
Line 3: Here Zheng echoes several classical phrases.

20.

The Seasons

This and the following poem are about the passing of the seasons, with intimations both of their relentlessness and of the possibility of radical change.

To the tune of 'Dear Niannu'

The weather is abnormal.
Autumn has begun,
but it's hotter than before.
When the sun lies overhead, heat gusts –
for three weeks now without a break.
Fanning furiously with fan-palm fans
and towelling the sweat away,
we slake our thirst.
At dead of night we wake up with a start,
reeking of sweat and soaking wet.

All of a sudden, blue smoke spirals up,
tacking and twisting in the sky.
A cool breeze blows,
depleting the summer heat, prefiguring
fall winds and dew-bespangled webs.
The Earth spins for no apparent reason at its poles.
The seasons pass in orderly progression,
while the autumn tiger pointlessly roars.
The high skies are fresh and crisp. The tilting moon
slips slantwise through the prison bars.

Line 18: In China the 'autumn tiger' is a hot, summer-like spell after the start of autumn, like Europe's Indian summer.

念奴娇

反常天气，
已交秋，
翻比秋前炎热。
烈日当空腾热浪，
连续二旬未歇。
蒲扇狂摇，
毛巾频拭，
白水解深渴。
夜阑惊觉，
浑身臭汗犹滴。

今日高突青烟，
顿移方向，
习习凉风发。
暑气都消，
正好是玉露金风时节。
地轨无端，
四时有序，
秋虎空猖獗。
高天爽气，
铁窗时透斜月。

Niànnú jiāo

Fǎncháng tiānqì,
yǐ jiāo qiū,
fān bǐ qiū qián yánrè.
Lièrì dāngkōng téng rèlàng,
liánxù èr xún wèi xiē.
Púshàn kuáng yáo,
máojīn pín shì,
báishuǐ jiě shēnkě.
Yèlán jīng jué,
húnshēn chòuhàn yóu dī.

Jīnrì gāotū qīngyān,
dùn yí fāngxiàng,
xíxí liángfēng fā.
Shǔqì dōu xiāo,
zhèng hǎo shì yùlù-jīnfēng shíjié.
Dìguǐ wúduān,
sìshí yǒuxù,
qiū hǔ kōng chāngjué.
Gāotiān shuǎngqì,
tiěchuāng shí tòu xiéyuè.

21.

When *Yin* Attains Its Limit

Zheng Chaolin and the Chinese Trotskyists were 'netted in one fell swoop' on 22 December 1952 – by a grim irony, the winter solstice, when the period of light is shortest and the night longest. Seven years later, on the anniversary of the arrest, Zheng starts by noting that it is again midwinter, when *yin* attains its limit. This line echoes the *Yi jing* ('Book of Changes', 9th century BCE), which presents *yin* (feminine, dark, cold and negative) and *yang* (masculine, light, hot and positive) as the two opposing and complementary principles of nature. Their interplay in the form of *qi* (vital energy) provides the primordial energy of the universe and upholds the rotation of the world, the theme of this *ci*. Hence the passage from cold to heat (and back again) noted in the following line, in which Zheng goes on to remind himself that the day will slowly lengthen and daylight will, in the course of time, prevail – 'if winter comes, can spring be far behind?'

When Yin Attains Its Limit

To the tune of 'Song of the South'

The light today dies soonest,
tonight's the longest night.
Looking back to seven years ago,
I recall the night that broke our hearts in two.

When *yin* attains its limit, *yang* begins to grow,
and heat and cold eventually swap place.
The years spin at an ever quicker pace,
and I plough my lonely furrow.

南歌子

今日光明短，
今宵黑暗长。
七年回首耐思量，
记得年时此夜断人肠。

阴极阳生长，
寒回暑在望。
年年岁岁转轮忙，
独有吾生从此永凄凉。

Nán gē zǐ

Jīnrì guāngmíng duǎn,
jīnxiāo hēi'àn cháng.
Qī nián huíshǒu nài sīliang,
jìdé nián shí cǐ yè duàn rén cháng.

Yīnjí yáng shēngzhǎng,
hánhuí shǔ zàiwàng.
Niánnián suìsuì zhuǎnlún máng,
dúyǒu wú sheng cóngcǐ yǒng qīliáng.

'To the tune of':   A *ci* by Xin Qiji.
Line 4:   This line draws on a *ci* edited by Zeng Zao.

22.

The Host

The host at the drinking party is a very strong man but at the same time studious – something of which few people are aware. The poet sees many similarities between himself and the host. Zheng implies that people only know the host as a brave warrior, and cannot imagine that he is also studious. Zheng too was both a fighter and a poet – like his host, a master of both pen and sword.

To the tune of 'The Water Song'.

Adapting Li He's 'Bearded Shen Playing His Tartar Horn'

My face is red – your wine does this to me.
Shen holds the horn reed in his mouth, chewing on its gentle sound.
My host has such a generous heart.
He has his servant play the pipe and fill the cup.
5   As notes sound out
spring winds begin to rise,
clouds to go scudding overhead,
buds to burst forth.
I doze, dreaming of a prostitute
10   while leaning on a silver screen.

'To the tune of': A *ci* by Su Shi.
Line 8:   A slightly reconfigured line from a poem by Li Qunyu.

The Host

I'm an old man
with bushy brows
who leads a sorry life.
The waves are billowing,
my mind is troubled at this gathering, as your guest.   15
I envy my hale and agile host,
galloping ahead and swinging his broad sword
with its blue-plumed handle.
Few know he leaves the city after dusk,
to gather fireflies in the grass.

Li He's 'Bearded Shen Playing His Tartar Horn'

My face is red – your wine does this to me.
Shen holds the horn reed in his mouth, chewing on its sound.
Her hairpin hanging carelessly awry,
Huaniang wakes behind the lotus screen.
Who cut the flute of peace,   5
who drilled it with these holes like stars?
Suddenly, spring winds pick up, and shake the flowers,
chasing clouds across the sky.
Tonight the flowers of our years cascade,
and I regret their passing.   10
My feelings break like waves,
seated here in constant shock.
The northerner astride his snow-white horse
swinging his blue-plumed sword
is agile and hale as a *yuannao* ape,   15
yet gathers fireflies in the grass.

Line 15:   A monkey mentioned in ancient literature.
Line 18, *The Host*:   In this poem, Zheng borrows frequently from Li He.
Line 20, *The Host*:   The poem draws on the biography of Che Ying in the *Jin shu* ('The Book of Jin'), an official history of the Jin dynasty (265–420), compiled in 648 by the imperial Tang court and edited by Fang Xuanling. In it, Che Ying, the son of poor parents, has no money to buy oil for his lamp, so he collects fireflies in order to read at night by their light. Similarly, Sun Kang studies in light reflected by snow, despite the cold. The idiom 'light reflected by snow or collected from fireflies' describes those who study hard in difficult circumstances.
Line 3:   Huaniang is the name of the host's beloved courtesan.
Line 15:   A monkey mentioned in ancient literature.

The Host

水歌头头
檃括李贺《申胡子觱篥歌》

颜热感君酒,
含嚼软芦声。
主人情重,
命仆吹管进瑶觥。
一弄春风复发,
再弄花枝开彻,
天上逐云行。
惊醒花娘梦,
坐起倚银屏。

庞眉客,
伤老大,
惜平生。
波涛起伏,
中坐心事不能平。
堪羡主人俊健,
驰马提携长剑,
剑靶系兰缨。
薄暮归郊野,
肯拾草中萤。

李贺《申胡子觱篥歌》

颜热感君酒,
含嚼芦中声。
花娘篸绥妥,
休睡芙蓉屏。
谁截太平管,
列点排空星。
直贯开花风,
天上驱云行。
今夕岁华落,
令人惜平生。
心事如波涛,
中坐时时惊。
朔客骑白马,
剑靶悬兰缨。
俊健如生猱,
肯拾蓬中萤。

Shuǐdiào gētóu
Yǐnkuò Lǐ Hè 'shēn húzi bì lì gē'

Yán rè gǎn jūn jiǔ,
hán jué ruǎn lú shēng.
Zhǔrén qíng zhòng,
mìng pū chuī guǎn jìn yáo gōng.
Yī nòng chūnfēng fùfā,
zài nòng huāzhī kāichè,
tiānshàng zhú yún xíng.
Jīngxǐng huāniáng mèng,
zuò qǐ yǐ yínpíng.

Páng méi kè,
shāng lǎodà,
xī píngshēng.
Bōtāo qǐfú,
zhōng zuò xīnshì bù néng píng.
Kān xiàn zhǔrén jùn jiàn,
chí mǎ tíxié chángjiàn,
jiànbǎ xì lányīng.
Bómù guī jiāoyě,
kěn shí cǎo zhōng yíng.

Lǐ Hè 'shēn húzi bì lì gē'

Yán rè gǎn jūn jiǔ,
hán jué lú zhōng shēng.
Huāniáng cǎn suí tuǒ,
xiū shuì fúróng píng.
Shéi jié tàipíng guǎn,
liè diǎn pái kōng xīng.
Zhí guàn kāihuā fēng,
tiānshàng qū yún xíng.
Jīnxī suì huá luò,
lìng rén xī píngshēng.
Xīnshì rú bōtāo,
zhōng zuò shíshí jīng.
Shuò kè qí báimǎ,
jiànbǎ xuán lányīng.
Jùn jiàn rú shēng náo,
kěn shí péng zhōng yíng.

23.

Loneliness

In this *ji* or assemblage,[1] Zheng creates a new poem out of lines from work by Li Shangyin (c. 813–858), a poet of the late Tang Dynasty. The first stanza mentions his literary ambition and anxiety about the outcome. The second describes the poet's yearning and isolation. Like Li He, another of Zheng's favourite poets, Li Shangyin was greatly admired by twentieth-century Chinese for his sensuous style and difficult, allusive imagery, whose meaning became the subject of much speculative interpretation among them. Anglo-American imagist poets like Ezra Pound, who favoured clear, sharp images and economy of expression, were attracted to Chinese and Japanese classical poetry and drew on translations of it, including of poems by Li Shangyin, while Chinese poets were, in turn, influenced by the Western imagist movement. Some Chinese appreciated Li Shangyin as a sort of Chinese precursor of imagism. A notable example of a Chinese intellectual's imagist turn was the philosopher and poet Hu Shi (1891–1962), the leader with Chen Duxiu of China's New Culture Movement in the late 1910s, who 'saw in the visual imagery and simple diction of Western imagist poetry a similarity to Song dynasty lyrics, and sought to transform what he found in the images into a modernized kind of Chinese verse.'[2] Perhaps Zheng Chaolin, whose writing was closely policed by the prison authorities, felt a special affinity with the cryptic and enigmatic Li.

---

1   For our definition of this term, see p. 65.
2   *The Flowering of Modern Chinese Poetry: An Anthology of Verse from the Republican Period,* trans. Herbert J. Batt and Sheldon Zitner, introductions by Michel Hockx, Montreal: McGill-Queen's University Press, 2016, p. 28.

Loneliness

To the tune of 'Bodhisattva Strength'

An assemblage of lines from poems by Li Shangyin

Innumerable lamps glow dimly in the dark,
while a madman poet pens his mighty lines as if by crossbow,
painting a tiger but ending up with – what?
My heart is troubled to the core.

Complex sentiments rely on so few letters.
Homesick, I weep unending tears. Once wiped,
they rise to fleck the autumn clouds.
Heaven is so high – how can my voice be heard there?

'To the tune of': The name is Pusa-man in Chinese – a *ci* tune, or processional dance, first performed in Tang times. It can be translated as either Bodhisattva Barbarian or Boddihisattva String of Jewels (from Sanskrit *mālā*, 'garland'). The title was associated with liaisons with beautiful women.
Line 1: See 'When my good friend charioteer Weipan could not visit me at the Shizi Stream, when he was living at Guo Binning's villa on the waterside' *(Zheng Chaolin's note, as are the following)*.
Line 2: See 'Seventy-two verses given to four fellow officials.'
Line 3: See 'A forty-verse five-syllable lyric verse humbly and wholeheartedly offered to my noble seventh brother'. According to a popular saying, you try to paint a tiger and end up with a dog.
Line 4: See 'Untitled' [no. 10].
Line 5: See 'Letter to Pei Heng.'
Line 6: See 'Lost its title: Former emperor granted his imperial favour.'
Line 7: See 'One hundred verses on the expedition to the western suburbs.'
Line 8: See 'Weeping for Registrar Liu: Two poems.'

菩萨蛮·集李商隐句

漆灯夜照真无数,
狂来笔力如牛弩,
画虎意何成,
中心最不平。

杂情堪底寄?
断续殊乡泪。
挥泪连秋云,
天高不为闻.

Púsà mán: Jí Lǐ Shāngyǐn jù

Qīdēng yèzhào zhēn wúshù,
kuáng lái bǐlì rú niúnǔ,
huà hǔ yì hé chéng,
zhōngxīn zuì bùpíng.

Záqíng kān dǐ jì?
Duàn xù shūxiāng lèi.
Huī lèi lián qiūyún,
tiāngāo bù wéi wén.

Line 1: 见'十字水期韦潘侍御同年不至时韦寓居水次故郭邠宁宅'
Line 2: 见'偶成转韵七十二句赠四同舍'
Line 3: 见'五言述德抒情诗一首四十韵献上杜七兄仆射相公'
Line 4: 见'无题:照梁初有情'
Line 5: 见'寄裴衡'
Line 6: 见'失题:昔帝回冲眷'
Line 7: 见'行次西郊作一百韵'
Line 8: 见'哭刘司户二首'

24.

Where Is the Warmth?

To the tune of the 'Tang Duo Song'

I have a worn-out cotton gown,
a woollen shirt, a hat, a pair of shoes – you see, I want for nothing.
I take it easy, as the years slip by.
But now my sickness reappears,
alas as if on purpose,
in these hard winter months.

'Where is the warmth?' I ask,
pointing my question upwards at the sky.
The moon hangs as a wheel of ice beyond the window bars,
lighting up the hoarfrost on the lovebird tiles on nearby roofs.
Where can I go
to escape this cold?

唐多令　　　　　　　　　Táng duō líng

依旧一袍棉，　　　　　　Yījiù yī páo mián,
绒衫帽履全。　　　　　　róngshān mào lǚ quán.
满轻松度过多年。　　　　Mǎn qīngsōng dùguò duō nián.
争奈新来添老病，　　　　Zhēng nài xīnlái tiān lǎobìng,
今特地，　　　　　　　　jīn tèdì,
过冬难。　　　　　　　　guòdōng nán.

温暖在谁边？　　　　　　Wēnnuǎn zài shéi biān?
举头欲问天。　　　　　　Jǔ tóu yù wèn tiān.
见冰轮窗外高悬。　　　　Jiàn bīnglún chuāng wài gāoxuán.
照得千家鸳瓦冷，　　　　Zhào dé qiānjiā yuān wǎ lěng,
何处减，　　　　　　　　héchù jiǎn,
此间寒！　　　　　　　　cǐjiān hán!

Line 10: This is a line from *Chang hen ge* ('Song of Everlasting Regret') by Bai Juyi. Lovebird tiles are pairs of tiles embossed with images of lovebirds.

25.

A Revolution without Breaks or Interruptions

Here, the poet summarises his understanding, from a Trotskyist point of view, of the course of the Chinese Revolution after 1921. The revolutionary high tide in the mid 1920s and the gains achieved by the Northern Expedition in 1926–27 were reversed by Chiang Kai-shek's attack on his erstwhile Communist allies in April 1927. Zheng notes that the Chiang 'bandits' were wrongly taken by the Communists as 'in-laws' during the First United Front (1924–27), forced on them by Moscow. For obvious reasons he never mentions Trotsky in the poem, but the argument in 'court and commonality' is a clear reference to the Stalin–Trotsky split, during which Trotsky spoke out loudly for a return to Marx's teachings. Zheng's realisation of the truth of Trotsky's analysis had come like a thunderclap, as the poem implies. The 'different tune sung with equal skill' suggests that the Chinese Revolution is no exception to the general pattern of world revolution described by Trotsky – only a particular realisation of it.

When Zheng wrote this poem, probably at around the time of the Great Leap Forward of 1958–61 or in its immediate aftermath, China's rural and industrial economy had begun a sudden steep decline after a short-lived 'high tide' of apparently bumper harvests and rapid industrial growth. Both urban and rural Chinese (but especially the latter) experienced famines and disasters as the Party-state stepped up the rate of extraction from the villages to unprecedented and unsustainable levels. The references in the first stanza to Chiang's crimes might also have served as a hidden reference to the ebbing of Mao's high tide after 1958 and Mao's cruel treatment of China's workers and peasants. The second stanza talks about the course the Chinese Revolution should have followed after Chiang's betrayal: a revolution without breaks or interruptions, one that would not pause for protracted periods at the discrete 'stages' that underpinned Stalin's and the Chinese Communists' own previous prescription.

A Revolution without Breaks or Interruptions

But does Zheng's comment have a further, hidden meaning? Starting in the late 1950s, Mao and his supporters began emphasising the need for what Mao's English-language translators called 'continuous' or 'uninterrupted' revolution (although the standard translation in Marxist literature of the Chinese word [*buduande*] Mao used in this context is 'permanent'). At around that time, the Maoists had suddenly started arguing that the revolution in China (considered by them to be still in progress) should proceed without interruption (as the Chinese Trotskyists had argued) rather than by stages (as Stalin and Mao had argued). However, the Maoists were loath to signal to the world Communist movement (which Mao hoped to eventually lead) any connection between their new concept of revolution and Trotsky's tainted theory of permanent revolution, so their translators avoided rendering *buduande* as 'permanent'. In prison, Zheng saw that Mao had changed his tune and he naturally felt vindicated, though he probably had little confidence that Mao and his choir of singers knew the words to it. But he could not resist sneaking into the poem's cryptic last two lines a reminder that the Chinese Trotskyists had put forward the same strategy thirty years before, at the time of their Founding Congress in Shanghai in 1931, and had been denounced for it in the 1930s as agents of Japan.

To the tune of 'Congratulating the Bridegroom'

The tide is sucked back down the stream.
Painful years
for workers and peasants everywhere,
with blood-stained snowflakes swirling in the gale.
The fruit will soon be gathered in –
but thieves will rally in the dead of night
to plunder the peasants' fields and homes.
Drawing lessons from the bitter past,
I detect a deviation from the old true path:
welcoming bandits
as if they're in-laws.

'To the tune of': The He Xin Lang are a series of *ci* poems by Xin Qiji.

A Revolution without Breaks or Interruptions

An argument splits court and commonality.
A loud voice calls
for a return to the essential teachings
of Lenin, Marx, and Engels:
a revolution without breaks or interruptions,
until the building's up and ready.
A different tune but sung with equal skill, for China's sake.
The scales have dropped from people's eyes,
but however loud the song, few really know the words.
Thirty years
seem like a day.

贺新郎   Hè xīnláng

潮退江河下。   Cháo tuì jiānghé xià.
痛年来,   Tòng niánlái,
工农处处,   gōngnóng chùchù,
雪花飘洒。   xuěhuā piāosǎ.
果实累累收获近,   Guǒshí lěilěi shōuhuò jìn,
大盗突临深夜,   dàdào tū lín shēnyè,
强占取田园庐舍。   qiáng zhànqǔ tiányuán lúshè.
痛定追思沉痛处,   Tòng dìng zhuīsī chéntòng chù,
觉原先指向生偏岔: jué yuánxiān zhǐxiàng shēng piānchà:
认寇盗,   Rèn kòudào,
作姻娅。   zuò yīnyà.

一场争辩分朝野。   Yī chǎng zhēngbiàn fēn cháoyě.
有宏音,   Yǒu hóngyīn,
重申遗教,   chóngshēn yíjiào,
列宁恩马: Lièníng Ēn Mǎ:
革命连绵无绝处,   Gémìng liánmián wú juéchù,
直至落成新厦。   zhízhì luòchéng xīnshà.
纵异曲同工华夏。   Zòng yìqǔ-tónggōng huáxià.
茅塞顿开眸乍展,   Máosè-dùnkāi móu zhà zhǎn,
但高歌不管相和寡。   dàn gāogē bùguǎn xiānghè guǎ.
三十载,   Sānshí zǎi,
一朝也。   yīzhāo yě.

26.

My Career

If this poem was written around 1961, Zheng is probably counting the 'second half' of his career from 1931, when the Chinese Trotskyists set up their organisation. (He was born in 1901, so he is reckoning in units of thirty years.) By 1961, Zheng had spent fifteen years in prison, first under the Guomindang, then under Mao – half of his thirty years as a Trotskyist. The poem makes this point too.

To the tune of 'Riverside Immortals'

Now is the thirtieth year of the second half of my career –
I think back sadly on missed chances.
Half the time was wasted
and the prisons kept on changing –
5   Cao River prison was the worst of all.

Flames of war raged everywhere, but life went on.
In the tenth year, I returned to my old haunts,
shocked to see the mansions flattened.
No more snarling jailers,
10   broken bricks on every side.

Line 5: Cao River is a reference to the Guomindang's Second Model Prison at Caohejing in Shanghai, known as a 'prison hell' to its inmates, with a sky-high annual death rate. Fortunately, Zheng was transferred after two months to Hangzhou and from there to the Suzhou Military Prison in Panmenwai. (The poem 'Suzhou Gardens (1)' records Zheng's time in Panmenwai.) After a further two months, Zheng was moved to the Central Military Prison in Nanjing, where he worked with Lou Shiyi and others as a prisoner-translator (see Lou Shiyi's memoir of Zheng, in *An Oppositionist for Life*, pp. xi–xiv).
Line 7: Zheng here borrows words from a poem written by the Southern Song Dynasty poet Liu Guo (1154–1206) after returning to his native place and finding it devastated by war. Zheng adds an extra observation to Liu Guo's description of the devastation – 'but life went on.' Ten years may be a reference to the period between the start of the Anti-Japanese Resistance in January 1932 and Zheng's return to Shanghai from Anhui in 1940, when the city still bore signs of the Japanese bombing in 1937.

临江仙

后半生涯今卅载,
追思堪叹蹉跎。
就中半数枉消磨。
牢监时更换,
最苦在漕河。

烽火连天人未死,
十年旧地重过。
却惊广厦变平坡。
咆哮无狱吏,
满地碎砖多。

Lín jiāng xiān

Hòu bàn shēngyá jīn sà zǎi,
zhuīsī kān tàn cuōtuó.
Jiù zhōng bànshù wǎng xiāomó.
Láo jiān shí gēnghuàn,
zuì kǔ zài Cáohé.

Fēnghuǒ-liántiān rén wèi sǐ,
shí-nián jiùdì chóngguò.
Què jīng guǎngshà biàn píngpō.
Páoxiào wú yùlì,
mǎndì suì zhuān duō.

27.

Meeting Liu Jingzhen

Zheng meets his beloved Liu Jingzhen and they take their first walk together in Shanghai. He pictures her first as a celestial Daoist nymph and then, after her suffering and dramatic ageing, as the Queen Mother of the West.

> To the tune of 'River Story'

> Christmas,
> a banquet,
> a painted tower, a small garden.
> A host of wise and virtuous old men
> in a well-lit, heated room,
> enjoying the laughter and the chatter,
> ispirits as lofty as rainbows.
>
> E Hua visits Yang Quan for the first time in his home.
> In the darkness of the night,
> lit by the moon, they walk out together.
> A young girl,
> instantly transformed
> into the Queen Mother of the West at Jasper Lake,
> iher earlocks into white silk.

Line 4: Those present included Chen Duxiu and other Party notables.
Line 8: E Hua (short for E Lühua) was a Daoist celestial nymph who lived in a cave in the Jiuyi Mountains. She visits the handsome Yang Quan, a man of the Jin Dynasty (265–420), on a magic cloud in the dead of night, and they fall in love. E Hua teaches Yang Quan Daoist rites and doctrines. Their story is told in the *Shishuo xinyu* and in a poem by the Tang poet Cao Tang (no dates).
Line 10: Zheng Chaolin and Liu Jingzhen walk together after the party.
Line 13: The Queen Mother of the West, a celestial immortal, lives at the Jasper Lake in the mythical Kunlun Mountains. The poet imagines the transformation of his adored wife, in reality over many years but seemingly in a trice, into a goddess, and pictures her having aged as a result of her suffering during his long imprisonment and her years of separation from him. She herself spent five years in jail, until her release in 1957. For a description of her suffering, see Wang Fanxi's obituary, reprinted in Benton, *Prophets Unarmed*, pp. 1170–3, where she goes under the name Wu Jingru.
Line 14: Both Li Bai and Du Fu used this line in poems.

Meeting Liu Jingzhen

河传

圣诞,
开宴,
画楼小苑。
一老群贤,
灯辉室暖。
席上谈笑风生,
气如虹。

萼华初探羊权舍,
将阑夜,
共步蟾光下。
妙龄少女,
转瞬王母瑶池,
鬓成丝。

Hé zhuàn

Shèngdàn,
kāi yàn,
huàlóu xiǎoyuàn.
Yī lǎo qún xián,
dēng huī shì nuǎn.
Xí shàng tánxiào-fēngshēng,
qì rú hóng.

È Huá chūtàn Yáng Quán shě,
jiāng lán yè,
gòng bù chán guāng xià.
Miàolíng shàonǚ,
zhuǎnshùn Wángmǔ Yáochí,
bìn chéng sī.

28.

Christmas

In this *ci* Zheng recalls, from his prison cell, a joyous Christmas in the Zheng–Liu family, probably in a village in the Anhui mountains in the first years of the war, where Zheng went to recover his health with the help of contacts of Chen Duxiu. Their only child was born there in 1938. The couple called their son Frei, meaning 'free' in German – a gesture of revolutionary internationalism. Frei died in Shanghai of tuberculosis in 1945.

To the tune of 'Wind in the Pine'

> Fur coat, fur hat, white whiskers,
> the cap dyed red.
> A reindeer sleigh speeds through the snow,
> amid green pines lit by the setting sun.
> The sleigh brings presents
> for our son tonight.
>
> His little eyes and little heart are set to burst.
> Before we sleep, I gaze towards the fire.
> I have my present too:
> beside the fireplace, a cherished heart,
> true love, unwavering affection.

'To the tune of': A *ci* by Wu Wenying.
Line 6: Christmas was important for Zheng as the time when he and Liu Jingzhen declared their love for one another. Zheng had lived for some years in France and Russia, and was familiar with Christmas celebrations.

风入松

皮裘皮帽白须翁,
裘帽染猩红。
鹿车独驾驰驱急。
斜阳照白雪苍松。
车上载来节礼,
今宵付与儿童。

小心小眼乐融融,
临睡望烟囱。
当年我亦蒙恩赐,
壁炉畔礼物玲珑:
珍重芳心一颗,
缠绵蜜意千重。

Fēng rù sōng

Píqiú pímào báixū wēng,
qiú mào rǎn xīnghóng.
Lù chē dú jià chíqū jí.
Xiéyáng zhào báixuě cāngsōng.
Chēshàng zàilái jiélǐ,
jīnxiāo fùyǔ értóng.

Xiǎoxīn xiǎoyǎn lè róngróng,
lín shuì wàng yāncōng.
Dāngnián wǒ yì méng ēncì,
bìlú pàn lǐwù línglóng:
Zhēnzhòng fāngxīn yīkē,
chánmián mìyì qiān chóng.

29.

Moonrise

To the tune of 'Prelude to the Song of Six States'

Sunset. Red glow licks
the tower top.
A star or two
twinkles now
in the blue.
Her dear face levitating
up from the East,
floating smooth and rounded as an *oeil de sorcière*,
her slow ascent
pushing the halo of the sun below the rim.
Brightly, clearly,
glittering, translucent,
bearding the buffeting west wind,
she deigns to shed her social standing
and drops straight through the lattice grate
into the cell to tell the old and ailing lag:
'The best time of the year,
Moon Palace night tonight!'
See how time flies,
it's already harvest month!

When I was young,
the autumn night as if eternal,
I shared my rapturous delight
with a beautiful young girl.
Few voices could be heard,

'To the tune of': Originally a drum song popular in the Tang and Song Dynasties.
Line 14: Quoting a line attributed to Emperor Jianwen of Liang (503–551).
Line 18: The Moon (or Guanghan) Palace is the home of the Goddess of the Moon.
Line 22: This phrase is said to have first appeared in a poem in Chinese by Heo Nanseolheon (1563–1589), born Heo Chohui, a prominent Korean woman poet of Korea's mid-Joseon dynasty.
Line 25: Echoing a line in the poem 'Deer Park' by Wang Wei.

the evening breezes had died down,
window screens were raised,
the view was wrapped in haze.
Cakes were laid out on tiny stands,
bright lanterns decked with festive frill,   30
and bitter tea was sipped.
At the corner of the rail,
bathed in the clear moon's light,
two hearts were joined.
We vied to call up lines of verse   35
to limn its lovely curvature,
gambling gaily on our bowls of tea.
Today, I grieve to see the moon as ever round,
while human affairs are like a rainbow –
gone in a trice!   40

六州歌头　　　　　　　　　Liù zhōu gētóu

高楼一角，　　　　　　　　Gāolóu yījiǎo,
落日敛余红。　　　　　　　luòrì liǎn yúhóng.
碧空净，　　　　　　　　　Bìkōng jìng,
疏星映，　　　　　　　　　shūxīng yìng,
见娇容，　　　　　　　　　jiàn jiāoróng,
出天东。　　　　　　　　　chū tiāndōng.
丰满如圆镜，　　　　　　　Fēngmǎn rú yuánjìng,
渐升起，　　　　　　　　　jiàn shēngqǐ,
退红晕，　　　　　　　　　tuì hóngyùn,
添皎洁，　　　　　　　　　tiān jiǎojié,
更晶莹，　　　　　　　　　gèng jīngyíng,
对西风。　　　　　　　　　duì xīfēng.
降贵纡尊，　　　　　　　　Jiàngguì-yūzūn,
直入窗棂铁，　　　　　　　zhírù chuānglíng tiě,
来探衰翁。　　　　　　　　lái tàn shuāiwēng.
道：'一年最好，　　　　　　Dào: 'Yī nián zuì hǎo,
今夕广寒宫。'　　　　　　　jīnxī guǎngghángōng.'
岁月匆匆，　　　　　　　　Suìyuè cōngcōng,
九秋中！　　　　　　　　　jiǔqiū zhōng!

Moonrise

记年少日，	Jì niánshào rì,
秋宵永，	qiūxiāo yǒng,
发清兴，	fā qīngxìng,
玉人同。	yùrén tóng.
人语静，	Rényǔ jìng,
晚风定，	wǎnfēng dìng,
卷帘栊，	juǎn liánlóng,
影朦胧。	yǐng ménglóng.
小几陈圆饼，	Xiǎojǐ chén yuánbǐng,
华灯暝，	huádēng míng,
苦茶浓。	kǔchá nóng.
栏角凭，	Lánjiǎo píng,
清光浸，	qīngguāng jìn,
两心通。	liǎngxīn tōng.
竟记诗词，	Jìng jì shīcí,
搜索团栾句，	sōusuǒ tuánluán jù,
笑赌茶钟。	xiào dǔ cházhōng.
叹月圆如旧，	Tàn yuèyuán rújiù,
人事类霓虹，	rénshì lèi níhóng,
瞬息成空！	shùnxī chéngkōng!

30.

To My Wife and Child

Zheng Chaolin dedicated this poem to his wife Liu Jingzhen and their son Frei. It describes the couple's wartime flight to the mountains of southern Anhui after Zheng's release from prison in 1937, and Frei's death from TB in 1945. According to local archivists in his native Longyan, it was written on the back of a family photograph.[1]

To the tune of 'Catching Fish in Your Hands'

In my mind's eye, a pair of swallows perching on a beam,
one newly fledged.
In Ganquan war flames light the night,
war fog blankets miles and miles of countryside.
Alas the anguish!   5
The birds swoop gracefully on scissor-tails
without the slightest change in their demeanour.
A pert and clever chick,
bright and alert,
everything he said and did   10
was agreeable and kind.

Heaven, why did you take my boy?
Tender buds die quickest in the frost,
in storms the supple twig is soonest lost.
Tossing and turning in my bed, I moaned and groaned for three full years,   15
wordlessly weeping bitter tears,

---

[1] Zhang Dasen and Li Cui'e, 'Zheng Chaolin de liang ci hunyin' ('Zheng Chaolin's two marriages'), long1998.com/news (accessed 14 September 2017).
'To the tune of':   A *ci* by Xin Qiji.
Line 1:   A reworking of a line by Shen Quanqi.
Line 4:   Ganquan is probably a reference to the mountainous Ganquan area in Jiangsu, not far from Shanghai, where Zheng lived between 1940 and 1952.
Line 6:   A common image in Song poetry.

To My Wife and Child

but to what avail?
Like a meteor briefly flashing soot
across a clear night sky,
20 youthful beauty is never hard to overlook.
And when we fly not wing to wing but each apart,
the nest in ruins,
does not the tragedy augment?

摸鱼儿

记当年双栖梁燕，
一雏初展毛羽。
甘泉烽火频惊夜，
四野迷茫烟雾。
愁几许！
但双翦差池，
未改原风度。
雏儿颖悟，
便一笑一颦，
一言一动，
总有可人处。

天何意？
嫩蕊先凋霜露，
柔枝早折风雨。
呻吟宛转三年近，
泪眼无言漫注。
终莫补！
似清夜流星，
一闪随尘土，
韶华易误。
况比翼分飞，
故巢久破，
追想更凄楚。

Mō yú'er

Jì dāngnián shuāngqī liáng yàn,
yī chú chū zhǎn máoyǔ.
Gānquán fēnghuǒ pín jīng yè,
sìyě mímáng yānwù.
Chóu jǐxǔ!
Dàn shuāng jiǎn chāchí,
wèi gǎi yuán fēngdù.
Chú er yǐngwù,
biàn yīxiào-yīpín,
yīyán-yīdòng,
zǒng yǒu kěrén chù.

Tiān hé yì?
Nènruǐ xiān diāo shuānglù,
róuzhī zǎo zhé fēngyǔ.
Shēnyín wǎnzhuǎn sān nián jìn,
lèiyǎn wúyán màn zhù.
Zhōng mò bǔ!
Shì qīngyè liúxīng,
yī shǎn suí chéntǔ,
sháohuá yì wù.
Kuàng bǐyì-fēnfēi,
gù cháo jiǔ pò,
zhuīxiǎng gèng qīchǔ.

Line 21: A reference to Zheng's enforced separation from his wife after 1952.

31.

My Son's Death

Zheng grieves for Frei's death in 1945. The poem was written on New Year, but we do not know which year, although he has apparently only just arrived in prison (1952) or been moved to a new prison. The second stanza is based on a folk tale recorded in the Tang Dynasty by Pei Xing (825–880), in his *Chuan qi* ('Strange Tales'), about a scholar, Pei Hang, who fails the imperial examination and roams the land in misery and despair. He meets a shamaness who knows about his failure and takes pity on him. She sends her granddaughter Yunying to fetch him water. Pei Hang is struck by Yunying's beauty and asks to marry her. The shamaness says she has an elixir of black frost that will make her immortal if pounded with a jade pestle in a jade mortar – and that she will let Pei Hang marry Yunying if he finds one for her. Pei Hang finds such a device, and seeks out a Jade Hare (a companion of the Moon Goddess) at the Blue Bridge. After 100 days of pounding by Jade Hare, the shamaness swallows the powder and achieves immortality. Pei Hang marries Yunying and he too becomes immortal. As in the previous poem, in the second stanza Zheng starts talking about himself and his wife.

To the tune of the 'Water Dragon Chant'

A rooster crowing jolts me from my sleep,
to greet the New Year in my new abode.
Fern frost coats the windowpane,
the cell ice cold –
no sign as yet of spring.
My darling son lies cradled in my arms,
squeezed in my embrace,
but in a dream.
I think back
on how the sickness quickened –
in next to no time
he was gone.

'To the tune of':   A *ci* by Su Shi.

My Son's Death

Tender buds die quickest in the frost,
while old and ailing trees escape its wrath.
Using your slight frame
and nimble fingers,
you dodge and fend off the demon of disease.
Jade Hare at Blue Bridge
pounds the black frost
and gives it to Yun Ying.
'When will you return', she asks Pei Hang,
'to take me by the hand
to the pure land?'

水龙吟

闻鸡早起怔忪,
却惊新地迎新岁。
飞霜窗外,
凝冰室内,
全无春意。
又见娇儿,
依依怀抱,
适才梦里。
念那年此日,
病情转恶,
无多久,
离人世。

嫩蕊先凋风雨,
甚衰树尚饶生气。
腰肢轻便,
指头灵活,
病魔回避。
玉兔蓝桥,
玄霜捣就,
云英赠馈。
问裴航何日,
重临携手,
赴清都会?

Shuǐlóng yín

Wén jī zǎoqǐ zhēng sōng,
què jīng xīndì yíng xīnsuì.
Fēishuāng chuāng wài,
níngbīng shì nèi,
quán wú chūnyì.
Yòu jiàn jiāo ér,
yīyī huáibào,
shìcái mènglǐ.
Niàn nà nián cǐ rì,
bìngqíng zhuǎn è,
wú duōjiǔ,
lí rénshì.

Nèn ruǐ xiān diāo fēngyǔ,
shén shuāishù shàng ráo shēngqì.
Yāozhī qīngbiàn,
zhǐtou línghuó,
bìngmó huíbì.
Yùtù Lánqiáo,
xuánshuāng dǎojiù,
Yún Yīng zèng kuì.
Wèn Péi Háng hé rì,
chónglín xiéshǒu,
fù qīngdū huì?

32.

A Handsome Place

To the tune of 'West River'

A handsome place –
its kingly air once more restored:
the self-claimed party-state usurps authority
and roots out its opponents.
What the Six Dynasties achieved was brought to naught   5
by fops and coxcombs' villainy.

Beyond the city, to the west,
jail walls stretch
for miles on end.
Sima Xiangru wrote *Changmen fu* at Maoling   10
resulting in his rehabilitation.
For years, Wenjun awaited his return –
her wifely sorrow made a single day seem longer than a year.
By the side of Mochou Lake cicadas chirp.
Suddenly bombs come crashing down,   15
smashing our mountains and our rivers,
making the layered iron gates impossible to close
and speeding our reunion beyond the prison walls.

Line 4: The place is Nanjing, which was the capital during several dynasties and under the Guomindang starting in 1927.
Line 6: The emperors of the Six Dynasties (220–589) established their capitals in Nanjing, only to collapse into disunity, warfare, intrigue and hedonistic excess.
Line 10: *Changmen fu* is the title of a prose poem by Sima Xiangru, a gifted writer and a favourite at the court of Emperor Wu of Han. Sima later fell into disfavour and was dismissed by the emperor. After this, he lived in Maoling to the west of Chang'an. In 127 BCE, the empress asked him to write *Changmen fu* on her behalf. Emperor Wu was moved by the prose poem and restored Sima Xiangru to his original post.
Line 13: According to the *Shiji* ('Records of the Grand Historian', written around 91 BCE), Sima Xiangru fell in love 'at first sight' with Zhuo Wenjun, a rich man's daughter, and eloped with her. The two lived in poverty until Zhuo's father was finally shamed into acknowledging their marriage. The couple became an emblem of steadfast love.
Line 14: The Mochou Lake is in Nanjing, so this poem refers to Zheng's imprisonment by the Guomindang and his release at the time of the Japanese invasion in 1937, when Chiang Kai-shek emptied the jails.

A Handsome Place

西河

佳丽地,
当年又见王气:
自称党国擅威权,
铲除异己。
六朝裙屐旧风流,
可怜付与缇骑。

西郊外,
监狱起,
高墙绵亘多里。
茂陵倦客赋《长门》,
翻遭羁系。
文君望久未归来,
伤心度日如岁。
莫愁湖畔蝉声曳,
忽炸弹乱落空际,
故国山河破碎,
看层层沉重铁门难闭,
恰早重圆监门外。

Xī hé

Jiālì dì,
dāngnián yòu jiàn wángqì:
Zìchēng dǎngguó shàn wēiquán,
chǎnchú yìjǐ.
Liùcháo qún jī jiù fēngliú,
kělián fùyǔ tíjì.

Xījiāo wài,
jiānyù qǐ,
gāoqiáng miángèng duō lǐ.
Mào Líng juàn kè fù 'Chángmén',
fān zāo jīxì.
Wénjūn wàng jiǔ wèi guīlái,
shāngxīn dùrì rú suì.
Mòchóu húpàn chánshēng yè,
hū zhàdàn luànluò kōngjì,
gùguó shānhé pòsuì,
kàn céngcéng chénzhòng tiěmén nán bì,
qià zǎo chóngyuán jiānmén wài.

33.

Forever Dissident

Zheng later wrote of this poem:

> The line 'Like me, they spent these thirteen years in jail' shows that I wrote it in 1965. On one occasion, when my wife came to visit me in prison, three stools were set out. A prison guard sat to one side to supervise our conversation. Before the start of such meetings, the guard would inform the relatives that it was their duty to persuade the prisoner to admit his or her guilt and undergo reform. So, at the start of visits, relatives would deliver some such 'exhortation'. I replied to the 'exhortation' in the presence of the guard. I said that I, too, wanted to compromise, out of consideration for the general interest, but there were limits beyond which I would not go. And even if I did go beyond those limits, it would be to no avail. Quite a few of those jailed as a result of our case had admitted their 'guilt' and yet received no leniency, and, like me, had spent the previous thirteen years in prison.

Food imagery comes up: whereas another imprisoned revolutionary might see in the flying swan a symbol of unattainable liberty, Zheng sticks to the Chinese folk image of a missed meal – 'a toad wanting to eat swan meat' is a metaphor for wishful thinking.

To the tune of 'Mount Mo Creek'

> You kindly advise me to follow others' suit.
> Though I would love to compromise,
> there is a gulf that I can never cross.
> Seemingly just inches wide,
> actually it reaches for a thousand miles.   5
> It is the gulf between a human and a beast.
> Should I drink the sweet and not the bitter cup,
> I would disgrace my father and my mother!

Forever Dissident

10　　And even if I crossed this gulf,
my mind would be forever dissident.
Do you not see some old acquaintances of mine
bending their heads low
and saying yes when so required,
but all to no avail?
15　　Like me, they spent these thirteen years in jail,
hungrily looking upwards at the swan
that wings its way across the sky –
where is the leniency?

蓦山溪　　　　　　　　　Mò shān xī

婆心苦口，　　　　　　　Póxīn-kǔkǒu,
劝我随声和。　　　　　　quàn wǒ suí shēng hé.
委曲愿求全，　　　　　　Wěiqū yuàn qiúquán,
奈鸿沟未容越过。　　　　nài hónggōu wèi róng yuèguò.
毫厘千里，　　　　　　　Háolí qiānlǐ,
一念判人禽。　　　　　　yīniàn pàn rén qín.
辞苦盏，　　　　　　　　Cí kǔ zhǎn,
就甜杯，　　　　　　　　jiù tián bēi,
父母徒生我！　　　　　　fùmǔ tú shēng wǒ!

鸿沟纵越，　　　　　　　Hónggōu zòng yuè,
心计依然左，　　　　　　xīnjì yīrán zuǒ,
不见旧相知，　　　　　　bùjiàn jiù xiāngzhī,
竟低头，　　　　　　　　jìng dītóu,
然然可可。　　　　　　　ránrán kěkě.

徒劳争取，　　　　　　　Túláo zhēngqǔ,
照样十三年。　　　　　　zhàoyàng shísān nián.
抬望眼，　　　　　　　　Tái wàngyǎn,
企天鹅，　　　　　　　　qǐ tiān'é,
何处来宽大？　　　　　　héchù lái kuāndà?

Line 13:　　This line is copied from a poem by Xin Qiji.

34.

Human Bustle

To the tune of 'Jade Tower Spring'

In spring the Jade Maid shakes her chignon loose,
hiding on Peng Island and performing Daoist rites.
Like the sun and moon, immortals never die,
while human bustle ceases in the twinkling of an eye.

I've long forgotten grace and hate,
although my early goals remain intact.
Once a Han envoy came back from the West
and passed on the news to Chang'an.

玉楼春

玉妃峨髻春云鬓,
蓬岛修持环珮隐。
仙家日月自长存,
人世繁华都一瞬。

已拼忘却恩和恨,
无奈凡心销未尽。
一朝汉使自西来,
又向长安传息信。

Yùlóu chūn

Yùfēi éjì chūnyún bìn,
péngdǎo xiūchí huánpèi yǐn.
Xiānjiā rìyuè zì chángcún,
rénshì fánhuá dōu yīshùn.

Yǐ pīn wàngquè ēn hé hèn,
wúnài fánxīn xiāo wèijìn.
Yīzhāo hànshǐ zì xī lái,
yòu xiàng cháng'ān chuán xīxìn.

Line 1: Jade Maiden or Jade Concubine is either a female celestial or a stylised reference to Yang Guifei, a Tang Dynasty imperial consort considered one of China's four great beauties.
Line 2: The Daoist search for longevity and immortality focused on the mythical Islands of the Blessed, including Penglai, believed to be off the coast of Jiangsu in the East China Sea, and on the mythical Kunlun Mountains in the West.
Line 8: Zheng borrowed this idea from 'Encountering an envoy who is returning to the capital' by Cen Shen, who was writing from a frontier battlefield. Zheng uses the line to indicate that his original goals remained unchanged despite his ordeals, the 'news' being that he is safe.

35.

Magpie Bridge

On the seventh day of the seventh lunar month, magpies form a bridge to reunite separated lovers for a single day. Zheng is thinking of his wife.

To the tune of 'Immortals at the Magpie Bridge'

Crossing the river to renew our tryst,
we whisper in the secret palace after dark,
back together in each other's arms.
The magpies scatter and the hairpins come undone –
so close, yet worlds apart, as in a mist.

The clear blue sky cannot be real –
there is no evidence of a life to come.
Peng Island is mere make-believe.
And even if, years hence, Heaven should bring me back to you,
who's to say that love will not have grown old too?

鹊桥仙   Quèqiáo xiān

斜河旧约,   Xiéhé jiùyuē,
深官私语,   shēngōng sīyǔ,
此夜总萦怀抱。   cǐ yè zǒng yíng huáibào.
如今鹊散宝钗分,   Rújīn què sàn bǎochāi fēn,
但咫尺天涯缥缈。   dàn zhǐchǐ tiānyá piāomiǎo.

碧空虚幻,   Bìkōng xūhuàn,
来生无据,   láishēng wújù,
谩说浮槎蓬岛。   mánshuō fúchá Péngdǎo.
纵然天遣得相逢,   Zòngrán tiānqiǎn dé xiāngféng,
怕情意似人衰老。   pà qíngyì sì rén shuāilǎo.

'To the tune of':   A *ci* by Qin Guan.
Line 1:   A line from a *ci* by Jiang Kui.

36.

Guttering Candles

To the tune of 'Bodhisattva Strength'

They say we're candles guttering in the wind –
in just one year I've written countless *ci*.
I started with 'Water Dragon Chant'
and ended with 'Overlapping Gold'.

A palindrome is like a picture drawn on silk –
you want to send a message from the heart.
Alas, we're separated by a heavy drape.
How can we expect the swallows to return to build their nest?

菩萨蛮

谩言身似风前蜡,
一年积得词盈箧。
年始《水龙吟》,
年终《重叠金》。

回文如织锦,
欲寄知心品。
争奈隔重帘,
难凭归燕衔。

Púsà mán

Mányán shēn sì fēng qián là,
yī nián jī dé cí yíng qiè.
Niánshǐ 'Shuǐlóngyín',
niánzhōng 'chóngdiéjīn.'

Huí wén rú zhījǐn,
yù jì zhīxīn pǐn.
Zhēng nài gé chónglián,
nán píng guīyàn xián.

37.

The Waxing and the Waning Moon

Writing in 1961, Zheng plays on the waxing and waning of the moon to describe his release under the Nationalists and his reunion with his wife Jingzhen in 1937, followed fifteen years later by his return to jail under the Communists, for what would turn out to be a far longer number of years.

To the tune of 'Remembering Times Past in the Peach Orchard'

'When autumn starts, the heat begins to die.'
At noon, the heat retains its fire.
At first light, and at last, small breezes stir,
while in the trees cicadas chirp.

Twenty years ago today and four,
at around this same time of the year,
the moon was full and I stepped out of jail –
who would have thought that after waxing it would wane again?

桃源忆故人

'立秋日后无多热。'
近午炎威未歇。
早晚凉风微发,
枝上蝉声咽。

计年廿四从头说,
正是这般时节,
出狱重圆明月,
岂料圆还缺。

Táoyuán yì gùrén

'Lìqiū rìhòu wú duō rè.'
Jìnwǔ yánwēi wèixiē.
Zǎowǎn liángfēng wēifā,
zhī shàng chánshēng yàn.

Jìnián niànsì cóngtóu shuō,
zhèngshì zhěbān shíjié,
chūyù chóngyuán míngyuè,
qǐliào yuán hái quē.

'To the tune of':   The title of a *ci* by Qin Guan.

38.

Wartime Sojourn in Anhui

In 1996, Zheng commented on the background to this poem:

> This poem records my life in Southern Anhui, escaping from the war. When the war broke out and the Japanese bombed Nanjing, the Guomindang decided to move its capital [first to Wuhan and then to Chongqing to the west] and to 'evacuate the prisons'. Starting in around August, the Central Military Prison began freeing inmates. The Guomindang explained that 'evacuating the prisons' was common practice in modern states in extraordinary times. Most people said it was one of the conditions put forward by the Communist Party during the second period of cooperation with the Guomindang,[1] I don't know if that's true. Whatever the case, the Central Military Prison released not just political prisoners but common criminals and military prisoners, and eventually even some long-term non-political prisoners were released and sent to the [Guomindang] rear.
>
> At the time, I was in a single cell with He Zishen,[2] who only had a few months left to serve. On 20 August, he underwent various prison formalities and was released the next day. He found out where my wife was living, and she took him to Huqiao Prison where Chen Duxiu and other comrades were being kept. They had not yet been released. Chen Duxiu had already arranged for He Zishen and my wife to go not to

---

[1] The Second United Front between Nationalists and Communists, inaugurated in 1937.
[2] He Zishen (1898–1961), who had succeeded Mao as Secretary of the CCP's Hunan Provincial Committee, became a Trotskyist in 1929. He spent several years in gaol under the Guomindang and then again under the Communists, starting in 1952. According to Zheng, he had collapsed in both body and spirit before dying of a stroke.

Wartime Sojourn in Anhui

Shanghai but to Jixi in Anhui, where Wang Mengzou's[3] great-nephew lived, to recover. I was freed on 29 August. Chen Duxiu had already been freed on 23 August, and was staying with Chen Zhongfan. We went to see him, and slept the night on his floor. The next morning we left Nanjing for Wuhu, and spent the night in Wang Mengzou's Science Book Club. The next day, we took a long-distance bus to Jixi. I was not happy to go to Jixi to recover, I wanted to go back to Shanghai and resume long-term work there. But then I heard that Shanghai's South Railway Station had been bombed and the trains had stopped running, so I gave up the Shanghai idea for the time being.

Who would have thought that I would stay in Jixi for almost three years? At first we stayed with Wang Mengzou's family, but later we rented a house from Wang Mengzou's nephew, said to be the best private house in town. Japanese planes bombed the town, and the rich fled to the countryside. We followed the Wang family to a nearby village and stayed there until after the lunar New Year. He Zishen went back to Hunan.

Just before the Festival of Pure Brightness,[4] it was rumoured that the Japanese were about to advance from Xuancheng to Huizhou, so the rich families took to the mountains. Wang Naigang set up a primary school in the village and let my wife teach at it, so that the children would not miss out on their education and we could make a meagre living. To pay the bills, I intended to do some translating, but my wife fell pregnant and I had to take over from her. I taught by day and translated by night. During the summer, I opened a cramming school. After the summer holidays, things settled down. The rich people moved back into the town, and so did we, in September. On 5 November, our son Frei was born.

In 1939, in a place southwest of Jixi, a rural school needed a maths teacher, so I had to put aside my translation work and start teaching. I later learned that the headmaster, Zhu Dading, a returned student from Japan, was a member of the Communist Party. Some of the teaching

---

3 Wang Mengzou was a publisher friend of Chen Duxiu and a supporter of all progressive movements in China since the start of the twentieth century. See Benton, *Prophets Unarmed*, pp. 1046–7.
4 In early April.

Wartime Sojourn in Anhui

staff were members of the Guomindang and even of the CC Clique. They turned against the headmaster and encouraged the students to boycott classes. The school lacked funding, so I taught for one or two months without pay. According to government provisions, every teacher had to give a written guarantee that he or she would 'not violate the Three People's Principles', so I decided to quit the job.

After resigning, I concentrated on my translation work. I translated Trotsky's masterpiece *The Revolution Betrayed*, Victor Serge's *L'an 1 de la révolution russe* ('Year One of the Russian Revolution'), Gide's *Voyage au Congo* ('Voyage to the Congo'), Hedin's *Durch Asiens Wüsten* ('Through Asia's Deserts'), and other books. I did some of the translating in the town and some in a village, where I again went to escape the bombing. When I returned to the town from the village, I lived for two-and-a-half years rent-free in the home of Chen Xiaoqing, a partner in [Wang Mengzou's] Oriental Book Company. I only learned afterwards that Chen Xiaoqing was an old revolutionary who had taken part in the Revolution of 1911, helped sponsor the May Fourth Movement, and joined the Communist organisation, although he never told anyone, not even his two sons. When our Trotskyist Comrade Chen Qichang was captured by the Japanese, Chen Xiaoqing rushed to tell me, and warned me that spies might be living nearby.[5]

In late March 1940, [the Trotskyists in] Shanghai needed my presence and sent us the money for tickets. I, my wife, and our newborn child Frei crossed rivers and mountains, by way of Tunxi, Lanxi, Jinhua, Yiwu, Xikou, and Ningbo, and eventually caught the boat back to the lonely island of Shanghai.[6]

---

5 On Chen Qichang and his murder by the Japanese, see Benton, *Prophets Unarmed*, passim.
6 These passages are excerpted from Zheng Chaolin, *Yu Yin shici benshi* ('Literary source materials on Yu Yin's [Zheng Chaolin's] poems'), pp. 10–12. No printed source is given.

Wartime Sojourn in Anhui

To the tune of 'Sand of the Silk-Washing Brook'

(One)

Above Stone City fly surrender flags.
Like swallows flying out from falling towers,
we take in desperation to the hills.

Heaven put us back as one, but flames of war
stand in the way of our return by boat.
We while away our autumn days high in the Maoling hills.

(Two)

The year is nearly up and cold sets in, while fresh troops join the fight.
Bombs and snow fall side by side upon the mountain town,
and after dark we cling together in sheer mortal fright.

We skim the stream and stamp the bank,
and see the Suzhou bridges, clogged with reeds.
At dawn we reach the outskirts of the town.

(Three)

Small disasters drive us from the town,
while big disasters drive us from the fields.
The two of us build shelters in the hills and live like monkeys there.

Spring rains turn the tea bush green.
In the bamboo groves the francolins call out –
the mountains cast their spell.

(Four)

On hot and humid days, the mountain breezes blow.
Few students attend classes out of term,
and my belly swells.

Intent on climbing right up to the top,
we pause to lean on lone pines.
Clutching each other tight, we watch the geese's northward flight.

'To the tune of': A song by the statesman and poet Yan Shu.
Line 1: This line is modelled on a line in a well-known poem by Liu Yixi. Nanjing is also known as the City of Stone, especially in literary works.

(Five)

Below us, fewer hostile planes wheel through the sky.
A west wind strips the branches of their leaves.
Reluctantly, we leave the hills. 27

We cut cloth, sew, and make our things ourselves –
Frei's coats, his shoes, his wraps and hat.
Before dawn breaks, we wake up to his crying in his cot. 30

(Six)

The winter has been harsh, and spring is late.
Enemy planes turn up without respite,
driving us back into the countryside. 33

Our suckling child at six months has a winning smile.
It's two years since we fled the chaos for this vale of tears:
we're now three people – father, mother, and a baby child. 36

(Seven)

Behind the village tiered hills climb towards the sky.
At night wolves howl and tigers roar,
stealing and killing local dogs and pigs. 39

Sometimes we arrive home late,
when the flaming maple's flame is all but spent
and the crosspiece fastened to the village gate. 42

(Eight)

In the hills we pluck wild flowers.
Loyal to our old ideals, we ride the bus
back across hills, and sail the sea, and celebrate arriving home. 45

Out on the Huangpu River for the first time in nine years,
the two of us drink Ceylon tea –
now no longer two but three. 48

Line 46: Zheng and Liu returned to Shanghai (and its Huangpu River) in 1940, nine years after Zheng's imprisonment in 1931.

浣 溪 沙（八首）

(其一)

忆昔降幡出石头，
人如双燕弃危楼，
山中萧索暂迟留。

才敢天官圆破镜，
又惊烽火阻归舟，
客中闲度茂陵丘。

(其二)

岁暮天寒更遇兵，
炸弹和雪落山城，
双栖连夜梦魂惊。

犟水滩头留足迹，
来苏桥畔挽枯藤，
日高人已出郊坰。

(其三)

小乱避城大避乡，
万山深处有村庄，
夫妻聊作猰㺄王。

春水生时茶树绿，
鹧鸪啼处笋梢长，
山居况味不寻常。

(其四)

溽暑高山有好风，
假期课室少儿童，
腹中块肉渐膨膨。

游兴未阑攀绝顶，
四肢无力倚孤松，
相扶同望北归鸿。

(其五)

山下新来少敌机，
西风吹叶剩空枝，
出山回望尚依依。

自剪自缝还自制，
孩鞋孩帽更孩衣，
侵晨忽听小儿啼。

(其六)

过尽残冬又晚春，
敌机连日往来频，
出城另觅一山村。

半岁乳儿能巧笑，
二年离乱叹艰辛，
相依亲子共三人。

(其七)

村后群山步步高，
夜深时听虎狼嗥，
几回豚犬吻馋膏。

数度入城归已晚，
丹枫残照映长袍，
到村门户早拴牢。

(其八)

又见山头拆野花，
提携抱负共登车，
越山渡海庆还家。

九载重临黄浦岸，
两人再饮锡兰茶，
却多身畔一娃娃。

Wartime Sojourn in Anhui

Huán xī shā (bā shǒu)

(Qí yī)

Yìxī jiàngfān chū shítou,
rén rú shuāngyàn qì wēilóu,
shānzhōng xiāosuǒ zàn chí liú.

Cái gǎn tiāngōng yuán pòjìng,
yòu jīng fēnghuǒ zǔ guīzhōu,
kè zhōng xián dù Màolíng qiū.

(Qí èr)

Suìmù tiānhán gèng yù bīng,
zhàdàn héxuě luò shānchéng,
shuāngqī liányè mènghún jīng.

Huīshuǐ tāntóu liú zújì,
Láisū qiáopàn wǎn kūténg,
rì gāo rén yǐ chū jiāojiōng.

(Qí sān)

Xiǎoluàn bìchéng dà bìxiāng,
wànshān shēnchù yǒu cūnzhuāng,
fūqī liáozuò róngsūn wáng.

Chūnshuǐ shēngshí cháshù lǜ,
zhègū tíchù sǔnshāo zhǎng,
shānjū kuàngwèi bù xúncháng.

(Qí sì)

Rùshǔ gāoshān yǒu hǎofēng,
jiàqī kèshì shào értóng,
fùzhōng kuàiròu jiàn péngpéng.

Yóuxīng wèilán pān juédǐng,
sìzhī wúlì yǐ gūsōng,
xiāngfú tóngwàng běiguī hóng.

(Qí wǔ)

Shānxià xīnlái shǎo díjī,
xīfēng chuīyè shèng kōngzhī,
chūshān huíwàng shàng yīyī.

Zìjiǎn zìfèng hái zìzhì,
háixié háimào gèng háiyī,
qīnchén hūtīng xiǎo'ér tí.

(Qí liù)

Guòjǐn cándōng yòu wǎnchūn,
díjī liánrì wǎnglái pín,
chūchéng lìngmì yī shāncūn.

Bànsuì rǔ'ér néng qiǎoxiào,
èr nián líluàn tàn jiānxīn,
xiāngyī qīnzǐ gòng sān rén.

(Qí qī)

Cūnhòu qúnshān bùbù gāo,
yèshēn shítīng hǔláng háo,
jǐhuí túnquǎn wěn chángāo.

Shùdù rùchéng guī yǐwǎn,
dānfēng cánzhào yìng chángpáo,
dàocūn ménhù zǎo shuānláo.

(Qí bā)

Yòujiàn shāntóu chāi yěhuā,
tíxié bàofù gòng dēngchē,
yuèshān dùhǎi qìng huánjiā.

Jiǔzǎi chónglín huángpǔ àn,
liǎngrén zàiyǐn xīlán chá,
quèduō shēnpàn yī wáwá.

39.

'Memorial to Ding'

In prison under Mao, Zheng Chaolin celebrated his love for Trotsky in a poetic rebus he wrote after reading in the Chinese press that Khrushchev had proposed building a memorial to the victims of Stalin's terror; and that the Fourth International had written to tell Moscow that Trotsky's name should be on it 'in gold letters'.

In 1988, Zheng wrote as follows about this poem:

> On 1 July this year, Reuters announced that 'on Friday Soviet leader Gorbachev proposed the establishment of a monument in Moscow to mourn the millions of victims of Stalin's dictatorial rule.' Gorbachev said: 'Many people have proposed a monument, and we can only agree.' He added that 'this monument must be built in Moscow. I am sure the people of the Soviet Union will be well disposed to the idea.'
>
> This followed a proposal by the Soviet leaders, twenty-seven years earlier, at the time of the Twenty-Second Congress in 1961, by the then leader Khrushchev, to put up a monument in Moscow to commemorate the victims of Stalin's terror. This was reported in the Chinese press. But what left an indelible impression on me was not the report itself but the Chinese Party's 'exposure', later, in 1963, during the Sino–Soviet dispute. The Soviet Party denounced the Chinese Party as 'modern-day Trotskyists', while the Chinese Party hit back with the same charge, and even provided evidence: after Khrushchev had made his proposal, the [Trotskyist] Fourth International's Secretariat sent Moscow a telegram saying that when you set up such a monument in Moscow, Trotsky's name should be 'engraved on it in gold letters.'
>
> Others might have forgotten this, but I have not. At the time I had been in prison for ten years, waiting to be dealt with. I had had no news of the Fourth International – did it still exist? Now I knew not only that it still survived but that it was able to respond quickly to world events.

'Memorial to Ding'

I had been waiting for ten years, and could have been taken out at any time and shot. I thought to myself, if there is life after death, where will my spirit go? First, it will go to Moscow, to put a bouquet of flowers on that memorial.

Zheng wrote on another occasion:

Not until after I was released from jail in 1979 did I learn that the memorial proposed by Khrushchev had not been built. So even if the disembodied soul in my poem really had taken flowers to Moscow, it would have had to lay them before a disembodied stone. Today, there is every chance that the memorial of my dreams will finally be built, regardless of whether Trotsky's name appears on it in gold. As for myself, I am still not yet a wandering ghost. Now [after my release from prison], I do not need to write about my dreams in ways that will fool the censor, for it is no longer a crime to speak out against Stalin. But I have no wish to write a new poem to voice my feelings, so I shall let the poem I wrote twenty-odd years ago stand, under its original title 'Memorial to Ding', as a record of the events of those days.

The Chinese character *ding* 丁 is close in shape to the Western letter T, and in his prison poem Zheng uses it to stand for Trotsky. The prison authorities failed to see through this thin disguise and took the poem to be nonsense.

'Memorial to Ding'

The north wind gusts, the snowflakes dance,
vast buildings tower along the way.
Red flags on rooftops dapple white,
crowds surge like tides through subway gates.
5 This stubborn shade, this wisp of smoke,
will face God with its granite brain:
clutching fresh blooms it treads the snow,
enquiring of each passer-by,
'Where is the grand memorial?'
10 When last here, I was very young.
Bullet scars could still be seen
around the university.
Yet people rose above the mean
and narrow streets to dwarf the gods.
15 Now poverty has given way
to affluence, unlettered night
to dawning of the lettered light.
Sapling of my youth, you've grown
into a tree where people take
20 shade from the sun and pick fresh fruit;
those who planted it are dead,
the earth beneath is stained jade green.
See, the marble comes in sight
clean and white as frozen fat.
25 Flowers bedeck the steps and plinth.
With spinning eyes I scan the stone
line by line for words of gold.
Framed in the blurred names' giddy ring,
whichever way I look I see
30 nothing but *ding*, *ding*, *ding*, and *ding*.

Line 1: This line echoes some phrases in Mao's poem 'Snow'.
Line 4: Zheng imagines a new Moscow, different from the one he left behind in 1924.
Line 6: Mao Zedong once said of his opponents who refused to give up their positions: 'Let them go to see their God with their granite brains.'
Line 22: Zhuangzi told a story about Chang Hong, a high official wrongly killed by a prince in Shu (now Sichuan). Chang Hong's blood, after being stored for three years, changed colour from red to emerald, whence the popular saying that the blood of those wrongly killed turns green, and even becomes green jade.

'Memorial to Ding'

丁字碑

朔风猎猎白雪飘,
道旁层楼百丈高。
楼顶红旗褪颜色,
地道人出势如潮。
游魂躯体烟缥缈,
顽固未化花岗脑。
鲜花在手踏雪行,
逢人问讯丰碑道。
忆昔来游正少年,
弹痕尚见学官前。
楼低街窄称简陋,
人物风流胜神仙。
昔穷今富文易白,
大树遮荫果可摘。
不见种树当时人,
树下藏血斑斑碧。
行行渐次见丰碑,
碑身洁白如凝脂。
鲜艳花枝碑前置,
碑上试寻黄金字。
累累名姓有若无,
纵行横行尽丁字。

Dīngzì bēi

Shuòfēng lièliè báixuě piāo,
dàopáng cénglóu bǎizhàng gāo.
Lóudǐng hóngqí tuì yánsè,
dìdào renchū shì rúcháo.
Yóuhún qūtǐ yān piāomiǎo,
wángù wèihuà huāgāng nǎo.
Xiānhuā zàishǒu tàxuě xíng,
féngrén wènxùn fēngbēi dào.
Yìxī láiyóu zhèng shàonián,
dànhén shàngjiàn xuégōng qián.
Lóudī jiēzhǎi chēng jiǎnlòu,
rénwù fēngliú shèng shénxiān.
Xīqióng jīnfù wén yìbái,
dàshù zhēyīn guǒ kězhāi.
Bù jiàn zhǒngshù dāngshí rén,
shù xià cángxuè bānbān bì.
Hángháng jiàncì jiàn fēngbēi,
bēishēn jiébái rú níngzhī.
Xiānyàn huāzhī bēiqián zhì,
bēi shàng shìxún huángjīn zì.
Lěilěi míngxìng yǒu ruòwú,
zòng háng héng háng jìn dīngzì.

40.

Two Birthday Poems

Zheng wrote in 1988:

> I spent my sixtieth birthday in prison [in 1961], and on that same day I wrote a *guti* poem[1] titled 'The Poet's Trade'. For fear of getting into trouble, I did not write at length, just a few things about my life as an ordinary poet. My seventieth birthday fell during the Cultural Revolution [in 1971]. I had to attend struggle meetings, and [on that occasion] I didn't dare write a poem. By my eightieth birthday I'd got some of my courage back, but, to be blunt, day had not yet dawned and the revolution had not yet happened. When you can't speak clearly, you have to fall back on mythology, so that people can't understand what you're saying. Now, those myths need to be brought back into human words. The *ci* was in the style of 'Congratulating the Bridegroom' ('He xin lang'). The darkness symbolises reaction, the brightness symbolises revolution. Xihe is the messenger of the sun, she drives the sun's chariot. Her driving towards the East represents waiting for the arrival of the revolution. Jinwu (the Golden Crow) is the sun, Yuxiao the place the sun reaches after it has gone down the mountain. The Golden Crow dropping down on Yuxiao means the sky is dark again. The last sentence says that socialist revolution will finally gain victory.

---

[1] A form of pre-Tang poetry, usually with five or seven characters (and therefore syllables) per line.

The Poet's Trade

Self-Congratulations on My Sixtieth Birthday

I wanted as a child to be a poet,
squinting through tears at autumn moon and springtime bloom,
belting out songs of joy and gloom,
swooning, groaning, moaning.
But my teachers taught me to see things as they are, 5
so I lost my appetite for Lady Love.
Instead I strove to understand what's right and wrong
rather than to laugh and cry.
I fought for decades for the cause,
cheating by happy chance the Yellow Springs. 10
Clinging as ever to the human world,
in soughing winds my grey head wears the southern crown.
But still I can't resist the urge to scratch the itch
to scribble off a melancholy line or two.
Young people's worries rarely weigh them down, 15
but mine reach up unto the very sky.
The sexagenary cycle is complete.
Fondly I hold the goblet to my lips:
scores of poems for a birthday feast,
here's to my youthful elegant ideals. 20
No one is around to appreciate my poems,
so I'll leave them for the ghosts of autumn grave to sing.

Line 8: Zheng paraphrases Spinoza: '*Sedulo curavi, humanas actiones non ridere, non lugere, neque detestari, sed intiligere*' ('I have laboured carefully, not to mock, lament or detest human actions, but to understand them').
Line 10: The world of the dead.
Line 12: A reworking of a line by Su Shi. The 'southern crown' was the classical marker of a prisoner.
Line 16: A reworking of two lines by Xin Qiji.
Line 23: A reworking of a line by Li He.

Self-Congratulations on My Sixtieth Birthday

诗人行

六十自寿

少年有志作诗人，
秋月春花学怆神。
不写欢心写愁思，
明知无病谩呻吟。
现实严师督促忙，
无心再访浪漫娘。
但求理解是与非，
不愿欢笑不悲伤。
斗争数十年，
幸未赴黄泉。
尚占人间一席地，
萧萧华发戴南冠。
吟诗不觉旧技痒，
轻弄笔头写惆怅。
少时每恨愁无多，
如今愁大如天样。
今年甲子恰重周，
捧觞称寿有温柔：
诗篇数十作寿酒，
少年雅志今得酬。
诗成无人赏，
留与秋坟听鬼唱！

Shīrén xíng

Liùshí zì shòu

Shàonián yǒuzhì zuò shīrén,
qiūyuè-chūnhuā xué chuàngshén.
Bùxiě huānxīn xiě chóusī,
míngzhī wúbìng mán shēnyín.
Xiànshí yánshī dūcù máng,
wúxīn zàifǎng làngmàn niáng.
Dànqiú lǐjiě shì yǔ fēi,
bùyuàn huānxiào bù bēishāng.
Dòuzhēng shùshí nián,
xìng wèi fù huángquán.
Shàngzhàn rénjiān yīxí dì,
xiāoxiāo huáfà dài nánguān.
Yínshī bùjué jiùjìy ǎng,
qīngnòng bǐtóu xiě chóuchàng.
Shǎoshí měihèn chóu wú duō,
rújīn chóudà rú tiān yàng.
Jīnnián jiǎzǐ qià chóngzhōu,
pěngshāng chēngshòu yǒu wēnróu:
Shīpiān shùshí zuò shòujiǔ,
shàonián yǎzhì jīn dé chóu.
Shīchéng wúrén shǎng,
liúyǔ qiūfén tīng guǐchàng!

Self-Congratulations on My Eightieth Birthday

This poem was written on 12 April 1980, a few months after Zheng's prison days. But this is still, essentially, a prisoner writing, and Zheng describes it in the same comment as on the poem he wrote for his sixtieth. It therefore appears here out of sequence.

> Can surviving chaos be a boon?
> This is a matter for debate.
> The yeti leaves its footprints in the mountain snow,
> the lotus in the mineshaft leaves its faint scent on the air.
> The redwood lends charm to the park,
> the panda in a circus ring, in panic and distress.
> See how the silent turn to stone –
> those who are speechless also speak
> about the trees and seas.

八十自寿

劫余生命岂祯祥?
惹得纷纷议论扬。
山上雪人留足迹,
矿中莲实发清香。
水杉婀娜庭园际,
班达凄惶竞技场。
何若无声诸化石,
不言亦足话沧桑。

Bāshí zì shòu

Jiéyú shēngmìng qǐ zhēnxiáng?
Rědé fēnfēn yìlùn yáng.
Shān shàng xuěrén liú zújì,
kuàng zhōng liánshí fā qīngxiāng.
Shuǐshān ēnuó tíngyuán jì,
bāndá qīhuáng jìngjì chǎng.
Héruò wúshēng zhū huàshí,
bùyán yìzú huà cāngsāng.

Line 3: Zheng has adapted the idea that life is as short and transient as a random footprint left in the snow from the poet Su Shi, who wrote: 'What can our life be likened to? It should be likened to a swan stepping on the snow. The flying swan does not care about its footprint, which will soon disappear under fresh snow.'
Line 6: Both perform to please the audience.
Line 9: The vicissitudes of life, and the prospect of massive change. See Poem 5, 'How the Mighty Fall'. Stone fossils preserve traces of past life.

41.

'Sending Off the Stove God'

In Chinese folk religion and popular Daoism, the Stove (or Kitchen) God protects the hearth and family. This poem traces the passage in the Chinese countryside from small-scale tyranny carried out by local bullies and corrupt officials, pictured by Zheng as Stove Gods, to large-scale tyranny exercised by the 'cadreist' state, as in the replacement during the Great Leap Forward of 1958–61 of a household-based domestic economy (and private kitchens) to a rural economy run by communes (with public canteens).

Cadreism (*ganbu zhuyi*) was Zheng's term for the type of state he believed had been established by the revolution of 1949 – one that was neither capitalist nor of the workers. Unfortunately, the book in which he had set out, while in prison, his ideas on cadreism was confiscated by the prison authorities, and no copies of it seem to have survived. Cadreism was akin to another current that emerged in world Trotskyism in the late 1930s and early 1940s – James Burnham's theory of 'managerial revolution' (describing a society in which a new 'managerial class' had assumed power) and Max Shachtman's position (similar in some respects to Burnham's) on the question of the class nature of the Soviet Union. Zheng and his comrades had loose, semi-active ties to Max Shachtman's organisation in the mid to late 1940s.

Most of the public canteens this poem talks about had closed by 1961–62 (mainly because the peasants hated them). However, the cadreist state remained intact, even after 1961. It was not until the 1980s that the Small Gods won back some of the power they had lost – during the Three Red Banners period – to the One Big God, representing the Communist Party. In 1988, Zheng wrote the following commentary on this poem:

> When these poems were about to be printed, I decided not to include this one, for fear of causing offence. Friends disagreed. They said the poem satirised public canteens, and that they too thought public canteens had

'Sending Off the Stove God'

been a mistake and that the poem would not get me into trouble. So I reluctantly agreed to publish it.

In fact, satirising public canteens is a superficial issue – this poem is about the essence of the state, a modern state sustained by spies and secret agents, an organisation more important than the standing army, which is itself controlled by spies and special agents. The Soviet Union under Stalin was a typical example of such a state. The activities of every household and every individual were recorded, and all opposition was nipped in the bud.

Stalin did not invent this sort of state – it's been around since ancient times. He simply perfected it. The subject people, in accordance with their life experience, used 'fairy tales' to explain the nature of the state. In their view, the reason the Jade Emperor knows so much about a family's or an individual's situation, his or her merits and demerits, was that the spirits send a Stove Lord into a family to live with them and collect information about them and pass it on to Heaven. Intelligence is concentrated in Heaven's hands and there's no way to stop that happening. So the Stove Lord sits between two parts of a couplet on hanging scrolls: 'When you go up to Heaven / Report good things', meaning that if we do anything bad, please don't tell on us, allow us to live our lives safely and in peace. Sometimes people don't use 'fairy talk' to explain the nature of the state but instead use 'human talk'. It's said that when China was under Mongol rule, each household had a *dazi* ('barbarian')[1] quartered with it, and if the members of the household did anything wrong, the *dazi* would report them. Towards the end of Mongol rule, the people were no longer prepared to put up with this and were planning to revolt. And so one year, at the Mid-Autumn Festival, everyone agreed to make cakes and to give them to each other, having baked the plan for the uprising into the cake. When the day came, they rose up and chased away the Mongols. This is said to be the origin of moon cakes.[2] But it's just a legend, not a fact. The Mongols didn't have

---

[1] Han Chinese saw the Mongol Yuan Dynasty (1271–1368) as an alien occupation.
[2] At the end of the Yuan Dynasty, Liu Bowen, a Han Chinese general, is said to have ordered his soldiers to tell people that disease was about to break out and eating moon cakes was the only remedy. His soldiers put pieces of paper into the cakes announcing an

'Sending Off the Stove God'

enough people to station one Mongol in each Han family. Still, the legend proves that the Chinese people understood the nature of the state. The rulers, on the other hand, were not happy about this.

Today there is something else that needs to be understood about this poem: the state system is determined by the mode of production. The Soviet Union under Stalin set up that sort of national system, and supported it with an organisation of spies and special agents. After the Second World War, however, the traditional capitalist mode of production suddenly took off, eclipsing the mode of capitalist production (cadreism) that had developed in the Soviet Union, so that the Soviet Union easily collapsed and 'peacefully evolved' into traditional capitalism. The perfected system of spies and secret agents was no longer needed – something that I, in the early 1960s, could not know would happen in the early 1990s. This confirms a basic tenet of Marxism, that the superstructure is determined by the economy, and the mode of production determines the form and nature of the state.

But if that state can conform to the prevailing mode of production, then the power that maintains its existence and development must be an organisation of spies and secret agents. Today's Russia under Yeltsin still needs spies and secret agents to support it.

> On the twenty-fourth day of *la*
> Stove God informs Jade Emperor in the Sky,
> in writing and by word of mouth,
> about all household matters great and small:
> 5   'Old Lady prays to Buddha but complains behind his back.
> Young Master gambles in the fan-tan shack.
> In public, Widowed Daughter gets ready for the life beyond,

---

uprising at the Mid-Autumn Festival. The uprising led to the end of Mongol rule. According to legend, this is why the Chinese eat moon cakes at mid-autumn.
Line 1:   *La*, the 'preserved month', is the twelfth month in the Chinese lunar calendar, corresponding roughly to December and followed by the Spring Festival.
Line 2:   On the twenty-fourth day of that month, Zaojun the Stove God goes to report to the Jade Emperor in Heaven on the family's behaviour over the past year, so that the Jade Emperor can reward or punish the family accordingly in the year to come. The family prepares offerings to Zaojun to secure his goodwill.

'Sending Off the Stove God'

but privately placates the Dipper Stars with food and wine.'
Heaven holds hearings on the household's merits and misdeeds.
The Southern Wain grants favours, the Northern Wain spreads woe.   10
The common folk are crafty when it comes to playing tricks.
At year's end when its members pass around the pigs and hens
they place a lump of sugar in the Stove God's gob
to stop him telling tales on them when reporting on his job.
What does Fat Guts do when household members grease his palm?   15
He says whatever's needed to preserve his folk from harm.
But his reports are usually quite flawed,
with the result that Heaven loses face abroad.
One year Sky God gets a mighty shock
when Stove God fails to show up for his meeting in the spheres.   20
Thousand Mile Eyes and Wind Borne Ears
peer down onto the world from Heaven's Gate:
the households have thrown Old Stovie out,
communal village gods now serve the big canteens.
No one burns incense for Old Stovie any more –   25
instead, he gathers dust behind the door.
Jade Emperor emits a sorry sigh,
for his Sky-God powers have gone awry.
Wain's assured a life of ease –
but Heavenly Official won't be pleased.   30
So it goes for three or four bleak years.
But Sky God's taken by surprise
as suddenly through clouds and mist to Heaven's Gate there plies
pell-mell a Stove-God cavalcade.
Haggard-faced and shedding bitter tears,   35
the Stove Gods sob their sorrows and blurt out their fears:
'Joss sticks are no longer lit.
Family kitchens are allowed again,
and the canteens have all been shut.
Even so, we still don't get our wine and meat,   40

Line 8: The Dipper or Wain mansion is one of twenty-eight mansions of the Chinese constellations. In Daoist texts, the Dipper stars cast a black light and are inhabited by female deities.
Line 21: Two martial figures with fierce expressions who protect the gods.
Line 30: In the celestial bureaucracy of Daoism, the asterisms or constellations of the celestial sphere are known as 'officials'.
Line 31: The crisis years of the Great Leap Forward (1958–61).

'Sending Off the Stove God'

and households rarely sprinkle incense at our feet;
today, intelligence is concentrated in another place,
where fortune and misfortune are dealt out case by case;
people must now beg New Master to be kind,
and put Old Stovie's gossip out of mind.'

送灶歌

年年腊月二十四,
灶君上天奏玉帝。
口头汇报笔头呈,
一家人事无巨细:
'老妪念佛心怨天,
小主偷闲学赌钱;
亦有孀媳修来世,
拜神礼斗丰杯盘。'
天廷据此判功过,
南斗施恩北斗祸。
世人亦有小聪明,
岁暮鸡豚相送迎,
大块饴糖塞神口,
求神天上抬贵手。
灶君满脑复肠肥,
上奏果然善说辞。
往往情报无凭准,
天堂从此失威信。
一年天上大惊奇,
云端不见灶君驰。
千里眼呼顺风耳,
急出天门看尘世:

家家私灶荡无存,
一方公灶一个村。
村灶无奁供香火,
灶君神像委埃尘。
玉帝闻言长叹息,
天堂权力从此毕!
双斗清闲惟弈棋,
仙官个个蹙愁眉。
如斯冷落三四载,
今年天上又惊怪:
腾云驾雾向天门,
灶君忽见来纷纷。
面黄肌瘦双泪堕,
泣诉:'人间断香火,
今年私灶幸重光,
处处村民散食堂;
今朝依旧无酒肉,
平时亦欠一炉香;
情报集中另有处,
祸福操持另有主;
但求新主发慈悲,
不畏小神搬是非!'

'Sending Off the Stove God'

Sòng zào gē

Niánnián làyuè èrshísì,
zàojūn shàngtiān zòu yùdì.
Kǒutóu huìbào bǐtóu chéng,
yījiārén shìwú jùxì:
'Lǎoyù niànfó xīn yuàntiān,
xiǎozhǔ tōuxián xué dǔqián;
yìyǒu shuāngxí xiū láishì,
bàishén lǐdòu fēngbēi pán.'
Tiāntíng jù cǐ pàn gōngguò,
nándǒu shī'ēn běidǒu huò.
Shìrén yìyǒu xiǎo cōngmíng,
suìmù jī tún xiāng sòngyíng,
dàkuài yítáng sāi shénkǒu,
qiúshén tiānshàng tái guìshǒu.
Zàojūn mǎnnǎo fù chángféi,
shàngzòu guǒrán shàn shuōcí.
Wǎngwǎng qíngbào wú píngzhǔn,
tiāntáng cóngcǐ shī wēixìn.
Yī nián tiānshàng dà jīngqí,
yúnduān bùjiàn zàojūn chí.
Qiānlǐyǎn hū shùnfēng'ěr,
jí chū tiānmén kàn chénshì:

Jiājiā sīzào dàng wúcún,
yī fāng gōngzào yī gè cūn.
Cūnzào wú kān gōng xiānghuǒ,
zàojūn shénxiàng wěi āichén.
Yùdì wényán cháng tànxí,
tiāntáng quánlì cóngcǐ bì!
Shuāngdǒu qīngxián wéi yìqí,
xiāngguān gègè cù chóuméi.
Rú sī lěngluò sānsì zǎi,
jīnnián tiānshàng yòu jīngguài:
Téngyún jiàwù xiàng tiānmén,
zàojūn hūjiàn lái fēnfēn.
Miànhuáng jīshòu shuāng lèi duò,
qìsù: 'Rénjiàn duàn xiānghuǒ,
jīnnián sīzào xìng chóngguāng,
chùchù cūnmín sàn shítáng;
jīnzhāo yījiù wú jiǔròu,
píngshí yìqiàn yī lú xiāng;
qíngbào jízhōng lìng yǒu chù,
huòfú cāochí lìng yǒu zhǔ;
dànqiú xīnzhǔ fā cíbēi,
bù wèi xiǎoshén bān shìfēi!'

42.

But for His Unyielding Character

Zheng wrote this poem in response to a poem presented to him on his birthday by his cellmate Yu Shouyi, an alias of Yu Shuoyi.[1] It belongs to a poetic genre known as 'presentation and response' (*zengda*), in which the recipient writes a 'companion piece' (*he*) to the poem received. We do not have Yu's poem, but Zheng's response would have made frequent references to the text he had received from Yu, answering its ideas and replicating parts of its structure, including its rhyme scheme. Response poems were part of a poetic transaction that usually expressed and deepened the writers' bonds, but in this case Zheng used the exchange to signal discord, not alliance, and to mark his break with Yu.

On 20 March 1996, Zheng wrote as follows about this poem:

I wrote this poem in 1965 in Tilanqiao Prison. The cellmate mentioned in the Preface who wrote me a birthday poem was Yu Shouyi. At the time, Yu Shouyi, like me, was one of the Trotskyists 'not yet dealt with', so he, [like me], did not attend the study group. In order to study 'anti-revisionist documents', we four prisoners who had 'not yet been dealt with' (Zheng Chaolin, Yin Kuan, Yu Shouyi, and Huang Jiantong[2]) were put in a special group. Our cell was segregated from that of the other Trotskyists, but soon Yin Kuan fell ill and was admitted to hospital, and we three continued studying the documents. Then Huang

---

1 Yu Shuoyi was a leader of the Shanghai young Trotskyists. He was the first to be arrested after 1949 and died in an asylum where he had been sent after developing schizophrenia
2 Yin Kuan (1897–1967) joined the Chinese Communist Party in France around 1920. He was active in the Shandong Provincial Committee, the Anhui Provincial Committee and the Jiangsu-Zhejiang Regional Committee in 1925–27, and became a Trotskyist in 1929. He was twice arrested by the Guomindang, and then by the Maoists in 1952. Huang Jiantong (1918–1987) was a leader of the Guangxi Trotskyists. He was released from prison together with Zheng Chaolin in 1979. His story is told in Benton, *Prophets Unarmed*, pp. 118–25.

But for His Unyielding Character

Jiantong also fell ill and had to go to hospital, and the two of us remaining were too few to form a group. We could chat about everything. We weren't worried about the authorities finding out.

Yu Shouyi had been arrested in Wuhan. At first, [like me], he refused to say he was guilty, but after a while he pleaded guilty. However, I learned from our conversation that his 'confession' was fake, and that he still stood with Trotsky against Stalin.

I agree that Yin Kuan told me in private that his guilty plea was fake, so he could still be regarded as an old friend, as a Trotskyist; but I couldn't regard Yu Shouyi as a Trotskyist, for his case differed from that of Yin Kuan. Yin Kuan never advised me to plead guilty, but Yu Shouyi repeatedly did so. He thought I was in great danger. He knew it was my birthday (I'd told him so), so he wrote a *qilü*,[3] partly to celebrate my birthday, partly to badger me into pleading guilty. The poem was no good, but the basic rhyme scheme was consistent.

At the time, I was reading *Shi guangchuan* ('The Propagation of Poetry') by Wang Fuzhi,[4] in which Wang quotes the line 'He who does not know me says that I am arrogant' and ends by asking: 'Who on earth enjoys being arrogant? If it is true that no one does, must we think that refusing to be arrogant is honourable?' What he meant was: obviously it's important not to think yourself head and shoulders above others, but you must do what you have to do. If others think you see yourself as head and shoulders above them, so be it. Wang Fuzhi's words were about his personal situation, but I was able to use them to respond to Yu Shouyi's advice.

In my response poem, the first line is about Chen Zhongzhi,[5] the second about Bao Jian,[6] the third about Liu Xiang,[7] the fourth about

---

3 An eight-line poem with seven characters in each line.
4 Wang Fuzhi (1619–1692) was a thinker and literary theorist of the late Ming and early Qing dynasties.
5 Chen Zhongzhi (c. 300 BCE) was an aristocrat from the state of Qi who starved himself to death in order to remain 'clean'.
6 Bao Jiao, a recluse of the Zhou Dynasty, opposed government corruption and chose to live in the mountains, eating nothing he had not grown himself and wearing only clothes woven by his wife.
7 Liu Xiang (79–8 BCE) was an official of the Han Dynasty stripped of office for remonstrating with the Emperor. He was famous for collating bamboo slips and silk scrolls in order to establish sound texts of Confucian and other writings.

But for His Unyielding Character

Yue Fei,[8] the fifth about the brothers Yi and Qi,[9] the sixth about [Xie Ao and] Zheng Sixiao,[10] and the eighth about Park Gate, which is what we called the prison. The rhyme class is that of the original poem, but that poem has been lost. The line ending in *zong* was originally in response to [a line ending with] Tang [Emperor] Taizong in [Yu Shouyi's] original poem, but only when I remembered that Zheng Sixiao's family name was Zheng was I able to solve the problem.

Preface to the Response

In the forty-second year of the sexagenary cycle [1965], on my birthday, a fellow-prisoner presented me with a *qilü*. In it, he urged me to be less stubborn and to accept reform, and cited the example of Emperor Taizong who had the humility to take counsel from others. At the time, I happened to be reading Wang Fuzhi's *The Propagation of Poetry*, where I came across the following paragraph: 'But for their unyielding character, Uncle Yi and Uncle Qi would not have starved to death. But for his unyielding character, Bao Jiao would not have held fast to a withered tree and died. But for his unyielding character, Shen Tudi would not have drowned himself.[11] But for his unyielding character, Liu Xiang would not have been dismissed. But for his unyielding character, Yue Fei would not have been killed. But for their unyielding character, Xie Ao and Zheng Sixiao would not have grieved. Is a sense of pride or unyielding spirit deliberately sought? Immense indignation explodes when worries and anxieties escape control. The unrestrained explosion of indignation does not yield to human force, it is as bright as the sun and moon. There are few in the world on whom it will not shine. A lofty and unyielding character is a natural thing. Anyone who pretends to be

---

8   Yue Fei (1103–1142) was a general in the Southern Song Dynasty, seen after his execution as the epitome of loyalty.
9   Uncle Yi and Uncle Qi were princes of the Shang Dynasty (c. 1600–1046 BCE). After the Shang's fall and the transition to the Zhou Dynasty, they refused to serve the Zhou and fled to the mountains, where they died of starvation.
10 Xie Ao and Zheng Sixiao were late Song Dynasty poets, who wrote poems mourning the fall of the Song and refused to serve under the new Mongol Yuan Dynasty.
11 Shen Tudi was an official in the Warring States period who held onto a stone and drowned himself when the king refused to accept his remonstration.

But for His Unyielding Character

unyielding for the sake of power is base. A person of honour does not delight in pride, nor does such a person refuse pride to achieve a false reputation. Base people's long-held jealousy of pride means little, just as stalks of grass cannot block the sounding of a big bell.' By using the *yinkuo* method,[12] I wrote a companion piece to Yu Shouyi's poem in accordance with its original rhyme scheme. I did not write Xie Ao and Shen Tudi into my poem, although Wang referred to them in his. Instead, I wrote in Chen Zhongzhi, to whom Wang did not refer.

1. Happily, he eats the maggots on the plum-tree by the well.
2. Spurning the dates and clinging to the withered tree, he holds fast to his purity.
3. In the Tianlu Pavilion, he treasures the ancient bamboo slips.
4. Under the Fengbo Pavilion, his outstanding work expires.
5. In the Western Hills, ferns feed men of virtue and integrity.
6. Orchids lack the soil in which to nourish errant thought.
7. Scratching your hoary head, you find your aspirations turn to nought.
8. The Park Gate inmates praise the ancient sages' style.

有答	Yǒu dá
不嫌井李蚀蟰虫，	Bùxián jǐnglǐ shí cáochóng,
弃枣身枯守素衷。	qìzǎo shēnkū shǒu sùzhōng.
天禄阁中珍古简，	Tiānlù gézhōng zhēn gǔjiǎn,
风波亭下败奇功。	fēngbō tíngxià bài qígōng.
西山有蕨供高士，	Xīshān yǒujué gōng gāoshì,
兰草无泥写敝宗。	láncǎo wúní xiě bìzōng.
壮志成灰搔白首，	Zhuàngzhì chénghuī sāo báishǒu,
园扉徒仰昔贤风。	yuánfēi túyǎng xī xiánfēng.

---

12 *Yinkuo* (literally 'a piece of wood used in straightening bent wood') is a way of rewriting a classical poem as a song lyric, quoting from another's poems or borrowing phrases from them without losing the original meaning, while at the same time changing some words in order to maintain the rhyme scheme of the new poem; or of rewriting a song lyric in another tune pattern or rhyme.
Line 4: Yue Fei was killed in the Fengbo Pavilion in Hangzhou.
Line 7: Zheng borrows part of a line from Du Fu, who wrote: 'Leaving the gate, you scratched your hoary head / as if having failed in your lifetime aims.'

43.

Buddha's Birthday

Laba is the eighth day of the twelfth lunar month, marking the Chinese version of Bodhi Day, the anniversary of the Buddha's enlightenment. Zheng wrote in a footnote that according to *Dongjing meng hua lu* ('Dream of Splendour in the Eastern Capital'),[1] on *laba* day monks and lay people in the Song Dynasty washed the Buddha's image in a big tub, using perfumed water, and begged alms from the public.

    Reading Gong's writings on the Tiantai School
got me thinking about *laba* day, which as a rule
is taken as the day of Buddha's birth, when people vie
to boil big vats of congee for the Buddha King.
The thriftless throw in ginkgo nuts and handfuls of red dates,
while the thrifty throw in vegetables and heed the ban
on chive and scallion.
A prison isn't quite the place for worshipping his Grace,
although we also get a bowl of vegetables and congee every meal.

腊八　　　　　　　　　　　Là bā

方从龚集溯台宗，　　　　　Fāng cóng Gōng jí sù tái zōng,
因忆年时腊八逢。　　　　　yīn yì nián shí làbā féng.
共说空王今日诞，　　　　　Gòng shuō Kōngwáng jīnrì dàn,
争熬佛粥案头供。　　　　　zhēng áo fózhōu àntóu gòng.
侈添白果兼红枣，　　　　　Chǐ tiān báiguǒ jiān hóngzǎo,
俭只园蔬戒韭葱。　　　　　jiǎn zhǐ yuánshū jiè jiǔcōng.
牢狱虽非供佛地，　　　　　Láoyù suī fēi gòngfó dì,
餐餐菜粥一瓯中。　　　　　cāncān càizhōu yīōu zhōng.

  1 A memoir by Meng Yuanlao (c. 1090–1150).
Line 1, 'Gong's': Gong Zizhen (1792–1841) was an essayist and poet who wrote on Buddhist themes.
Line 1, 'Tiantai School': A school of Buddhism.
Line 4: This image echoes a line by Chen Zhu.

44.

Autumn Thoughts

Zheng Chaolin thinks back on the early war years, which he spent in Anhui, and his taking leave of his friends in Anhui. He returned to Shanghai in the winter of 1940 on board a boat by way of Ningbo, to resume his political work.

To the tune of 'Autumn Meditations' (two of a suite of eight poems)

In the depths of autumn, among falling leaves,
the sumptuous feast for the first time sees the crescent brows,
natural white skin and bright red cheeks,
long dress, short coat, to put the final touch.   4
Walking at a steady pace along the moonlit street,
lingering on the riverbank to take the breeze,
we were in those years of one heart and mind,
but now our temple hairs are as white twine.   8

Taking up book and sword, I left behind my native place.
On the river, the autumn air turns slowly dull and drear.
We gather in the county town to hold a farewell feast –
my feelings for the island remain fervent and intense.   12
The October frost has not yet fallen on the southern peaks,
where the glow of the equator burns throughout the year.
The boat cuts through the foaming waters of the Red Sea –
only now do I rejoice, feeling the snow and bitter hail.   16

'To the tune of': The name of a set of eight poems by Du Fu.
Line 8: Bai Juyi has a line, to which Zheng here vaguely alludes, lamenting his white and stringy hair and his 'failure in life and in his cause'.
Line 10: There are echoes here of Du Fu's 'Autumn Meditations'.
Line 12: In Anhui, Zheng longs to return to his political base in Shanghai, which was known as the 'lonely island' until the outbreak of the Pacific War at the end of 1941.
Line 16: It is not clear what Zheng means here, unless this is a garbled reference to the Israelites' crossing of the Red Sea under Moses.

秋兴（八首之二）

正值深秋落叶时，
华筵初次见蛾眉。
素肌朱颊天然好，
短袄长裙结束宜。
月下街头同款步，
风前江畔共徘徊。
当年一结同心带，
直至如今两鬓丝。

书剑提携别故林，
江头秋气渐萧森。
郡城聚会离筵盛，
海岛停留感慨深。
十月岭南霜未降，
四时赤道热难禁。
一般冲浪过红海，
始觉严寒霰雪侵。

Qiū xìng (bā shǒu zhī èr)

Zhèngzhí shēnqiū luòyè shí,
huáyán chūcì jiàn éméi.
Sùjī zhūjiá tiānrán hǎo,
duǎnǎo chángqún jiéshù yí.
Yuèxià jiētóu tóng kuǎnbù,
fēngqián jiāngpàn gòng páihuái.
Dāngnián yī jié tóngxīn dài,
zhízhì rújīn liǎngbìn sī.

Shūjiàn tíxié bié gùlín,
jiāngtóu qiūqì jiàn xiāosēn.
Jùnchéng jùhuì líyán shèng,
hǎidǎo tíngliú gǎnkǎi shēn.
Shí yuè lǐngnán shuāng wèi jiàng,
sìshí chìdào rè nán jìn.
Yī chuán chōnglàng guò hónghǎi,
shǐ jué yánhán sǎn xuě qīn.

45.

Autumn Night

Zheng Chaolin misses his wife so badly that he cannot sleep. This poem reflects on their painful separation and their frustrated lives.

The wall lamps are extinguished to save power.
Disconsolate, I toss my book aside.
The din of autumn insects overlays the quiet of the night,
while Spying Moon briefly rests its bright light on a distant gate.
The metal lattice morphs into a checkerboard,
the pillow blotches with my fitful tears.
At Dingrao tonight I will dream of south bank sorrows,
and regret my having plucked the pear of paradise.

秋夜

灯因节电墙头灭，
惆怅轻抛一卷书。
聒耳秋虫鸣静夜，
窥人明月照疏扉。
纵横铁影成棋局，
断续啼痕染枕衣。
今夜定饶南浦梦，
当年悔摘乐园梨。

Qiū yè

Dēng yīn jié diàn qiángtóu miè,
chóuchàng qīng pāo yī juàn shū.
Guō'ěr qiūchóng míng jìngyè,
kuīrén míngyuè zhào shūfēi.
Zònghéng tiěyǐng chéng qíjú,
duànxù tíhén rǎn zhěnyī.
Jīnyè Dìngráo Nánpǔ mèng,
dāngnián huǐ zhāi lèyuán lí.

Line 4   An allusion to a line by Su Shi.
Line 7:   A reworking of lines by Qu Yuan and Jiang Yan.
Line 8:   A reference to Adam and Eve, but substituting a pear for an apple, for the sake of rhyme.

46.

A Poem for New Year's Day

This poem was apparently written in 1964.

> A joyless start this New Year morn,
> after twelve heartbreaking years behind these bars.
> I eagerly await signs that the blushing clouds of dawn
> will bathe me in bright light, red
> will be the colour of this old white head.

元旦和诗

岁首无欢只有愁,
可怜一纪作羁囚。
殷勤为感朝霞意,
迸发红光照白头。

Yuándàn hè shī

Suìshǒu wúhuān zhǐyǒu chóu,
kělián yī jì zuò jīqiú.
Yīnqín wèi gǎn zhāoxiá yì,
bèngfà hóngguāng zhào báitóu.

47.

Qingming

Qingming, known in English as Tomb-Sweeping Day, Ancestors' Day, or the Festival of Pure Brightness, is the day Chinese visit the graves and pray to their ancestors.

> No flowers, no wine on the Day for Sweeping Graves,
> just kitchen scraps – an egg, some sugar – in case the rain stops.
> The wandering ghosts are routed at the ruined tomb,
> where they can only envy the three sacrifices.

清明

无花无酒过清明，
剩蛋残糖对晚晴。
终胜游魂墟墓上，
祭盘徒羡足三牲。

Qīngmíng

Wúhuā wújiǔ guò qīngmíng,
shèngdàn cántáng duì wǎnqíng.
Zhōng shèng yóuhún xūmù shàng,
jìpán tú xiàn zú sānshēng

Line 4: Pig, sheep and cow.

48.

Intoning History (Three of Six Poems)

In a comment dated 21 March 1996, Zheng wrote:

> There were originally six poems, but I can't remember the other three. Before this book came out, the Hong Kong journalist Luo Fu saw a manuscript of my poems somewhere or other, and published a review in which he said that these three poems were a case of pointing at the mulberry tree and abusing the locust, and those who read them would know what they were really about and would need no explanation. It's true, these three poems use the past to satirise the present. The first poem is ostensibly about Qin Hui,[1] but actually it's about Stalin. The second poem is ostensibly about the 'party stele' set up in the Northern Song Dynasty at the time of the struggle between the new party and the old. At the time, the new party was in power. Its supporters weren't content with excluding Sima Guang's faction: they also raised a stele on which they engraved the names of the members of the opposition, and they called them 'the party', the 'bad people'. Later, when the situation changed, the stele was destroyed. The people named on it became 'good people' and their descendants were glorified. The third poem is about a phenomenon [corruption] difficult to avoid after victory in a peasant war, which Guo Moruo talked about in his article 'The Three-Hundredth Anniversary of the Jiashen Year [1644]';[2] at the time [1944], Mao Zedong called on his people to study this article, but it didn't stop corruption. During the Cultural Revolution, it was revealed in the press that the mayor of Shanghai, Cao Diqiu, had nine houses and each of his children had a piano.

---

1 Qin Hui (1090–1155) was a chancellor of the Song Dynasty, widely despised as a traitor for his part in the execution of Yue Fei, a patriotic general.
2 Guo Moruo (1892–1978), a well-known author and government official under Mao, published his article in 1944. The Manchus' Qing Dynasty began ruling China in 1644.

Intoning History (Three of Six Poems)

(One)

Chancellor Qin did not plan far ahead.
He weeded out dissidents and killed the pure.
Alive, much power rested in his hands:
dead, he was judged to rate the headsman's blade.　　　　　4

(Two)

Warnings of the ups and downs at court are hard to find,
but don't forget the towering party stele:
raised to list dissidents accused of crime,
toppled to right a wrong, forever and throughout all time.　　　　　8

(Three)

Console the people by punishing the bad, rise up among the wormwood groves –
a general owes his victory to ten thousand bleaching bones.
I have not yet seen the common people sleeping in the rice-straw bowers,
but I've heard the new elite is raising canopies and towers.　　　　　12

Line 9:　Zheng borrowed the wormwood image, symbolising a wild place, from Chen Zi'ang.

Intoning History (Three of Six Poems)

Yín shǐ (liù shǒu cún sān)

(其一)

秦相专权乏远图,
锄除异己杀无辜。
生前纵保崇高位,
死后难逃斧钺诛。

(Qí yī)

Qínxiāng zhuānquán fá yuǎntú,
chúchú yìjǐ shā wúgū.
Shēngqián zòngbǎo chónggāo wèi,
sǐhòu nántáo fǔyuè zhū.

(其二)

政海升沉消息微,
巍峨一座党人碑:
立时名恶毁时美,
付与千秋论是非。

(Qí èr)

Zhènghǎi shēngchén xiāoxī wēi,
wéi'é yī zuò dǎngrén bēi:
Lìshí míng è huǐshí měi,
fùyǔ qiānqiū lùn shìfēi.

(其三)

吊民伐罪起蒿莱,
一将功成万骨埋。
未见黎民登衽席,
但闻新贵筑楼台。

(Qí sān)

Diàomín-fázuì qǐ hāolái,
yījiāng gōngchéng wàngǔ mái.
Wèi jiàn límín dēng rènxí,
dàn wén xīnguì zhù lóutái.

49.

Memories of Deep Autumn (Six of Fourteen Poems)

(1)

Reed catkins have a special charm,
dangling fine and slender on the branches near the garden gate.
How could I forget the late autumnal snow
filling the hill streams in my native place?

(2)

The chrysanthemums by the fence are dusted thick with frost,
in soil on which five scarlet petals of the blooming plum-tree snap apart.
No poet sings the praises of integrity in old age,
for the creed come from the West has not outgrown its infant stage.

(3)

Amid the falling leaves, I visited my beauty.
Still the vase held fresh blooms in its slender flute.
Dimly I recall her sweet face and its lustrous tone,
memories of a long-gone spring.

(4)

Fresh persimmons, fat as ripe tomatoes, diced and splayed
by slender fingers, served by hands of jade.
Dried in the sun, flattened, caked and strung
up by the stove, to deliver honey to the tongue.

(5)

Late autumn – when my son was born,
an anniversary on which I can only weep and mourn.
I wonder if the fragile urn
still holds his ashes, nine years on?

(6)

The quail is plump and stout when fall winds bite,
vigilant but good at gliding flight, and good as well at keeping out of sight.
I wouldn't have believed it if you'd told me
that people raise this rare and precious bird in pens, as poultry.

Memories of Deep Autumn (Six of Fourteen Poems)

深秋杂忆(十四首存六)　　Shēnqiū zá yì (shísì shǒu cún liù)

(其一)　　(Qí yī)

芦花别有好丰姿，　　Lúhuā biéyǒu hǎo fēngzī,
仅见园门袅数枝。　　jǐnjiàn yuánmén niǎo shùzhī.
因忆故山溪水上，　　Yīn yì gùshān xīshuǐ shàng,
年年飞雪晚秋时。　　niánnián fēixuě wǎnqiū shí.

(其二)　　(Qí èr)

霜稠篱菊委尘埃，　　Shuāngchóu líjú wěi chén'āi,
忽有红花五瓣开。　　hū yǒu hónghuā wǔ bàn kāi.
未得诗人吟晚节，　　Wèidé shīrén yín wǎnjié,
只缘新自泰西来。　　zhǐyuán xīn zì tàixī lái.

(其三)　　(Qí sān)

落叶声中访丽人，　　Luòyè shēngzhōng fǎng lìrén,
胆瓶犹插菊花新。　　dǎnpíng yóu chā júhuā xīn.
花容粉面相辉映，　　Huāróng fěnmiàn xiàng huīyìng,
往事依稀数十春。　　wǎngshì yīxī shùshí chūn.

(其四)　　(Qí sì)

鲜红柿子似番茄，　　Xiānhóng shìzi shì fānqié,
玉手擘来味倍佳。　　yùshǒu bāi lái wèi bèijiā.
更有晒干平若饼，　　Gèngyǒu shàigān píng ruò bǐng,
炉边细嚼蜜沾牙。　　lúbiān xìjiáo mì zhān yá.

(其五)　　(Qí wǔ)

殇儿本是晚秋生，　　Shāng ér běnshì wǎnqiū shēng,
每逢生朝老泪零。　　měiféng shēngzhāo lǎolèi líng.
知否骨灰今尚在？　　Zhīfǒu gǔhuī jīn shàngzài?
九年空对小花瓶！　　Jiǔ nián kōngduì xiǎo huāpíng!

(其六)　　(Qí liù)

鹌鹑肥壮待秋深，　　Ānchún féizhuàng dài qiūshēn,
性警飞高不易寻。　　xìng jǐng fēigāo bùyì xún.
如此尊前珍美品，　　Rúcǐ zūnqián zhēnměi pǐn,
居然驯养作家禽。　　jūrán xúnyǎng zuò jiāqín.

50.

Stamps (2)

Again, the poet delights from the confines of his cell in the design on the stamps Liu Jingzhen has attached to her letter to him.

On Postage Stamps Showing Bridges
(three poems out of four)

Anji Bridge

Outside Zhaozhou City, the soil where the bridge abuts the bank
is stained and perfumed by the seas of alcohol libated on it.
The master builders, famed for their prowess, are long since gone.
At nighttime, jostling herdsmen drive their sheep across the arch.

The Precious Belt Bridge

A fine place known for one thousand years as Hanging Arc,
where hills and water set each other off.
Does the temple by the bridge still stand
for the Three Hermits – Tao Zhu, Lu Guimeng, and Zhang Han?

(continued on the next page)

Title 1: The world's oldest stone arch bridge, said to have been designed by the craftsman Li Chun and built in 595–605 during the Sui dynasty.
Line 2: Here, Zheng borrows a phrase from Gong Zizhen.
Title 2: The Precious Belt Bridge or Baodai Bridge is a stone arch bridge near Suzhou, at the intersection of the Grand Canal and Tantai Lake. It was last reconstructed in 1446. Zheng adds a note to say that this is not the same as the Hanging Rainbow (Chuihong) Bridge.
Line 4: Tao Zhu, known as Tao Zhu Gong, originally called Fan Li (born 517 BCE), was a statesman, soldier, Daoist and successful trader, worshipped after his death as the God of Wealth. Zhang Han and Lu Guimeng were known as 'men of high character and integrity', Zhang in the Western Jin and Lu in the Tang Dynasty. They are the patron saints of the three temples Zheng mentions.

Stamps (2)

Chengyang Bridge

I'd never heard of Chengyang or its bridge,
its five pavilions astride the sky.
Interfolding roof-tiles block the wind and rain,
while roaring waves and hill views beckon to the ear and eye.

题桥邮票(四首之三)

安济桥

赵州城外石为梁,
尊酒频浇土亦香。
巧匠声名久埋没,
世人争道夜驱羊。

宝带桥(按宝带桥不是垂虹桥)

千年绝景说垂虹,
掩映山光水色中。
桥畔三高祠在否?
陶朱张翰陆龟蒙。

程阳桥(按程阳桥在广西)

未识程阳何处桥,
五亭如盖立岧峣。
瓦檐相接遮风雨,
山色波声槛外招。

Tí qiáo yóupiào (sì shǒu zhī sān)

Ānjì qiáo

Zhàozhōu chéngwài shí wéi liáng,
zūnjiǔ pínjiāo tǔ yì xiāng.
Qiǎojiàng shēngmíng jiǔ máimò,
shìrén zhēng dào yè qū yáng.

Bǎodài qiáo (àn Bǎodài qiáo bùshì chuíhóng qiáo)

Qiānnián juéjǐng shuō chuíhóng,
yǎnyìng shānguāng shuǐsè zhōng.
Qiáopàn Sāngāocí zàifǒu?
Táo Zhū Zhāng Hàn Lù Guīméng.

Chéngyáng qiáo (àn Chéngyáng qiáo zài Guǎngxī)

Wèishì Chéngyáng héchù qiáo,
wǔtíng rúgài lì tiáoyáo.
Wǎyán xiāngjiē zhē fēngyǔ,
shānsè bōshēng kǎnwài zhāo.

Title: The Yongji Bridge of Chengyang in Guangxi is a covered bridge completed in 1912.

Post-Prison Poems

51.

Boat Trip

23 November 1979, sailing on the Yangtze River

To the tune of 'The Water Song'

Fifty-three years –
how the scenery has changed.
A bluebeard then,
but now a white-haired man with tinted brows.
Visiting the new bridge at Wuhan,
dashing ashore, dashing aboard again,
along a fairway through nine provinces.
I would like to be the Liaocheng crane,
standing on my marble plinth.

West wind,
autumn sun,
East Lake.
Our kind host
treats us to wine-soaked Wuchang bream.
After thirty years of exile near the coast
my sudden rehabilitation into national life
left me, like Qu Yuan, chagrined and abashed.
However beautiful the setting sun,
clouds are likely in the days to come.

'To the tune of': A *ci* by Su Shi.
Line 1: Zheng Chaolin had first sailed up the Yangtze to Wuhan in April 1927, as an official of the Communist Party's Propaganda Department. Now he returns on an official tour, after his release from prison.
Line 5: Across the Yangtze.
Line 9: Modelled on lines by Wang Wei and Li He. See the annotation to Zheng's poem 'My Native Place', Poem 6 in this volume.
Line 14: Mao also ate Wuchang fish, before swimming the Yangtze in 1956, and wrote about about it in his poem 'Swimming'.
Line 17: Qu Yuan, a poet, political idealist and patriot, responded to the fall of his country's capital by walking into a river carrying a rock and drowning himself.
Line 18: Zheng cites a line from a poem by Li Shangyin.

Boat Trip

水调歌头

五十三年事,
风物古今殊。
昔时青须,
今日霜雪染眉须。
新见长桥横水,
上下车船奔竞,
九省此通衢。
愿作辽城鹤,
华表立斯须。

西风紧,
秋日暖,
泛东湖。
主人情重,
款我良酝武昌鱼。
卅载海滨逐客,
一旦赐环归国,
屈子愧难如。
无限夕阳好,
前景惜模糊。

Shuǐdiào gētóu

Wǔshísān nián shì,
fēngwù gǔjīn shū.
Xīshí qīngxū,
jīnrì shuāngxuě rǎn méixū.
Xīn jiàn chángqiáo héngshuǐ,
shàngxià chēchuán bēn jìng,
jiǔ shěng cǐ tōngqú.
Yuànzuò Liáochéng hè,
huábiǎo lì sī xū.

Xīfēng jǐn,
qiūrì nuǎn,
fàn dōnghú.
Zhǔrén qíngzhòng,
kuǎn wǒ liángyùn wǔchāng yú.
Sà zǎi hǎibīn zhúkè,
yīdàn cì huán guīguó,
Qūzi kuì nánrú.
Wúxiàn xīyáng hǎo,
qiánjǐng xī móhú.

52.

A Playful Four-Line Poem Echoing Yang Muzhi

Commissioner Yang Muzhi
twirled his beard and recited Gaozu verse.
In Gaozu's reign, Lü Zhi minced Han and Peng to bits,
taking her cue from Liu Bang's bag of tricks.

APPENDIX

Yang Muzhi's original poem

Supported by a galaxy of skills
Liu Han replaced Ying Qin by wiping out the generals,
any one of whom was fit to found a state.
A pity Liu Bang overlooked the actions of his mate.

The empire of Liu Han was on the road to its collapse
when Han and Peng were killed and minced to bits.
How did the Lü clan reap such tribute from its vassal kings?
One trembles to imagine the dark deeds performed.

Line 1: Yang Muzhi (1901–1999) was Zheng's colleague when they both worked for the Party organ *Guide Weekly* in the mid 1920s. Yang was a member of the People's Political Consultant Conference of Changzhou City when Zheng wrote this poem.
Line 2: Verse from the period of the rule of Emperor Gaozu (Liu Bang), founder of the Han Dynasty (reigned 202–195 BCE).
Line 3: An ancient form of execution and retribution. The outstanding generals Han Xin (231–196 BCE) and Peng Yue (?–196 BCE) were both appointed by Gaozu as vassal kings for their extraordinary contribution to the establishment of the Han Dynasty. However, they were accused of treason and executed by Empress Lü Zhi (241–180 BCE), with the tacit agreement of her husband Liu Bang. Their execution was a classic example of the (often tragic) demise of outstanding officials under a brutal ruler, after contributing to the establishment of new dynasty. According to the *Records of the Grand Historian*, 'When birds disappear, pack the bows away; when hares have been killed, stew and eat the hounds.'
Line 4: Yang Muzhi and many others likened Mao's wife Jiang Qing (1914–1991) to Lü Zhi and blamed her for the suffering during the Mao years. Zheng refutes the suggestion and blames Mao instead.

A Playful Four-Line Poem Echoing Yang Muzhi

读羊牧之吟史诗戏成一绝

羊牧委员字牧之,
捻须吟出汉高诗。
韩彭菹醢生前事,
吕雉何曾别有师。

Dú Yáng Mùzhī yínshǐ shī xìchéng yījué

Yáng Mù wěiyuán zì Mùzhī,
niǎnxū yínchū hàngāo shī.
Hán Péng jūhǎi shēngqián shì,
Lǚ Zhì hécéng biéyǒu shī.

[Fù]

羊牧之吟史诗

解用当年人杰辰,
群雄得削代嬴秦。
安知将将能开国,
竟会纵容一妇人。

汉室垂危帝业颠,
韩彭菹醢剧堪怜。
王封诸吕何功德,
想见风高月黑天。

Yáng Mùzhī yínshǐ shī

Jiě yòng dāngnián rénjié chén,
qúnxióng dé xuē dài yíngqín.
Ānzhī jiāngjiāng néng kāiguó,
jìnghuì zòngróng yī fùrén.

Hànshì chuíwéi dìyè diān,
Hán Péng jūhǎi jù kānlián.
Wáng fēng zhūlǚ hé gōngdé,
xiǎngjiàn fēnggāo yuèhēi tiān.

53.

In Imitation of Yang Muzhi

Ask not the human world what's right and wrong,
or why its parties never can agree.
The shepherd searching for his missing sheep
marvels to find Duke Zhu where the path forks, and to hear him weep.

15 February 1980

仿羊牧之	**Fǎng Yáng Mùzhī**
不问人间是与非,	Bù wèn rénjiān shì yǔ fēi,
岂缘尘世久相违?	qǐ yuán chénshì jiǔ xiāngwéi?
牧童心切寻羊日,	Mùtóng xīnqiè xúnyáng rì,
却见朱公泣路岐。	què jiàn Zhūgōng qì lù qí.

Line 4: Echoing a line by Li Shangyin. Duke Zhu of Tao saved his native state of Zheng from invading Qin forces.

54.

Bide Not Your Time

A Collection of Lines from Old Poems in Response to Yang Muzhi

Bide not your time, for black hair soon turns white,
with petrels darting to and fro across the bight.
Do not claim rashly names that Xie owned in his time –
who cares if winter, summer, spring or fall?

23 February 1981

APPENDIX

Yang Muzhi's original poem

Spring in an eye's blink turns to fall,
hair in the mirror soon turns white.
A lost sheep on a byroad, a lamenting of past times.
The River Town as ever with the Yangtze as its pillow.

集古和羊牧之

等闲白了少年头,
海燕参差沟水流。
别有狂言谢时望,
管他冬夏与春秋。

Jí gǔ hè Yáng Mùzhī

Děngxián báile shàonián tóu,
hǎiyàn cēncī gōushuǐ liú.
Biéyǒu kuángyán Xiè shíwàng,
guǎntā dōngxià yǔ chūnqiū.

(continued on the next page)

Line 1: Yue Fei, 'Man jiang hong'.
Line 2: Li Shangyin, 'Gossiping and having fun with my fellow-graduate Li Dingyan at Qu Jiang'.
Line 3: Gong Zizhen, 'Poems from the Thirty-Sixth Year of the Sexagenary Cycle', no. 126. Xie is Xie An (320–385), a statesman and general.
Line 4: Lu Xun, 'A Satire on Myself'.

Bide Not Your Time

[附]

羊牧之原诗

驹光如驶度春秋,
今日灯前已白头。
歧路亡羊伤往事,
江城依旧枕寒流。

[Fù]

Yáng Mùzhī yuān shī

Jūguāng rúshǐ dù chūnqiū,
jīnrì dēng qián yǐ báitóu.
qílù-wángyáng shāng wǎngshì,
jiāngchéng yījiù zhěn hánliú.

55.

A New Guest on Deep Lane

In 1979, shortly after Zheng's release from prison, he received a visit from Ye Yonglie, a writer of science fiction and biographies. Ye wrote:

> I arrived at Zheng's out-of-the-way dwelling in a residential block in a remote neighbourhood. I knocked at the door. At the time, I was dressed in spring clothing, but he was wearing a thick brown ski shirt, a blue woollen cap, and a pair of clamshell cotton-padded shoes. He was bent nearly double, and his movements seemed slow. I had a long talk with him – it was our first meeting. When Zheng Chaolin heard my name, he said 'I know, I know.' He was surprised that I should interview him as a special person. I remember he immediately wrote this poem for me, on my notepad.

An assemblage rhyming with an original poem by Yang Muzhi

> Sat at home with a new guest in Deep Lane,
> idly conversing, bold like Su and Xin, and unconstrained.
> My southern voice, compelled for years to seek its own commúne,
> strikes up when chiming to his northern one a brisker tune.

3 March 1981

Line 2: Su Shi and Xin Qiji were representatives of a school of poetry known for its vividness, spontaneity and lack of inhibition.
Line 4: Zheng's original line copies a well-known line by Xu Wei.

A New Guest on Deep Lane

APPENDIX

Yang Muzhi's original poem

Xie, famed and hidden from the human world.
White heads confer to talk about life's ills.
The day that rumours even spread about the Duke of Zhou,
he too a survivor of the the great calamity.

步韵和羊牧之集古诗

深巷家居鲜客尘，
闲吟词句学苏辛。
老来敢作孤芳赏，
'一个南腔北调人！'

[附]

羊牧之原诗

谢却高名远俗尘（洪升），
白头闲坐话艰辛（汪中）。
周公亦有流言日（俞樾），
同是昆明劫后人（钱谦益）。

Bù yùn hè Yáng Mùzhī jí gǔshī

Shēnxiàng jiājū xiān kè chén,
xián yín cíjù xué Sū Xīn.
Lǎolái gǎnzuò gūfāng shǎng,
'yī gè nánqiāng-běidiào rén!'

[Fù]

Yáng Mùzhī yuān shī

Xièquè gāomíng yuǎn súchén (Hóng Shēng),
báitóu xiánzuò huà jiānxīn (Wāng Zhōng).
Zhōugōng yìyǒu liúyán rì (Yú Yuè),
tóngshì Kūnmíng jiéhòu rén (Qián Qiānyì).

Line 1: The Qing Dynasty playwright and poet Hong Sheng (1645–1704).
Line 2: The Qing Dynasty scholar Wang Zhong (1745–1794).
Line 3: The Qing Dynasty scholar and official Yu Yue (1821–1907).
Line 4: Qian Qianyi (1582–1664) was a Ming Dynasty official and scholar who surrendered and served the Qing Dynasty.

56.

The Firewood Cutter and the Taoyuan Spring

During the Jin Dynasty (265–420), Wang Zhi went out to collect firewood. He saw a child and an old man on a rock by a stream playing chess, and put down his axe to watch. After he had watched for a long time, the boy told him to go home. Wang Zhi went to get his axe and found its handle rotted, while the blade had become jagged and twisted. On reaching home, everything had changed. No one recognised him, and when he mentioned what he had seen, some old men told him that these events had happened hundreds of years before. Wang Zhi had entered the land of the immortals, where one days equals 100 years.

An assemblage rhyming with an original poem by Yang Muzhi

> The handsome man has suddenly grown old,
> in a crowd ten thousand strong, one easily can hide.
> While the firewood cutter watched the chess, his axe-shaft turned to rot.
> Inwardly he smiled, at his enchantment by the game.   4
>
> 19 March 1981
>
> The lord is sage and wise, so his subjects always bear the blame.
> I was born into this world, of whatever name.
> Does the Wu River really cross the Taoyuan Spring?
> Given their provenance, the three households cannot but win.   8
>
> 22 March 1981

Line 1: This line includes a phrase from a poem by Gong Zizhen.
Line 2: This line is modelled on a phrase from a poem by Su Shi.
Line 5: A slightly rewritten line by Han Yu.
Line 7: The fable of the Peach Blossom (Taoyuan) Valley (or Spring), written by Tao Yuanming in 421, tells of a hidden utopia of peace and prosperity.
Line 8: According to the *Records of the Grand Historian*, 'even if Chu had only three households, if Qin is destroyed it must be the work of the Chu' (under Xiang Yu in 207 BCE). The word *ying* means 'win', but it also denotes Ying Qin.

The Firewood Cutter and the Taoyuan Spring

The path to the bronze camels is wild and overgrown,
but the brambles can be slashed and cleared from sight.
Far ahead, there shines a light,
the lake and hills as if drawn, the grass as if a carpet.

23 March 1981

In the transient joy of the balmy breeze of spring
I forget that I'm no longer young.
Catching the dragon and the tiger is no longer my concern,
braving the hail of bullets is a matter of the past.

23 March 1981

APPENDIX

Yang Muzhi's original poem

Youthful beauty has turned white and old,
who greets the spring breeze with a smiling face?
So old, how many still are left in place
who witnessed the alterations of four dynasties?

Emerald sea, blue sky, lunar light,
do not build empty reputations on a person's failure or success.
The axe-helve rotted while the woodman watched the chess,
who said immortals are invariably right?

Line 9: The Han bronze camels in the Golden Valley near Luoyang.
Appendix, line 4: The four 'dynasties' Zheng witnessed were the Qing, the Northern Warlords, the Nationalists, and the Communists.
Appendix, line 5: This line contains an image from a poem by Wen Tingyun.
Appendix, line 6: This idea crops up in reflections on the Chinese revolution by other Chinese Trotskyists, who refused to accept that their defeat negated the truth of their theories and projects.

The Firewood Cutter and the Taoyuan Spring

Wishing to cut a small path through the thorns,
Duke Zhu, having toiled in vain, stood weeping by the road.
The Buddha said, 'Look back and you will see the shore.'
Everyone recites it – how could it be to no effect? 12

Spring is more fragrant the further back you go,
how many people reach one hundred years?
There is no point in chiding an old horse.
Fu Sheng at ninety still retrieved the texts. 16

步韵和羊牧之赠诗　　　　　Bù yùn hè Yáng Mùzhī zèng shī

惨绿年华倏已翁，　　　　　Cǎnlǜ niánhuá shū yǐ wēng,
万人如海只身容。　　　　　wànrén rúhǎi zhīshēn róng.
观棋樵子烂柯客，　　　　　Guānqí qiáozǐ lànkē kè,
自笑心迷棋局中。　　　　　zìxiào xīnmí qíjú zhōng.

臣罪当诛主圣明，　　　　　Chénzuì dāngzhū zhǔ shèngmíng,
生逢斯世世何名。　　　　　shēngféng sīshì shì hémíng.
乌江可是桃源渡？　　　　　Wūjiāng kěshì táoyuán dù?
三户由来不避嬴。　　　　　Sān hù yóulái bu bì yíng.

铜驼大道满荆榛，　　　　　Tóngtuó dàdào mǎn jīngzhēn,
斩伐能辞事苦辛。　　　　　zhǎnfá néng cí shì kǔ xīn.
远望前方光照处，　　　　　Yuǎnwàng qiánfāng guāngzhào chù,
湖山如画草如茵。　　　　　húshān rúhuà cǎo rúyīn.

婆娑春梦正温馨，　　　　　Pósuō chūnmèng zhèng wēnxīn,
忘却如今异幼龄。　　　　　wàngquè rújīn yì yòulíng.
缚虎擒龙非我事，　　　　　Fùhǔ qínlóng fēi wǒ shì,
枪林弹雨旧曾经。　　　　　Qiānglín-dànyǔ jiù céngjīng.

Appendix, line 11:   The Buddha said the sea of suffering is boundless, but if you look back you will see the shore behind you.
Appendix, line 16:   Fu Sheng (260–161 BCE), known as Master Fu, was a Confucian scholar who defied the anti-Confucian Qin Dynasty by hiding and later retrieving Confucian texts, which the Qin ruler sought to burn. He lived until one hundred.

The Firewood Cutter and the Taoyuan Spring

[附]

羊牧之原诗

朱颜白发已成翁,
莫看春风带笑容。
此老人间能有几?
沧桑阅尽四朝中。

碧海青天月自明,
莫将成败定浮名。
烂柯樵子看棋局,
那有仙人都是赢?

欲开小径斩荆榛,
泣路朱公枉费辛。
佛说回头是岸语,
人人能诵岂无因?

古春愈古愈芳馨,
多少人间近百龄。
谩道老骥无用处,
伏生九十尚传经。

[Fù]

Yáng Mùzhī yuánshī

Zhūyán báifà yǐ chéngwēng,
mòkàn chūnfēng dài xiàoróng。
Cǐlǎo rénjiān néng yǒu jǐ?
Cāngsāng yuèjìn sì cháo zhōng。

Bìhǎi-qīngtiān yuè zìmíng,
mòjiāng chéngbài dìng fúmíng。
Lànkē qiáozǐ kàn qíjú,
nàyǒu xiānrén dōushì yíng?

Yùkāi xiǎojìng zhǎn jīngzhēn,
qìlù Zhūgōng wǎng fèixīn。
Fó shuō huítóushì'àn yǔ,
rénrén néngsòng qǐ wúyīn?

Gǔchūn yùgǔ yù fāngxīn,
duōshǎo rénjiān jìn bǎi líng。
Mándào lǎojì wú yòngchù,
Fú Shēng jiǔshí shàng chuánjīng。

57.

Gong Zizhen Railed at Wrongs

An assemblage of Gong Zizhen's poetry as a gift for Yang Muzhi

In the southeast, high learning centred on Piling.
Gong railed at being thought less talented than Zhong Jun and Jia Yi.
He regretted having been the Prince's guest,
and that in his native place they know him only as a poet.

集龚一首赠羊牧之

东南绝学在毗陵，
终贾年华气不平。
悔向侯王作宾客，
流传乡里只诗名。

Jí Gōng yīshǒu zèng Yáng Mùzhī

Dōngnán juéxué zài Píling,
Zhōng Jiǎ niánhuá qì bùpíng.
Huǐ xiàng hóuwáng zuò bīnkè,
liúchuán xiānglǐ zhǐ shīmíng.

Line 1: Gong Zizhen, *Jihai zashi* ('Various Poems from the Thirty-Sixth Year of the Sexagenary Cycle'), p. 59. In this line, Gong Zizhen is referring to the Qing Dynasty scholar Liu Fenglu (1776–1829), whom he held in high regard. Piling is an old name for Changzhou.
Line 2: Ibid., p. 47. During the Han Dynasty, Zhong Yun and Ya Yi were promoted to important positions at a young age.
Line 3: Ibid., p. 79.
Line 4: Ibid., p. 178. Gong Zizhen aspired to be a social reformer, and regretted being known in his birthplace first and foremost as a poet.

58.

The Waking of the Insects

This poem is rich in political imagery and implications – the revolutionary tide at ebb (after 1927), unrealised hopes, doctrinal consolation and the hint of a new spring.

Rhyming a Poem with Comrade Xie Shan

Hurtling nonstop to my demise, remembering my spring –
what point is there in digging up the buried texts?
'Ox-Demon's writings mourned Li He,
a shovel borne upon a deer-drawn cart interred Liu Ling.'

Woken insects ride the wind,
can truth be grasped from what our fathers preach?
The ebbtide etched deep marks while dropping down the beach –
as fishes stranded in a drying rut spout damping jets,
still we discuss the sacred texts.

11 October 1984

Title: Xie Shan, who appeared earlier in this section, was a Chinese Trotskyist jailed in 1952.

Line 4: Cao Xueqin (1715–1763), author of the classical novel *Dream of the Red Chamber* and of these two lines, admired Li He. Cao avoided a 'living death' – turning into a 'walking corpse', a careerist without conscience or integrity – by becoming a devil in the eyes of officialdom, spurning rank and fame. Like the dissipated and eccentric poet Liu Ling, he disdained etiquette and drank heavily. Liu Ling practised nudity and was followed around by a servant carrying a bottle of wine for him to drink and a shovel with which to bury him when he fell dead.

Line 5: The Waking of the Insects (*jingzhe*) by the sound of thunder marks the third of the twenty-four solar terms (6–10 March). The implication is that the weather is getting warmer and spring is about to start.

Line 6: A reference to Kong Li, Confucius's only son, to whom he passed down instructions.

Line 8: A classical idiom that describes stranded fishes moistening each other with water jets.

The Waking of the Insects

步韵和谢山同志

无端垂老忆年青,
简册沉埋未宜醒。
'牛鬼遗文悲李贺,
鹿车荷锸葬刘伶。'

乘风原是虫惊蛰,
悟道何曾鲤过庭?
潮退尚留砂砾上,
相濡涸鲋亦谈经。

Bù yùn hè Xiè Shān tóngzhì

Wúduān chuílǎo yì niánqīng,
jiǎncè chénmái wèiyí xǐng.
'Niúguǐ yíwén bēi Lǐ Hè,
lùchē héchā zàng Liú Líng.'

Chéngfēng yuánshì chóng jīngzhé,
wùdào hécéng lǐ guòtíng?
Cháotuì shàngliú shālì shàng,
xiāngrú héfù yì tánjīng.

59.

Requesting Criticism from Comrade Xie Shan

The Monkey King, Sun Wukong, was born from a magic stone. (*Wukong* means 'to awaken to the nihility or emptiness of life'.) A Daoist immortal, Sun is a main character in the sixteenth-century Chinese novel *Journey to the West*. He is supernaturally strong, knows seventy-two transformations, and commands the elements. He defeats Heaven's army and creates havoc in its kingdom. But although he can somersault around the earth, he cannot escape the Buddha's palm. Even when he thinks he has leapt to the farthest boundary of Heaven, the Mountain of the Five Elements turns out to be the Buddha's fingers.

To the tune of Lady Yu

Soon ninety, but still basking in life's spring,
aspiring to be a second Monkey King.
Wielding a golden rod to put the Sky God's court to fright,
smashing the network, setting the whole world to right!

I calmly withstand the raging flames in Taishang Laojun's stove,
but how to escape the Buddha's palm?
Seek quiet and isolation in the Mountain of Five Elements
and, after a long hard journey to the West, bear back the sacred texts.

10 November 1986

Title: A *ci* by Li Yu.
Line 6: Sun Wukong the Monkey King burned in the stove of Taishang Laojun, the supreme Daoist deity, for forty-nine days and became even stronger as a result.

Requesting Criticism from Comrade Xie Shan

虞美人·就正于谢山同志

九旬未至犹年少,
敢企悟空老。
一枝金棒闹天庭,
争奈网罗难破事难平。

老君炉内终无恙,
怎脱如来掌?
五行山下幸幽栖,
绝胜西天跋涉护经归。

Yú měirén: jiù zhèng yú Xiè Shān tóngzhì

Jiǔxún wèizhì yóu niánshào,
gǎn qǐ Wùkōng lǎo.
Yī zhī jīnbàng nào tiāntíng,
zhēng nài wǎngluó nánpò shì nánpíng.

Lǎojūn lúnèi zhōng wúyàng,
zěn tuō Rúlái zhǎng?
Wǔxíng shān xià xìng yōuqī,
jué shèng xītiān báshè hù jīng guī.

60.

Reflections on a Tour of the Historic Site of the *Buersaiweike* [Bolshevik] Editorial Department

In the mid 1920s, Zheng Chaolin edited the Central Committee organ *Guide Weekly*, which became *The Bolshevik* in 1927. After Zheng's release from prison in 1979, when historians were encouraged by Party authorities to 'seek truth from facts' and prejudice against Trotskyism had begun to abate, Zheng was often consulted by scholars about events and issues in Party history of the 1920s, a period of which he was by then an increasingly rare survivor. This poem describes his lively encounter with historians during a tour of the site of his old workplace, perhaps during his river-trip to Wuhan or in Shanghai (Zheng worked for the Party in both cities at various times).

To the tune of 'The Sand of the Silk-Washing Brook'

An old man up against a younger throng
of sage and virtuous questioners whose shining spears
and armoured horses clash and clang ding-dong.

As with each dying day my old friends pass away,
I watch the sunset flood the painted tower with light.
'Washed by the moon, an overpowering sight!'

27 October 1988

Line 5: The painted tower or hall, a frequent image in classical Chinese poetry, can refer to a boudoir in which a heroine lives. Here, it might symbolise Zheng's wife Liu Jingzhen, who died in 1979.
Line 6: A line from a poem by Li Yu, to whose tune the present poem was written.

Reflections on a Tour of the Historic Site of the Buersaiweike

浣溪沙
游《布尔塞维克》编辑部旧址有感

济济明贤对一翁,
高谈雄辩气如虹,
金戈铁马响丁冬。

旧友尽随流水逝,
画楼犹恋夕阳红。
'不堪回首月明中!'

Huán xī shā
Yóu *Bùěrsāiwéikè* biānjíbù jiùzhǐ yǒugǎn

Jǐjǐ míngxián duì yīwēng,
gāotán xióngbiàn qì rúhóng,
jīngē-tiěmǎ xiǎng dīngdōng.

Jiùyǒu jǐn suí liúshuǐ shì,
huàlóu yóuliàn xīyáng hóng.
'Bùkān huíshǒu yuè míng zhōng!'

61.

An Assemblage of Gong Zizhen's Poetry for Self-Consolation

After his release from prison, Zheng Chaolin spent much time reflecting on his life. In this poem, he borrows four lines from four separate poems by Gong Zizhen to compare himself with Gong. Both men were broad-minded, unconventional, and denied the chance to apply their talent.

> This body has become a mountain spring,
> an old tree in the hills.
> In the vicissitudes of life, my mind's set on an even course,
> though my pen still rolls to wilder waves.

集龚自嘲

此身已作在山泉，
又作山中老树看。
世事沧桑心事定，
文章合有老波澜。

Jí Gōng zìcháo

Cǐshēn yǐ zuò zàishānquán,
yòu zuò shānzhōng lǎoshù kàn,
shìshì cāngsāng xīnshì dìng,
wénzhāng héyǒu lǎo bōlán.

Line 1: A line from Gong Zizhen, who goes on to say that not much can be done by an isolated, powerless individual to affect the fate of a country, just as 'a tiny drop of water cannot replenish a great river'.
Line 2: Gong Zizhen perceives himself as a man rich in experience.
Line 3: Gong complains about the vicissitudes of life but congratulates himself on enjoying freedom and peace of mind.
Line 4: Gong regrets the Qing court's failure to adopt his bold proposals on a number of topical issues.

62.

Landscape Painting

Rong Sun sent me a New Year's card depicting an autumn scene and wrote a new-style poem to accompany it. Here, I turn it into an old-style poem.

> In the depths of autumn, the leaves drop one by one,
> as I hike alone along the city limits on my cane.
> Trees throw their shadows on the lake,
> where I look out for fishing boats.
> The sparse woods set off the cloudless sky,
> a sandspit blocks the waterflow.
> Today seeds sown in spring and summer are in fruit,
> but winter quickly brings the blooming to an end.

题风景画

纷纷落叶正深秋,
策杖城郊独自游。
树映水中呈倒影,
目横湖面觅渔舟。
疏林掩映天无翳,
沙嘴沉浮水不流。
春夏耕耘今结实,
隆冬转眼物华休。

Tí fēngjǐng huà

Fēnfēn luòyè zhèng shēnqiū,
cèzhàng chéngjiāo dúzì yóu.
Shù yìng shuǐzhōng chéng dàoyǐng,
mù héng húmiàn mì yúzhōu.
Shūlín yǎnyìng tiān wúyì,
shāzuǐ chénfú shuǐ bù liú.
Chūnxià gēngyún jīn jiēshi,
lóngdōng zhuǎnyǎn wùhuá xiū.

63.

A Response to Rong Sun

A *qilü*   27 January 1988

Rong Sun says that even in the winter cold the earth spins on, and tells me not to be so glum, to which I answer with these lines.

> Immediately the blooming ends, new life begins again,
> in shoots and leaves formed in the snow.
> Gradually on the pond the dream of spring awakes.
> The willow lightly casts its scent.
> Cuckoos call the peasants to the fields,
> which turn to green with shoots of rice.
> The seasons follow their eternal wheel,
> how many turns can an ailing man behold?

答 荣 孙

物华休后一阳生,
雪地冰天万象萌。
池上渐醒春草梦,
陌头行见柳烟轻。
声声布谷催耕急,
处处秧苗染地青。
时序轮回又一遍,
衰翁能见几回程!

Dá Róng Sūn

Wùhuá xiū hòu yīyáng shēng,
xuědì-bīngtiān wànxiàng méng.
Chíshàng jiàn xǐng chūncǎo mèng,
mòtóu xíng jiàn liǔyān qīng.
Shēngshēng bùgǔ cuīgēng jí,
chùchù yāngmiáo rǎndì qīng.
Shíxù lúnhuí yòu yī biàn,
shuāiwēng néngjiàn jǐ huí chéng!

64.

Response to Mr Chen Jingxian's Gift of a Poem

5 February 1988

Is it so hard to find your forebear's house?
Step through the East Gate, then go north.
The town wall serves you as a screen,
your back to Pure Creek, listening to the waves.
Two families' fathers once were bosom friends,
known for three generations for their verse.
The scene remains the same, but the modern and the old diverge.
When will we drink again in old Jing Town?

答陈竞先先生赠诗

君居旧宅岂难寻?
步出东门向北行。
面对高城当照壁,
背临清涧听波声。
两家父辈原知己,
三世诗书享盛名。
风景不殊今昔异,
何时共饮古菁城?

Dá Chén Jìngxiān xiānshēng zèng shī

Jūnjū jiùzhái qǐ nánxún?
Bùchū dōngmén xiàngběi xíng.
Miànduì gāochéng dāng zhàobì,
bèilín qīngjiàn tīng bōshēng.
Liǎngjiā fùbèi yuán zhījǐ,
sānshì shīshū xiǎng shèngmíng.
Fēngjǐng bùshū jīnxī yì,
héshí gòngyǐn gǔ Jīngchéng?

Line 8: Jingcheng (Jing Town, now Jingcheng District) in Longyan County (now Longyuan City) was Zheng's hometown in Fujian Province.

Response to Mr Chen Jingxian's Gift of a Poem

APPENDIX

Mr Chen Jingxian's Original Poem: Affection

My admiration for you has increased with age,
I sought your view on 'Without Reason' purely for enlightenment.
To my surprise, I plant a wutong tree and get a phoenix,
as my old friend's footsteps echo through the empty dell.
You have long been versed in world affairs and know the classics well.
Your writing is a priceless gem.
I sincerely hope that you will let me visit you,
so that I can look towards the light and hear the plucking of the strings.

[附]陈竞先先生原诗

怀情

残年积慕益侵寻，
妄次《无端》寄素心。
引得高梧栖凤哕，
传来空谷故乡音。
穷经早报盈三径，
述作应能窖万金。
何日程门容立雪，
仰瞻山斗听鸣琴。

[Fù] Chén Jìngxiān xiānshēng yuán shī

Huái qíng

Cánnián jīmù yì qīn xún,
wàng cì 'Wúduān' jì sùxīn,
yǐndé gāowú qī fèng huì,
chuánlái kōnggǔ gùxiāng yīn.
Qióngjīng zǎobào yíng sān jìng,
shùzuò yīngnéng jiào wànjīn.
Hérì chéngmén róng lìxuě,
yǎngzhān shāndòu tīng míngqín.

Line 2: Perhaps the name of a poem.
Line 3: Phoenixes roost only on wutong trees, on which they bestow honour and nobility.
Line 7: Chen Jingxian alludes to a story from the Song Dynasty, in which Yang Shi, a pupil of the scholar Cheng Yi, visits his master on a snowy day. Cheng sits still, his eyes closed. Yang stands before the gate and waits. When Cheng awakes, the snow is a foot deep. This story is cited as an example of a pupil's reverence for his master.

196

65.

A Reply to Comrade Xie Shan

To the tune of 'The Butterfly Lingers over the Flower'

16 February 1990

On 4 June 1989, less than a year before Zheng wrote this poem, pro-democracy protests in Beijing and other major cities met with a brutal military crackdown. That same day, the Solidarity trade union won an election in Poland, leading to the peaceful fall of Stalinism in Poland in the summer. Hungary started dismantling its border controls, and in November 1989 the Berlin Wall came down. The upheavals excited Trotskyists throughout the world, but Zheng wondered whether the collapse would lead to true socialism and democracy. This exchange of poems conveys Zheng's mixed feelings. In it, Xie and Zheng invoke a poem by Xin Qiji celebrating the lunar New Year. Xin's poem was an expression of his anxiety at the fate of the Southern Song Dynasty, under hostile pressure at the time.

Today, at the start of spring and on lunar New Year's Day, Comrade Xie Shan has written a poem based on Xin Qiji's original. Here is my reply, written to the same tune.

> The *yang* is low, the *yin* is vigorous,
> the day is cold and swept by storms,
> and grey beards turn to white.
> Who still remembers darling spring?
> The old regret it to their dying day.
>
> When will spring return and where to ask?
> It's said that day by day
> she's drawing closer.
> My thoughts turn this way and then that,
> good news is hard to count on.

A Reply to Comrade Xie Shan

蝶恋花·答谢山同志

今年立春日, 恰值旧历元旦, 谢山同志以辛弃疾的《蝶恋花》词原韵作一首见示, 因步韵答之。

阳气消沉阴气盛,
苦雨凄风,
白了青青鬓。
似锦年华谁记省?
衰翁应抱终身恨。

何日春回何处问?
见说行踪,
逐日将临近。
心事翻腾浑未定,
者番喜讯仍难准。

Dié liàn huā: Dá Xiè Shān tóngzhì

Jīnnián lìchūn rì, qià zhí jiùlì yuándàn, Xiè Shān tóngzhì yǐ Xīn Qìjí de 'Dié liàn huā' cí yuányùn zuò yīshǒu jiànshì, yīn bùyùn dázhī.

Yángqì xiāochén yīnqì shèng,
kǔyǔ qīfēng,
báile qīngqīng bìn.
Sìjǐn niánhuá shéi jìxǐng?
Shuāiwēng yīngbào zhōngshēn hèn.

Hérì chūnhuí héchù wèn?
Jiànshuō xíngzōng,
zhúrì jiāng línjìn.
Xīnshì fānténg hún wèidìng,
zhěfān xǐxùn réng nánzhǔn.

APPENDIX

Xie Shan's original *ci*

Zang and Gu both lose a sheep – who will find it first?
Time presses,
as our hair turns grey.
It is unbearable to recall old times.
Once old, you no longer bear the grudge.

Appendix, line 1: Xie Shan cites a story from the Daoist philosopher Zhuangzi about Zang and Gu, each of whom loses a sheep. Zang had been reading bamboo tablets, Gu had been engrossed in a game. The sheep are hard to find, along forking roads. Zhuangzi adds: 'Nowhere has there been anyone who has not under [the influence of external] things altered [the course of] his or her nature. Small people for the sake of gain have sacrificed their persons; scholars for the sake of fame have done so; great officers, for the sake of their families; and sages, for the sake of the kingdom.' This story is used to describe unintended consequences and complicated choices.

A Reply to Comrade Xie Shan

Don't say that Heaven is too high to ask.
When winter passes,
spring will not be far behind.
'In the vicissitudes of life, my mind's set on an even course.'
Tides ebb and flow at the appointed hour.

藏榖亡羊知孰胜？
有限年华，
换却双青鬓。
雨雨风风常懒省，
老来不抱闲愁恨。

莫谓天高无处问，
过了严冬，
料是春期近。
'世事沧桑心事定'，
潮生潮落应仍准。

Záng Gǔ wángyáng zhī shú shèng?
Yǒuxiàn niánhuá,
huàn què shuāng qīng bìn.
Yǔyù fēngfēng cháng lǎn xǐng,
lǎolái bubào xián chóu hèn.

Mòwèi tiāngāo wúchù wèn,
guò le yándōng,
liào shì chūnqí jìn.
'Shìshì cāngsāng xīnshì dìng',
cháoshēng cháoluò yīng réngzhǔn.

APPENDIX

Xin Qiji's original *ci*

Who festoons with gauds the pepper plates?
The darling girls
vie to pin baubles to their hair.
It is unbearable to recall old times.
Spring, how I hate the briefness of your flowering.

I am keen to know when spring will come.
I hate its late arrival and the long wait for its buds,
just as I do an early spring and early loss of hue.
I have heard the news about the blooming months this year,
but storms do not, alas, depend on human will.

Line 2:   A line from Gong Zizhen that Zheng Chaolin used in Poem 61.
Appendix, line 3:   Those around Xin happily celebrate the festival, but the poet does not share their joy: he is deeply worried about the survival of the Southern Song Dynasty, racked by internal crisis and external threats.

A Reply to Comrade Xie Shan

谁向椒盘簪彩胜?
整整韶华,
争上春风鬓。
往日不堪重记省,
为花长把新春恨。

春未来时先借问,
晚恨开迟,
早又飘零近。
今岁花期消息定,
只愁风雨无凭准。

Shéi xiàng jiāopán zān cǎishèng?
Zhěngzhěng sháohuá,
zhēng shàng chūnfēng bìn.
Wǎngrì bùkān chóng jìxǐng,
wèi huā chángbá xīnchūn hèn.

Chūn wèi lái shí xiān jièwèn,
wǎn hèn kāichí,
zǎo yòu piāolíng jìn.
Jīnsuì huāqí xiāoxī dìng,
zhǐ chóu fēngyǔ wú píngzhǔn.

Chen Yi

Introduction

Chen Yi (1901–1976) was born in Chengdu in 1901, the same year as Zheng Chaolin, into a family headed by a bankrupt landowner and scholar. He died of cancer in 1972, after being sidelined and humiliated for criticising Mao's Cultural Revolution.

As a young child, he attended a small private school where he read the Four Confucian Books. After his father's death, he suffered at the hands of his grandfather, a harsh and usurious yamen chief.[1] He claimed to have learned compassion and class hatred as a result, sympathising with the oppressed and dreaming of becoming a soldier in the fight to change China. Having spent much of his childhood in a yamen, he was versed in the 'etiquette of official circles', which he later employed to charm local dignitaries during the guerrilla war and the Anti-Japanese Resistance War. At school he learned to write poetry in the classical style, a skill he would exploit to great effect while setting up a military base for the Party in eastern China.[2]

Physical descriptions of him differ according to the beholder. If the US envoy Colonel David Barrett thought he had a 'cruel hard face; the face of a killer', the Communist poet Xu Xingzhi saw nobility: 'sparkling strong eyes that radiated warmth; a high-bridged nose; a firm, resolute mouth; a fine voice; a shaved chin, as in France'.[3]

In 1919, Chen won a scholarship to France on a work-study programme,

---

1 A yamen was the administrative office or residence of a local mandarin.
2 The description of Chen Yi that follows is based on passages in Gregor Benton, *Mountain Fires: The Red Army's Three-Year War in South China, 1934–1938*, Berkeley: University of California Press, 1992, and *New Fourth Army: Communist Resistance along the Yangtze and the Huai, 1938–1941*, Berkeley: University of California Press, 1999.
3 Benton, *Mountain Fires*, p. 34.

where he met Zheng Chaolin. Like Zheng and many others who later became leaders of the CCP, he did not enrol on a formal course of higher education but instead learned about socialism and French culture in Paris, while earning his keep by loading barges, washing dishes and doing factory work. In late 1921, he and 103 other students were deported back to China for taking part in a protest movement, and he gave up his dream of personally saving China 'by learning science'.

For a while, he resisted joining the CCP and was in two minds about his future – politics and literature both beckoned, and so did the idea of a military career. In 1921 he rejected an invitation by Cai Hesen, who had founded the Chinese Communist movement among the Chinese students in France, to go to Russia and study – in this respect resembling Mao, who declared that he would not set foot in Russia until the revolution had prevailed in China. Chen finally joined the Party in 1923, after losing his job as editor of a Chongqing newspaper. But his Communist conversion did not put an end to his freethinking and individualism. Even after signing up as a professional revolutionary in 1925, setting aside his earlier hope of a literary career, he was criticised for his 'petty-bourgeois' attitude and sent to work in a factory to 'steel himself' politically. But he lost the factory job and went to Guangzhou to join the Whampoa Military Academy under the Communist Zhou Enlai, thus setting out on the military road he had imagined as a youth. He fought for the Party in the Northern Expedition (1926–27) and the Nanchang Uprising (1927), before joining Zhu De and Mao Zedong in the Jinggang Mountains. There he helped set up the Fourth Red Army and gained a Maoist label for himself, although it never completely stuck.

In October 1934, when the Chinese Red Army was defeated by the Nationalists and its main body set out on the Long March to the north from its rural base in south China, Chen Yi and his comrades stayed behind as part of a rearguard (better, a probable death-legion, for few expected them to survive) of scattered units, and began their Three-Year War as lone remnants of what had been the Chinese Central Soviet. In 1937, the survivors of this small war came down from the mountains to a heroes' welcome from Party leaders, who had established a new Red capital in Yan'an and more or less given up the 'staybehinders' for dead. In the years between the

Introduction

start of the Long March and the physical reunion of the southern rearguard (by then reorganised as the New Fourth Army) with the Eighth Route Army (formed under Mao in the north, around two years after the end of the Long March in October 1935), Chen Yi and his comrades were engaged in a lonely and supremely difficult struggle to survive, fighting a war quite different in nature from that waged by Mao and his Long Marchers. It was during these years that Chen wrote most of the poems here translated.

The differences between Chen's war and Mao's northward evacuation after October 1934 were as follows:

> The Long March symbolizes centralism, homogeneity, and the rise to power of the Party's historic leader; the Three-Year War represents polycentrism and regional diversity. The march is celebrated as a new turn after a wrong start [in the early 1930s]; the war exemplifies continuity and loyalty to the victims of Party failures. The march is primarily a feat of arms performed by men; the war combines military and civilian forms of struggle and enlists secret armies of women. The march unites the Party and brings its different factions into one political line; the war requires the creative adjustment of policy to varied circumstance, compromise, improvisation, flexibility and independent initiative. The march exemplifies urgency and haste, and, as a forced march to safety, has become a symbol of China's hopes for rapid progress toward wealth and power; the war is the tortoise to Mao's hare, the hedgehog to his fox, a symbol of patience and stoical endurance. The march is hailed as an act of immense will that miraculously snatches the Red Army from the jaws of ruin; the virtues of the war are tact, brains, moderation, and its human scale.[4]

During the Three-Year War – which was screened from sight for many years by the Maocentric bias in mainland-Chinese scholarship, not to say deplored and denounced for its anarchic nature – Chen Yi and his comrades in the south set up guerrilla bases after breaking through the ring of steel that Chiang Kai-shek had erected around the ruins of the old Central Soviet.

---

4 Ibid., p. 516.

Introduction

Chen and the other rearguard leaders, principally the worker-Communist Xiang Ying, were soldered by their experience into a quarrelsome intimacy that fell far short of the chemical fusion brought about by the experience of the Long March.

The collapse of the Central Soviet was practically total after the start of the Long March. Chiang's propagandists announced that 'there is not a tree that has not been felled [in the Soviet], not a fowl or dog that has not been killed, not an able-bodied man remaining; no smoke rises from the kitchen chimneys in the alleys and the lanes, the only noise in the fields is the wailing of ghosts.' But although Communist activities subsided to a flicker, they were never entirely extinguished.

On remote mountains throughout the huge territory inside and outside the old Central Soviet previously under Red Army rule, Chen and other Communists maintained bases that rested at first on personal followings and unorthodox alliances (dressed up as 'united fronts') with bandits, Daoist sect-leaders, pirates, 'mountain hegemons', opium barons, 'men of the greenwood', and other local strongmen. Some played hide-and-seek among the refugees loosed across the region by the collapse of the Soviet in 1934. Others climbed ever higher above the abandoned villages towards the summits, where they bivouacked out of reach of vengeful authorities. Isolated groups of Communists lived like *dharma* families in hermitages, under father-masters who preserved and transmitted Party doctrines. They refined a war of tricks and ruses, squatting motionless in the undergrowth when enemy troops approached. Fleetness was their great defence. They rarely stepped inside a house for most of the war, sleeping instead under giant paper umbrellas treated with persimmon gum and wood oil, lengths of cloth tied between branches, or in the open under the stars. They set up Party forest schools to teach literacy and a rough version of Marxist-Leninist thought to the guerrillas and their civilian supporters. As they stole through the mountains in the dead of night, they encountered snakes, tigers and leopards, with which the forests teemed, and fed on hornets' pupae, bullfrogs, wild vegetables, nuts, muntjac, hares and wild boar. Many limped around on sticks after suffering injuries. Scabies, ulcers, malaria and TB were rife among them.

Each of the separate rearguard groups marched down the mountains

Introduction

following the declaration of a new anti-Japanese united front between Communists and Nationalists at an all-China level in 1937. Few ignored the call – the great majority stayed loyal to the Party. After reorganising these groups into the New Fourth Army, Chen Yi, Xiang Ying and other southern leaders led their new detachments north, into Jiangnan (the region south of the Yangtze River, centred on Nanjing), whence – after regularisation – they gradually began to infiltrate Jiangbei (north of the Yangtze). Along the Yangtze, the guerrilla veterans were joined by new worker and student recruits from the cities of central China and the Yangtze plain, and by refugees.

The battleground onto which the guerrillas debouched was the polar opposite of the southern mountains they had left behind: a polished plain, fringed by gentle hills to the west and broken everywhere by a maze of ditches, dykes, streams, canals, rivers, lakes, swamps and inland seas on which the now waterborne Communists moved and fought.

Communist studies on the Chinese revolution emphasise class conflict as its primary engine, but the New Fourth Army specialised in co-opting the authority of rural elites, especially in the first few years of its existence. Chen Yi was particularly good at exploiting the particularistic ties that bound local society in Jiangnan and Jiangbei, and at drawing 'prominent personalities' into the Party's orbit by means of social relations and cultural resources. His main early target was Han Guojun, a former official and leading member of the Jiangbei gentry, well known locally as a poet. Han was a foremost representative of the traditional local elite, which, according to the Party's analysis of class relations, was in conflict with the new 'comprador capitalists' represented by the Guomindang, who had eroded Han's authority in the region.

To win Han Guojun over, Chen Yi deployed intermediaries and social relations, and conducted himself with tact and charm. After Chen's initial overture, Han sent him a patriotic couplet, to which Chen responded with a couplet of his own. Han praised Chen as 'having the demeanour of both a scholar and a general'. 'Their intimacy grew daily', thanks to Chen's mastery of scholarly bonding rituals. Han Guojun was not the only target of Chen Yi's poetry offensive. Chen also wrote poems to other members of the gentry, and enlisted the talents among his generals as well as Communist

Introduction

poets from nearby Nationalist areas to weigh in with their own verse. At around this time, he founded and ran the Lakes and Seas Art and Literature Society, which celebrated important moments in the Resistance War with verse. The Society had a big impact on the 'enlightened gentry' in Jiangbei and helped Chen win power in most of the region, by mobilising an extensive and deep-rooted gentry coalition. Han Guojun saw in the Communists a reflowering of the promise of his youth, when he had sought to restore his native region to political health (privately, however, the Communists did not reciprocate the esteem). The drama of Chen Yi's wooing of Han Guojun and disaffected sections of the Jiangbei gentry was by no means unique: Communists everywhere in China made use of gentry networks for their own ends. However, none achieved an outcome to match that in Jiangbei in the early 1940s, where gentry influence – roused by Chen Yi's inspired courting – was a decisive factor in the New Fourth Army's military advance.

Our selection of Chen Yi's poems is confined to the Three-Year War and the first four years of the Resistance War up to 1940. The New Fourth Army under Chen Yi and Xiang Ying, like its guerrilla forerunners in the Three-Year War, was no outgrowth or copy of the Chinese Communists' senior and better-known Eighth Route Army, but a force with its own origins, history and features. Not until 1941 did it begin to look like its more Maoist elder brother in the north, with which it soon became definitively aligned.

After 1941, Chen enjoyed a stellar military career in the Communist Party and its army, commanding the forces that defeated Chiang Kai-shek in the crucial Huaihai Campaign in 1948–49. Appointed mayor of Shanghai in 1949 and one of China's ten field marshals in 1955, he also served as vice premier and foreign minister until his death in 1972.

Chen Yi's accomplishments were unusual among his comrades in the Three-Year War and the early New Fourth Army: he was a horseman, a chess player, a poet (classical and modern) and a translator of poems from the French. A rebel long before he became a Communist, he told hostile Red Guard inquisitors during the Cultural Revolution that he would remain one to the end, 'even after death'. Here, he was simply repeating the sentiments expressed in 'Three Stanzas Written at Meiling' in the winter of 1936: 'What if my head falls now? ... I shall rally my old comrades in the

Introduction

netherworld, a mighty host to kill the King of Hell.' He was never rigidly wedded to Maoist ideas or Party structures, but rather a pliant thinker and a flexible strategist, under whom Communists with creative talents and the courage to take responsibility generally prospered.

A comrade-in-arms described him thus: 'Frank and open; big-hearted, bold, grand of vision; wise and far-sighted, with an eye to the whole; resolute and resourceful; well versed in both the polite letters and the martial arts ... warm and loving toward us ... skilful and patient; factual and rational; not given to slapping on labels and waving big sticks; good at uniting with other comrades.'

In times of crisis (of which there were many, especially in the years covered by this selection of Chen Yi's poems) he stayed calm and spoke of the need – a favourite theme of his – to 'be heroes in defeat'. He was good at holding people together of their own free will, as opposed to dragooning them. His childhood travails in his grandfather's yamen had taught him the need to compromise with authority and even to ally with the rich and powerful, when this was expedient.

In his poems, written in mountain bivouacs, command posts or the heat of battle, stored in notebooks or in his head, Chen Yi describes how it feels to fight. The poems deal with the entire span of events in the Three-Year War and the early Resistance War along the Yangtze: the collapse of the Soviet, living and fighting in the wilderness, coming down from the mountains, entering the plains, and meeting up again with old comrades after years of separation, as in the autumn of 1940 the Eighth Route Army and the New Fourth finally join forces in northern Jiangsu. These poems are not the 'cogs and wheels' of revolution that Stalin (and Mao following him) ordained as the role of literature, so much as private records of despair, hope and defiance alongside a public celebration of key events in the two wars. Chen Yi wrote free verse in the vernacular when he was young, before turning in middle age to an espousal of the classical style. His work nonetheless makes more use of the vernacular than that of other poets writing in that style, with less recourse to allusion, parallelism and other conventions.

1.

In Mourning for Comrades Ruan Xiaoxian and He Chang

A *wu*lü   April 1935

Chen Yi mourns two comrades killed when survivors of the rearguard in the old Central Soviet broke through the Nationalist encirclement in April 1935. Chen Yi and Xiang Ying slipped south with five others, disguised as refugees, and set up a new base on the nearby border between Jiangxi and Guangdong. Ruan Xiaoxian (1897–1935) was born in Guangdong and joined the CCP in 1921. Ruan was wounded in a battle during the breakout and subsequently died. He Chang (1906–1935) was killed on the battlefield while providing cover for Chen Yi and Xiang Ying's escape. The story of the breakout is told in Benton, *Mountain Fires*, pp. 57–63.

> Among our comrades
> Ruan and He Chang may be called virtuous and able.
> Ruan was well known in southern China,
> He Chang's name was famous in the north.
> In planning and checking they were diligent and tireless,
> in administering they had authority and weight.
> I am grieved that when we tried to crack the ring
> they fell, and only I survived.

哭阮啸仙、贺昌同志   **Kū Ruǎn Xiàoxiān, Hè Chāng tóngzhì**

环顾同志中，   Huángù tóngzhì zhōng,
阮贺足称贤。   Ruǎn Hè zú chēngxián.
阮誉传岭表，   Ruǎn yùchuán lǐngbiǎo,
贺名播幽燕。   Hè míngbō yōuyàn.
审计呕心血，   Shěnjì ǒu xīnxuè,
主政见威严。   zhǔzhèng jiàn wēiyán.
哀哉同突围，   Āizāi tóng túwéi,
独我得生全。   dú wǒ dé shēngquán.

2.

Climbing Dayu Mountain

A *qijue*   *Autumn 1935*

Chen Yi wrote this poem in the Dayu Mountains in his and Xiang Ying's new base, after abandoning the Central Soviet and getting news of the Tanggu Truce (the He-Umezu Agreement) signed in 1935 by China and Japan. The truce gave Chiang Kai-shek the chance to focus his efforts on destroying the Communists, most of whom were then on the final stages of the Long March to the north.

> The sky lours on Dayu Mountain,
> storms over Europe and Asia cloud my eyes.
> Traitors have sold the last handful of our soil.
> The sky fills with red banners raised among war's beacons.

登大庾岭   **Dēng Dàyǔ Lǐng**

大庾岭上暮天低，   Dàyǔlǐng shàng mùtiān dī,
欧亚风云望欲迷。   Ōu Yà fēngyún wàng yù mí.
国贼卖尽一抔土，   Guózéi màijìn yī póu tǔ,
弥天烽火举红旗。   mítiān fēnghuǒ jǔ hóngqí.

Title: On the border between Guangdong and Jiangxi.

3.

Bivouacking

Spring 1935

In his mountain hideouts, always on the run, Chen Yi was largely cut off from sources of information, but he sometimes received newspapers smuggled in from nearby towns. In one he read that the Long Marchers (a term not yet invented at the time) had crossed the Jinsha River, an upper stream of the Yangtze between Sichuan and Yunnan. The epic crossing took ten days to complete, using just a handful of small boats. The news confirmed the Red Army's continued survival, and buoyed Chen and his comrades hiding out in the wilderness.

> Storm-lashed and homeless,
> we sleep in the wild and every day change base,
> with nothing but cold food to still our hunger.
> Quietly we catch lice among the mountain flowers.
> Pebbles can fill the sea of blood,
> we rejoice that our distant army crossed the Jinsha.
> As we peer out into the long lampless nights,
> our hair grays with the anguish of our love for China.

Line 5: The mythical jingwei bird is determined to fill up the sea with pebbles.
Line 8: An allusion to the story of Shen Baoxu, a patriotic official of the Chu Kingdom in the Spring and Autumn period, who saved the Chu from subjugation by getting support from the Qin.

Bivouacking

野营

恶风暴雨住无家,
日日野营转战车。
冷食充肠消永昼,
禁声扪虱对山花。
微石终能填血海,
大军遥祝渡金沙。
长夜无灯凝望眼,
包胥心事发初华。

Yěyíng

Èfēng bàoyǔ zhù wújiā,
rìrì yěyíng zhuǎn zhànchē.
Lěngshí chōngcháng xiāo yǒngzhòu,
jìnshēng ménshī duì shānhuā.
Wēishí zhōngnéng tián xuèhǎi,
dàjūn yáozhù dù Jīnshā.
Chángyè wúdēng níng wàngyǎn,
Bāoxū xīnshì fā chūhuá.

4.

Guerrilla Fighting in Gannan

To the tune of 'Thinking of Jiangnan'

Summer 1936

Chen Yi describes life in the mountains under Nationalist siege. The line about Japan overrunning China is a reference to Japan's steady encroachment into Northeastern China (Manchuria) and Northern China in the mid 1930s, after establishing a puppet state of Manchukuo in 1932 and as a prelude to the full-scale invasion of China in July 1937.

First light nears, our troops wake early.
Dew soaks our shirts and quilts: it's summer, but still cold.
In the trees, cicadas sing.
4   Blades of grass cling to our clothes.

The sun is near its noontime peak, and our bellies beat like drums.
For three months the blockade has stopped supplies.
Counting the grains of rice,
8   we boil wild vegetables.

The sun is setting in the west, and we sit and talk of war.
We have no news of our liaison man.
He left at dawn, and should be back by now.
12   We strike camp.

Night marching is a test of fortitude, for two weeks now it has rained relentlessly.
Tentless we camp
beneath a spreading tree, waiting for dawn.
16   Sleep does not come easily.

The weather clears, we bivouac
under the beaming moon. Breezes speed our sleep.
Ten thousand pines shield us from the sky, like clouds.
20   We dream of the enemy.

Guerrilla Fighting in Gannan

Speak in whispers, do not laugh or joke.
Beyond the woods lurk spies.
Before, coughing betrayed our whereabouts.
By sincerely recognizing our mistakes, we can improve. 24

We sigh for lack of grain, for months on end we've fed on nature's store.
In summer months we eat wild strawberries, in winter months bamboo.
We chase wild boar across the mountains
and snare snakes deep into the night. 28

The mountain is surrounded and besieged, trees go up in flames.
The enemy slaughters us more ruthlessly than ever.
Our people resist with even greater confidence.
We shall fight and fight. 32

Be tactical, angle with confidence.
Fight when the enemy won't;
don't when he will;
then we're his master. 36

Depend on the people, never forget their support.
They are our parents,
we their good sons in the fight.
The revolution will advance from strength to strength. 40

Study hard and pity those who lag behind.
Let us refine our skills,
so that another year
we can march victoriously forward and advance without losing heart. 44

Do not complain; march steadily on.
Traitors have surrendered the Yu tripod to Japan, but our great force
has crossed the Jinsha River now.
The iron tree will bud and burst in flower. 48

Line 46: The legendary Yu the Great of the Xia Dynasty (2070–1600 BCE) made nine tripods as symbols of state power.
Line 47: By crossing the Jinsha, upstream of the Yangtze, the Red Army's main force finally broke through the Guomindang's encirclement and laid the foundations for the victory of the Long March.
Line 48: 'The iron tree in blossom' predicts hard-won victories against Japan.

忆江南•赣南游击词

天将晓,队员醒来早。
露侵衣被夏犹寒,
树间唧唧鸣知了。
满身沾野草。

天将午,饥肠响如鼓。
粮食封锁已三月,
囊中存米清可数。
野菜和水煮。

日落西,集会议兵机。
交通晨出无消息,
屈指归来已误期。
立即就迁居。

夜难行,淫雨苦兼旬。
野营已自无篷帐,
大树遮身待晓明。
几番梦不成。

天放晴,对月设野营。
拂拂清风催睡意,
森森万树若云屯。
梦中念敌情。

休玩笑,耳语声放低。
林外难免有敌探,
前回咳嗽泄军机。
纠偏要心虚。

叹缺粮,三月肉不尝。
夏吃杨梅冬剥笋,
猎取野猪遍山忙。
捉蛇二更长。

满山抄,草木变枯焦。
敌人屠杀空前古,
人民反抗气更高。
再请把兵交。

讲战术,稳坐钓鱼台。
敌人找我偏不打,
他不防备我偏来。
乖乖听安排。

靠人民,支援永不忘。
他是重生亲父母,
我是斗争好儿郎。
革命强中强。

勤学习,落伍实堪悲。
此日准备好身手,
他年战场获锦归。
前进心不灰。

莫怨嗟,稳脚度年华。
贼子引狼输禹鼎,
大军抗日渡金沙。
铁树要开花。

Guerrilla Fighting in Gannan

Yì Jiāngnán: Gànnán yóují cí

Tiān jiāngxiǎo, duìyuán xǐng lái zǎo.
Lù qīn yībèi xià yóuhán,
shù jiān jījī míng zhīliǎo.
Mǎnshēn zhān yěcǎo.

Tiān jiāngwǔ, jīcháng xiǎng rú gǔ.
Liángshí fēngsuǒ yǐ sān yuè,
nángzhōng cúnmǐ qīng kěshǔ.
Yěcài héshuǐ zhǔ.

Rì luòxī, jíhuì yì bīng jī.
Jiāotōng chénchū wú xiāoxī,
qūzhǐ guīlái yǐ wùqī.
Lìjí jiù qiānjū.

Yè nánxíng, yínyǔ kǔ jiān xún.
Yěyíng yǐzì wú péngzhàng,
dàshù zhēshēn dài xiǎo míng.
Jǐfān mèng bùchéng.

Tiān fàngqíng, duì yuè shè yěyíng.
Fúfú qīngfēng cuī shuìyì,
sēnsēn wànshù ruò yúntún.
Mèngzhōng niàn díqíng.

Xiū wánxiào, ěryǔ shēng fàngdī.
Línwài nánmiǎn yǒu dítàn,
qiánhuí késòu xiè jūnjī.
Jiūpiān yào xīnxū.

Tàn quēliáng, sānyuè ròu bùcháng.
Xià chī yángméi dōng bōsǔn,
lièqǔ yězhū biànshān máng.
Zhuōshé èrgēng cháng.

Mǎnshān chāo, cǎomù biàn kūjiāo.
Dírén túshā kōng qiángǔ,
rénmín fǎnkàng qì gènggāo.
Zàiqǐng bǎ bīng jiāo.

Jiǎng zhànshù, wěn zuò diàoyútái.
Dírén zhǎowǒ piān bù dǎ,
tā bù fángbèi wǒ piān-lái.
Guāiguāi tīng ānpái.

Kào rénmín, zhīyuán yǒng bùwàng.
Tā shì chóngshēng qīn fùmǔ,
wǒ shì dòuzhēng hǎo erláng.
Gémìng qiáng zhōng qiáng.

Qín xuéxí, luòwǔ shí kānbēi.
Cǐrì zhǔnbèi hǎo shēnshǒu,
tānián zhànchǎng huò jǐn guī.
Qiánjìn xīn bù huī.

Mò yuànjiē, wěnjiǎo dù niánhuá.
Zéizǐ yǐnláng shū Yǔdǐng,
dàjūn kàngrì dù Jīnshā.
Tiěshù yào kāihuā.

5.

On My Thirty-Fifth Birthday

A *qilü*   1936

Chen Yi wrote this poem on 1 August, to mark his thirty-fifth birthday. At the time he was leading the guerrilla struggle in the Wuling Mountains in southern Jiangxi and experiencing hardship, which he contrasts with what he imagines to be the smooth progress of the main body of the Red Army in the north following the victorious conclusion of the Long March. Like Zheng Chaolin in his poem 'When *Yin* Attains Its Limit (Poem 21)', he uses the image of the revolving Earth to argue the inevitability of revolution.

    Our main army has marched splendidly west,
    while for us in the south war breaks out again.
    Half the fatherland is drowned in blood,
    many of my good friends lie in their graves.
    Enemies track and attack us night and day.
    By luck I am still alive;
    ten thousand died as heroes.
    When carried to extremes, all things must change;
    the Earth will turn and redden.

三十五岁生日寄怀   Sānshíwǔ suì shēngrì jìhuái

大军西去气如虹,   Dàjūn xīqù qì rúhóng,
一局南天战又重。   yījú nántiān zhàn yòuzhóng.
半壁河山沉血海,   Bànbì héshān chén xuèhǎi,
几多知友化沙虫。   jǐduō zhīyǒu huà shāchóng.
日搜夜剿人犹在,   Rìsōu yèjiǎo rén yóuzài,
万死千伤鬼亦雄。   wànsǐ qiānshāng guǐ yìxióng.
物到极时终必变,   Wù dào jíshí zhōng bìbiàn,
天翻地覆五洲红。   Tiānfān-dìfù wǔzhōu hóng.

6.

Three Stanzas Written at Meiling

Winter 1936

Chen Yi wrote these lines while under siege, in the winter of 1936. He lay wounded in the bushes for more than twenty days. He later wrote in a note: 'Not expecting to escape, I wrote these three stanzas and kept them in my pocket. But the siege was lifted.'

>What if my head now falls?
>Revolution is hard; it takes a hundred battles.
>I shall rally my old comrades in the netherworld,
>a mighty host to kill the King of Hell. 4
>
>Beacons have blazed in the south for ten long years;
>this head of mine may dangle from the city gate,
>but you who live on must make redoubled efforts:
>news of your victories will be our paper coins. 8
>
>This revolution has been my home;
>though heaven rains blood, slaughter must sometime end.
>Today the just cause claims our lives,
>sowing flowers of freedom over all the earth. 12

Line 8: Chen Yi compares his own likely death as a staybehinder in the south with the victories he imagines the Long Marchers in the north will win, thus vindicating him.

Three Stanzas Written at Meiling

梅岭三章

断头今日意如何？
创业艰难百战多。
此去泉台招旧部，
旌旗十万斩阎罗。

南国烽烟正十年，
此头须向国门悬。
后死诸君多努力，
捷报飞来当纸钱。

投身革命即为家，
血雨腥风应有涯。
取义成仁今日事，
人间遍种自由花。

Méilǐng sānzhāng

Duàntóu jīnrì yì rúhé?
Chuàngyè jiānnán bǎizhàn duō.
Cǐqù quántái zhāo jiùbù,
jīngqí shíwàn zhǎn Yánluó.

Nánguó fēngyān zhèng shí nián,
cǐtóu xūxiàng guómén xuán.
Hòusǐ zhūjūn duō nǔlì,
jiébào fēilái dāng zhǐqián.

Tóushēn gémìng jí wéi jiā,
xuèyǔ-xīngfēng yīng yǒuyá.
Qǔyì chéngrén jīnrì shì,
rénjiān biànzhǒng zìyóu huā.

7.

To Friends

A *qilü*   Spring 1937

Subsequently Chen Yi wrote a note to this poem:

> The Japanese were daily stepping up their plans to invade China. At the same time, the Guomindang reactionaries conducted an even more frenzied 'campaign of annihilation' against us. I was leading the guerrilla struggle in the Wuling Mountains. The Red Army main force had marched west to Shaanxi and Gansu; news was hard to get. Comrades Ruan Xiaoxian, He Chang, and Liu Bojian had been sacrificed one after the other. Nightly they came into my dreams. In death as in life, our comradeship has never changed. My guerrilla comrades were dispersed here and there in small groups, so I wrote this poem to let them know my feelings.

> Wind and rain soak our clothes.
> We hide by day and march by night, scarcely ever meeting others.
> Whom can we ask for news of Shaanxi and Gansu?
> Ghosts of dead comrades reach me in my dreams.
> Even innocent relatives and friends
> among the common people suffer tyranny.
> Brother fights brother, while the invader waxes fat.
> Renegades and traitors should be put to death.
> On the southern front the nation's fate is in our hands.

Line 7:   Chen cites the story of the power struggle between two sons of Cao Cao during the Three Kingdoms period (220–280) as a reference to the continuing civil war, which prevents a unified resistance to Japan.

To Friends

七律·寄友

风吹雨打露沾衣,
昼伏夜行人迹稀。
秦陇消息倩谁问,
故交鬼影梦中归。
瓜蔓抄来百姓苦,
萁豆煎时外寇肥。
叛徒国贼皆可杀,
吾侪南线系安危。

Jì yǒu

Fēngchuī-yǔdǎ lù zhān yī,
zhòufú-yèxíng rénjì xī.
Qínlǒng xiāoxī qiàn shéi wèn,
gùjiāo guǐyǐng mèngzhōng guī.
Guāmàn chāolái bǎixìng kǔ,
qídòu jiānshí wàikòu féi.
Pàntú guózéi jiē kěshā,
wúchái nánxiàn xì ānwéi.

8.

Lines Improvised While Coming Down the Mountains on the Occasion of the Second United Front between the Guomindang and the Communists

To the tune of 'Fresh Berries'

August 1937

The Second United Front, so called to distinguish it from the First United Front in the mid 1920s, was the name of the alliance declared in July 1937 between Chiang Kai-shek's Guomindang and the Chinese Communists, which marked the end of ten years of civil war. Nominally, the alliance continued until 1945, but in effect it did not survive the Wannan Incident of January 1941, when Chiang's forces wiped out the headquarters of Chen Yi's New Fourth Army on the south bank of the Yangtze (the rest of the army remained intact). Chen Duxiu had been blamed by the official Party for the defeat in 1927 that ended the First United Front. He was accused of failing to stand up to the Guomindang by pursuing a distinct revolutionary policy, although in reality Chen Duxiu had simply (and reluctantly) been following a line forced on the CCP by Moscow. Chen Yi pledges not to repeat the mistake (falsely) attributed to Chen Duxiu.

> After ten years of war
> Nationalists and Communists collaborate again.
> As I recall past fallen comrades
> tears stain my sleeve.
> Our main task is to resist Japan,
> but our salvation hinges on democracy.
> We should insure ourselves by swearing that
> we won't behave like Chen Duxiu.

Line 8: Chen Duxiu and the other Trotskyists were branded as traitors by the Communists.

Lines Improvised While Coming Down the Mountains

生查子·国共二次合作出山口占

十年战争后,
国共合作又。
回念旧时人,
潸然泪沾袖。
抗日是中心,
民主能自救。
坚定勉吾侪,
莫作陈独秀。

Shēng zhā zǐ: guógòng èrcì hézuò chushān kǒuzhàn

Shí nián zhànzhēng hòu,
guógòng hézuò yòu.
Huíniàn jiùshí rén,
shānrán lèi zhān xiù.
Kàngrì shì zhōngxīn,
mínzhǔ néng zìjiù.
Jiāndìng miǎn wúchái,
mòzuò Chén Dúxiù.

9.

Arriving at Gaochun for the First Time during the Eastern Expedition

June 1938

After a decade fighting in the Jiangxi mountains, Chen Yi arrives for the first time at Gaochun in Jiangnan, 'the land of rice and rice', unrelievedly flat apart from a few hills to the west. There he spearheads the New Fourth Army's guerrilla war on the central and eastern plains, to chime with the efforts of the Eighth Route Army in the north.

Ripples reflect the sun's rays.
Countless creeks and rivers break the land.
A small boat floats slowly by, the people as if painted on it.
In the midst of war, peace.   4

Willows bending on the river lend pattern to the shafts of light.
Peasants take supper, talking of mulberry and jute.
When our soldiers' boat arrives, people suspect that we are Japanese.
When they learn that we are their compatriots, they talk and laugh with us.   8

This is my first time in Jiangdong.
For twenty years I've dreamed of Suzhou.
Today I sit beneath the sail and gaze
at hills and water everywhere.   12

I pass freely through the reeds and rushes,
fires of fishermen reflected in the waves.
Lookouts give the signal, men awake
happy to find themselves in Gaochun at midnight.   16

Line 9: The eastern part of Jiangnan.
Line 10: Chen uses the ancient name Wu for Suzhou.

Arriving at Gaochun for the First Time during the Eastern Expedition

东征初抵高淳	Dōngzhēng chūdǐ Gāochún
波光荡漾水纹平,	Bōguāng dàngyàng shuǐwén píng,
河汊沟渠纵复横。	héchà gōuqú zòng fù héng.
扁舟容与人如画,	Piānzhōu róngyǔ rén rúhuà,
抗战军中味太平。	kàngzhàn jūnzhōng wèi tàipíng.
堤柳低垂晚照斜,	Dīliǔ dīchuí wǎnzhào xié,
农家夜饭话桑麻。	nóngjiā yèfàn huà sāngmá.
兵船初过群疑寇,	Bīngchuán chūguò qún yí kòu,
及见亲人笑语哗。	jíjiàn qīnrén xiàoyǔ huā.
江东风物未曾谙,	Jiāngdōng fēngwù wèicéng ān,
梦寐吴天廿载前。	mèngmèi Wútiān niànzǎi qián.
此日一帆凭顾盼,	Cǐ rì yīfān píng gùpàn,
重山复水是江南。	chóngshān fùshuǐ shì Jiāngnán.
芦苇丛中任我行,	Lúwěi cóngzhōng rèn wǒ xíng,
星星渔火水中明。	xīngxīng yúhuǒ shuǐzhōng míng.
步哨呼觉征人起,	Bùshào hūjué zhēngrén qǐ,
欣然夜半到高淳。	xīnrán yèbàn dào Gāochún.

10.

Ten Years

30 March 1939

This is Chen Yi's draft of the New Fourth Army song. It is followed by the collectively rewritten and retitled official version.

In the glorious ranks of the Northern Expedition
people remembered our respected name.
Inheriting the revolutionary's martyr spirit
our isolated troops were tempered
and steeled in the Luoxiao Mountains of the south. 5
The voice of revolution, loud and dear,
was heard abroad and in the villages.
We saw the vanguard march ten thousand miles to fight Japan
and stayed behind to keep the struggle going
so that we could eventually reunify our land. 10
Like cocks at dawn we issued the great call to fight Japan.

We started amid the wind and snow and pitched our tent
in the deserted mountains, hardship tempered us;
for three years we were cut off from the world,
but this increased our courage and our will to carry on alone. 15
In long years of ambushes and manoeuvring
we linked guerrilla war with secret work.
Our only reliance is on the people,
we are the son, they the mother;
they are the furnace of our iron discipline. 20
Today we leave to fight Japan:
the bandit enemy is truly scared.

We flit to the north and the south of the Yangtze and penetrate enemy lines.
Our resistance banner flutters outside Nanjing's walls.
We are politically united, living and dying for each other. 25

Line 5: On the border between Jiangxi and Hunan.

It is this that inspires the people under enemy rule to confidence in final victory.
We slip through the Japanese blockade
and engage the enemy in his city forts.
We fight at night
30 hand-to-hand with bayonets,
torching the enemy lair.
Small wins accumulate and become great victories.
First stalemate, then on to the counteroffensive.
Strike with lightning speed, wipe out the Japanese!
35 March on, march on! We are the New Fourth Army Ironsides!
Lift high the flag of the new China, and march on!

十年〔新四军军歌初稿〕

光荣的北伐行列中,
曾记着我们的威名。
我们继承着革命者受难的精神,
在南国的罗霄山,
锻炼成为钢铁的孤军。
这里有革命的反帝的歌声烂漫,
飘扬海外,散播农村。
我们送出了抗日先遣的万里长征,
我们留下来坚持斗争,
招引那民族再团结,
雄鸡破晓,
伟大的抗日之声。

风雪饥寒,穷山野营,
磨炼我们艰苦奋斗的精神;
三年隔绝,四围孤立,
增添我们独立坚持的勇气。
长年累月的埋伏与周旋,
把游击战争与秘密工作结合在一起。

我们惟一的依靠就是广大的人民,
我们就是这个母亲的儿子,
我们铁的纪律就来源于此。
啊!这光荣的传统准备了十年,
今朝抗日,敌寇胆寒!

我们在大江南北,向敌后进军,
南京城外遍布抗战的旗旌。
我们有共生死的政治团结,
鼓舞着敌后人民的胜利信心。
在日寇封锁线上穿插,
在日寇坚城下纠缠,
我们惯长于夜间作战,
用白刃同日寇肉搏,
向敌人巢穴里投进烈火。
集小胜为大胜,由相持到反攻,
看我们风驰电掣,横扫千军。
前进,前进,我们是铁的新四军,
高举新中国的旗帜前进!

Shí nián (Xīnsìjūn jūngē chūgǎo)

Guāngróng de běifá hángliè zhōng,
céng jìzhe wǒmen de wēimíng.
Wǒmen jìchéng zhe gémìngzhě shòunàn
  de jīngshén,
zài nánguó de Luōxiāoshān,
duànliàn chéngwéi gāngtiě de gūjūn.
Zhèlǐ yǒu gémìng de fǎndì de gēshēng
  lànmàn,
piāoyáng hǎiwài,
sànbò nóngcūn.
Wǒmen sòngchū le kàngrì xiānqiǎn de
  wàn lǐ chángzhēng,
wǒmen liú xiàlái jiānchí dòuzhēng,
zhāoyǐn nà mínzú zài tuánjié,
xióngjī pòxiǎo,
wěidà de kàngrì zhī shēng.

Fēngxuě jīhán,
qióngshān yěyíng,
móliàn wǒmen jiānkǔ fèndòu de
  jīngshén;
sān nián géjué, sìwéi gūlì,
zēngtiān wǒmen dúlì jiānchí de yǒngqì.
Chángnián lěiyuè de máifú yǔ
  zhōuxuán,
bǎ yóují zhànzhēng yǔ mìmì gōngzuò
  jiéhé zài yīqǐ.

Wǒmen wéiyī de yīkào jiùshì guǎngdà de
  rénmín,
wǒmen jiùshì zhè ge mǔqīn de érzǐ,
wǒmen tiě de jìlǜ jiù láiyuán yúcǐ.
A! Zhè guāngróng de chuántǒng zhǔnbèi
  le shí nián,
jīnzhāo kàngrì, díkòu dǎnhán!
Wǒmen zài dàjiāng nánběi,
xiàng díhòu jìnjūn,
nánjīng chéngwài biànbù kàngzhàn de
  qíjīng.
Wǒmen yǒu gòngshēngsǐ de zhèngzhì
  tuánjié,
Gǔwǔ zhe díhòu rénmín de shènglì
  xìnxīn.
Zài rìkòu fēngsuǒ xiàn shàng chuānchā,
zài rìkòu jiānchéng xià jiūchán,
wǒmen guànchāng yú yèjiàn zuòzhàn,
yòng báirèn tóng rìkòu ròubó,
xiàng dírén cháoxué lǐ tóujìn lièhuǒ.
Jí xiǎoshèng wéi dàshèng,
yóu xiāngchí dào fǎngōng,
kàn wǒmen fēngchí diànchè,
héngsǎo qiānjūn.
Qiánjìn, qiánjìn,
wǒmen shì tiě de Xīnsìjūn,
gāojǔ xīn Zhōngguó de qízhì qiánjìn!

Ten Years

The New Fourth Army Song

In the battle of Wuchang, on the glorious Northern Expedition,
our names were written in blood.
We fought alone in the Luoxiao Mountains,
upholding the achievements of our martyrs.
5   We fought a hundred thousand battles
in the wind and snow, hungry and cold.
We marched a hundred thousand marches
through the bare mountains, camping in the wilderness.
We acquired a rich experience of war
10 and tempered our spirit of sacrifice.
For the welfare of society and the survival of our nation
we have persisted in the fight.
We rallied from eight provinces to form an iron current.
March east! March east!
15 We are the New Fourth Army Ironsides!

We march freely to and fro on both banks of the Yangtze and the Huai;
piercing deep behind enemy lines,
we have won a hundred fights.
Everywhere our battle cry is heard.
20 We must attack bravely to destroy the enemy;
we must raise our voices high to rouse the people.
Develop the excellent traditions of our revolution
and create a modern revolutionary new army
for the welfare of society and the survival of our nation.

25 We must consolidate our unity and persist in struggle!
Resist the invaders and reconstruct the country,
hold high the banner of independence and freedom!
March on! March on!
We are the New Fourth Army Ironsides!

Line 1: Provincial capital of Hubei. The Fourth Army of the National Revolutionary Army played a key role in capturing Wuchang in September 1926.
Line 16: The Huai River valley runs through Henan, Hubei, Anhui, Jiangsu and Shandong.

新四军军歌

血染着我们的姓名；
孤军奋斗罗霄山上，
继承了先烈的殊勋。
千百次抗争，风雪饥寒；
千万里转战，穷山野营。
获得丰富的战争经验，
锻炼艰苦的牺牲精神。
为了社会幸福，为了民族生存，
一贯坚持我们的斗争！
八省健儿汇成一道抗日的铁流，
东进，东进！
我们是铁的新四军！

扬子江头淮河之滨，
任我们纵横的驰骋；
深入敌后百战百胜，
汹涌着杀敌的呼声。
要英勇冲锋，歼灭敌寇；
要大声呐喊，唤起人民。
发扬革命的优良传统，
创造现代的革命新军。
为了社会幸福，为了民族生存，
巩固团结坚决的斗争！
抗战建国，高举独立自由的旗帜，
前进，前进！
我们是铁的新四军！

Xīnsìjūn jūngē

Xuèrǎn zhe wǒmen de xìngmíng;
gūjūn fèndòu Luōxiāo shān shàng,
jìchéng le xiānliè de shūxūn.
Qiānbǎi cì kàngzhēng, fēngxuě jīhán;
qiānwàn lǐ zhuǎnzhàn, qióngshān yěyíng.
Huòdé fēngfù de zhànzhēng jīngyàn,
duànliàn jiānkǔ de xīshēng jīngshén.
Wèile shèhuì xìngfú, wèile mínzú shēngcún,
yīguàn jiānchí wǒmen de dòuzhēng!
Bā shěng jiàn'ér huìchéng yī dào kàngrì de tiěliú,
dōngjìn, dōngjìn!
Wǒmen shì tiě de Xīnsìjūn!

Yángzǐ jiāngtóu Huái Hé zhī bīn,
rèn wǒmen zònghéng de chíchěng;
shēnrù díhòu bǎizhàn-bǎishèng,
xiōngyǒng zhe shādí de hūshēng.
Yào yīngyǒng chōngfēng, jiānmiè díkòu;
yào dàshēng nàhǎn, huànqǐ rénmín.
Fāyáng gémìng de yōuliáng chuántǒng,
chuàngzào xiàndài de gémìng xīnjūn.
Wèile shèhuì xìngfú, wèile mínzú shēngcún,
gǒnggù tuánjié jiānjué de dòuzhēng!
Kàngzhàn jiànguó, gāojǔ dúlì zìyóu de qízhì,
qiánjìn, qiánjìn!
Wǒmen shì tiě de Xīnsìjūn!

11.

Reunion with Comrades of the Eighth Route Army Sent South, Some of Whom I Have Not Seen for More Than Ten Years

A *qijue*   November 1940

After Chen Yi's victory over the Nationalists in northern Jiangsu in October 1940, a major step in the New Fourth Army's consolidation of its control over the region, Chen Yi met up with the Eighth Route Army's Huang Kecheng near Baiju.

This meeting, celebrated with joyous embraces, handshakes, smiles, songs, tears and group photos, was their first since the Jinggang Mountains [in the south] in the late 1920s. It was also the first step toward the reintegration of northern and southern Jiangsu [either side of the Yangtze], of the Eighth Route and New Fourth Armies, and of the Chinese Communist movement north and south. The meeting was one not just of two armies but of two styles, a northern and a southern style.[1]

> Few survived the ten years' war
> but now I am reunited with some comrades;
> we ride back side by side to camp.
> Who controls the Chang, Huai, Han and Yellow Rivers now?
> Red flags flutter throughout the October sky.

与八路军南下部队会师,
同志中有十年不见者

十年征战几人回,
又见吾侪并马归。
江淮河汉今属谁?
红旗十月满天飞。

Yǔ bālùjūn nánxià bùduì huìshī,
tóngzhì zhōng yǒu shí nián bùjiàn zhě

Shí nián zhēngzhàn jǐ rén huí,
yòu jiàn wúchái bìngmǎ guī.
Jiāng Huái Hé Hàn jīn shǔ shéi?
Hóngqí shí yuè mǎntiān fēi.

---

1 Benton, *New Fourth Army*, p. 485.

Mao Zedong

Introduction

Mao Zedong was born into a moderately well-off peasant family in the village of Shaoshan in Hunan province in 1893. In 1936, he told Edgar Snow that he had rebelled against his father, a strict disciplinarian. However, the father provided his favourite son Zedong with everything that a child from a peasant family could have expected in those days. Mao received several years of private tutoring before he was sent to a modern local primary school to study Chinese classics and knowledge (including maths, physics, chemistry, geography and world history). In 1907 or 1908, at the age of thirteen, he entered into an arranged marriage with an eighteen-year-old local girl, in accordance with a local custom of marrying younger husbands to older brides.[1] At the age of sixteen he enrolled in a higher primary school at the county seat. In 1911, when the Qing Dynasty fell to republican revolutionaries, he started high school. He graduated from Hunan's First Normal School in the provincial capital Changsha at the age of twenty-five in June 1919, the year of the radical May Fourth Movement, after moving around several schools and, at one point, spending six months in a local army unit.

During his school years, Mao did not cope well with the formal curriculum, but he read widely outside it. His reading included Chinese popular novels (such as *Romance of the Three Kingdoms*, *Water Margin* and *Journey to the West*) and translations of Western writers including Charles Darwin, Herbert Spencer, Friedrich Paulsen, Adam Smith, Jean-Jacques Rousseau, John Stuart Mill and Charles de Montesquieu. He also devoured fashionable publications by Chinese constitutional reformers, republican revolutionaries and thinkers associated with May Fourth, which promoted

---

[1] The girl, Luo Yixiu (1889–1910), died of dysentery.

Introduction

China's modernisation and enlightenment. Mao's formative years coincided with massive political and intellectual transformations and the emergence of a modern Chinese intelligentsia. The centuries-old classical school curriculum and the imperial examination system, designed to select candidates for civil and military posts, were abolished in 1905; the millennia-old imperial system was replaced by a democratic republic in 1912; and the New Culture Movement, starting with the publication of *New Youth* in 1915, set out to transform China. Mao's primary and secondary education provided him with a grounding in Chinese learning and a basic knowledge of the main elements of modern Western political thought.

A combination of factors, including personal disinclination and family misfortune, prevented Mao from going to university. His mother died in October 1919, his father in January 1920; Yang Changji, his mentor at the First Normal School, died in the same month. Yang had been appointed professor at Beijing University in 1917 and had taken Mao to work there as a part-time library assistant in 1919. In Beijing, Mao was quickly radicalised, and he soon became a professional activist and revolutionary. He returned to Hunan in 1920 to teach. While there, he married Yang Changji's daughter, Yang Kaihui. He devoted most of his energy to political activities informed by radical ideologies, first anarchism and then Bolshevism. In his anarchist phase, he published articles calling for a Great Union of the Popular Masses and for Hunan's independence from China. He also joined a campaign to drive out Zhang Jingyao, the military governor of Hunan appointed by the central government, and assisted Tan Yankai, a general close to Sun Yat-sen and his Nationalist Party (the Guomindang), to take over Hunan.

Mao was eventually recruited into the CCP, founded with Comintern help in 1921 by Chen Duxiu, Li Dazhao, and their associates. In July 1921, along with twelve other delegates, he was invited to attend its First National Congress in Shanghai, convened by the Comintern representatives Maring and Nikolsky. The CCP's two main founders, Chen Duxiu and Li Dazhao, did not attend, due to other pressing commitments. Chen Duxiu was elected general secretary. At the time, Mao and his comrades knew next to nothing about Marxism.

In 1922, acting on Comintern instructions, Mao and other Communists joined the Guomindang, thus forging a coalition with China's 'bourgeois democrats' in pursuit of democratic revolution. Thanks partly to his connections with Tan Yankai, Mao quickly rose to prominence in the Guomindang, becoming an alternate member of the Central Executive Committee and acting director of the Central Propaganda Department. The alliance between the CCP and the Nationalists ended in a bloody split in 1927, by which time the victory of the Guomindang's Northern Expedition against the central government in Beijing controlled by northern warlords was in sight. The new Guomindang leadership, dominated by Chiang Kai-shek, expelled the CCP and massacred thousands of Communists.

Stalin and the Comintern blamed Chen Duxiu for the disaster, even though the primary responsibility for it rested with Stalin, who had ordered the CCP to join the Guomindang in the first place. The CCP leadership split in the ensuing crisis. Chen Duxiu and his supporters stuck to orthodox Marxist theory, arguing that the CCP should focus on the labour movement and rely on urban workers to make a proletarian revolution. They were expelled, and some (including Chen and Zheng Chaolin) became Trotskyists. The majority, including Mao, resolved to take up arms against the Guomindang – rousing peasants and landless labourers in rural areas and among social strata defined by Marx as lumpenproletarian, including bandits and outlaws. In the hands of these leaders, Marxism was transformed into a tool for the mobilisation of rural discontent and the legitimation of the seizure of state power by military means.

In the two years after their descent into the countryside in 1927, the Chinese Communists created a Red Army that set up a score of revolutionary bases, known as Soviets, in mountainous areas around the country. The largest Soviet was in the Jinggang Mountains, where Mao's troops were joined by those of Peng Dehuai, Zhu De, Chen Yi, and others. In August 1927, Mao ended his relationship with Yang Kaihui (who had borne him three sons) and started a new relationship with He Zizhen, an eighteen-year-old guerrilla fighter. Initially, the Red Army expanded quickly, and defeated attempts by Guomindang armies to 'encircle and annihilate' its forces. Encouraged by their success, Red Army troops attacked the city of Changsha in 1930, but were driven back. The CCP's central leadership, which had been hiding in the International Concession in Shanghai for several years, moved to the Central Soviet in 1933, to escape the Nationalists.

Introduction

However, the Soviet fell to superior forces in 1934, after several bloody purges and loss of popular support due to the financial burden of sustaining the Red Army in its war against Chiang Kai-shek's National Revolutionary Army. In October 1934, Red Army columns escaped first west and then north, on a trek that would become legendary as the Long March.

The Long March led to the elevation of Mao's status from a local leader to a dominant figure in the CCP. The Red Army's 1934 defeat required a change in military strategy and leadership, formalised by a meeting in January 1935, shortly after the start of the Long March. At the meeting, Mao was promoted to a leading role in military affairs.

The Red Army eventually reached Shaanxi in the north, where the Communists set up their new capital in Yan'an. It was the Japanese invasion of China that saved the CCP and the Red Army from possible extinction at this point, and created circumstances in which it was able to revive and prosper. The Japanese had seized northeastern China in 1931 and continued to expand southward in subsequent years. The crisis of national subjugation strengthened Chinese nationalism, which greatly benefited the Communists. In the summer of 1935, partly in response to Comintern instructions, the CCP leaders started a process that culminated in August 1937 in a Second United Front with the Guomindang. Under its terms, the Red Army was rebadged as the Eighth Route Army in the north and the New Fourth Army in the south, although its leaders insisted on maintaining complete independence from the central government's military command.

The CCP and its armies grew phenomenally during the eight years of war against Japan, from 1937 to 1945. The Japanese invasion dealt a fatal blow to Chiang Kai-shek, enfeebling his main force, driving his government into the remote and backward southwest of the country, cutting his ties to the coastal areas, and ruining the Chinese economy. The Communists generally avoided major battles with the Japanese and focused on mobilising the peasantry and expanding their territory. According to Mao, speaking in October 1939, the Communists would win power by wielding their 'three magic weapons' – the united front, armed struggle, and party-building. By the time of the Japanese surrender in 1945, the Communists had 1.3 million soldiers and 2.6 million militia members, and ruled over a population of 100 million.

Introduction

During the war, Mao became supreme leader of the CCP. Despite the Party's apparently egalitarian ethic, Communist society in Yan'an was marked by deep inequalities. Food and clothing were differentiated according to a person's social and political status. Former wives were abandoned for better-educated, younger women. In 1938 Mao left He Zizhen, who had borne him five children, to marry Jiang Qing, a well-known actress. Between 1941 and 1945, Mao and his supporters carried out a Rectification Campaign designed to unify the CCP ideologically, by means of a system of indoctrination, confession and criticism, to secure the complete submission to it of each member and ensure Mao's ascendency. At the end of the Rectification Campaign in April 1945, Mao Zedong Thought was adopted as the CCP's guiding ideology.

After the Japanese surrender in August 1945, China descended into an all-out civil war that the Communists won in 1949, against a Guomindang beset by corruption, factionalism, economic failure and low morale. With the establishment of the People's Republic in Beijing, the Chinese state under Mao acquired the contours of a Party dictatorship run by a new Communist bureaucracy that sought to eliminate all opposition, real and potential, by means of never-ending campaigns and purges. Urban workers were officially the masters of the nation, yet they were not allowed to go on strike or form independent trade unions. The Party did its best to turn the intelligentsia, previously an important source of support and legitimation, into its cowed servants, by thrusting them into the furnace of thought reform.

In the late 1950s, an ill-advised, ill-executed campaign to accelerate the modernisation of the Chinese economy through a crash programme of industrialisation and rural collectivisation caused millions to die of hunger. A decade later, the Cultural Revolution led to years of political turmoil and successive purges of Mao's loyal followers and closest colleagues, including Lin Biao, Peng Dehuai and Liu Shaoqi. In 1976, the year of Mao's death, 90 per cent of Chinese continued to live in poverty in the villages, and the country was largely sealed off from the outside world. It is true that the Mao years laid the foundations for industrialisation, enabled wider elementary education and a longer life expectancy for ordinary Chinese, and freed women from some of their heaviest burdens – but it is now commonly

Introduction

accepted that these achievements came at a huge, and unnecessary, human and environmental cost.

Before 1949, Mao had unofficially published just four poems. In 1957, a poetry journal printed eighteen of them. Thirty-nine of Mao's poems appeared in his lifetime, most of them serving a clear political purpose. A collection of fifty poems appeared in 1986 to commemorate the tenth anniversary of his death. The number increased to sixty-seven in 1996, on the twentieth anniversary. Not all the pieces were necessarily Mao's exclusive creations. 'Changsha', dated 1925 and arguably among the finest poems claimed by Mao, is believed by some scholars to have been collectively written by Mao and fellow-students and teachers at the First Normal School during an excursion in 1920. Mao himself admitted that the poems that came out during his lifetime were repeatedly revised and polished before publication and republication (and therefore appear in different forms in different editions), either by himself, by poet friends such as Dong Biwu, Xie Juezai, Liu Yazi and Guo Moruo, or by his secretaries, Hu Qiaomu and Chen Boda. Some poems, including a few allegedly written during the struggle in the Jinggang Mountains, might have been composed later and backdated. ('The People's Liberation Army Captures Nanjing', dated 1949, may also have been written later, given that Mao did not include it among the eighteen poems published in 1957.) In this book, we present twenty-eight poems written while Mao was in power between the 1930s and the 1970s, together with the Changsha poem, which betokens his ambition as a young man. One was written on the Long March, another in the Party's wartime capital of Yan'an, twelve at the time of the Communist victory and in the early days of New China, nine in the late 1950s and the early 1960s, and three during the Cultural Revolution. Our selection includes six poems not translated in the official Foreign Language Press version.

Mao's poems in the classical style demonstrate his traditional learning and reflect his character and career. He was a tough revolutionary, an outstanding military tactician, an ideologist, a romantic visionary and a ruthless ruler. Chinese poems since the Tang Dynasty have been categorised into two broad schools, one bold and unrestrained, the other subtle and subdued. Mao's poems fall at the extreme end of the bold and unrestrained.

The Trotskyist Wang Fanxi, in a study on Mao Thought, wrote as follows about them:

Introduction

[They] reveal the 'innermost soul' not of a petty-bourgeois intellectual (of the sort Mao excoriated in his Yan'an Talks) but of a feudal general, brandishing his sword and shooting eagles with his stretched bow, while displaying an elegance of manner, attitude, and speech, as overlord of the hegemons. Everyone knows that writers exaggerate, although romantic fantasy has no place in revolutionary literature. However, boasting and romanticising can reveal unintended truths. A revolutionary leading an army out of battle who arrives at the Yellow River by the Great Wall ... might, like Mao, 'muse over things of the remote past' and spit out lofty ideals; but most would not. Most would mourn the countless thousands of abandoned wives, deserted villages, and commoners and dissident scholars forced to build the Great Wall, or conscripts like Chen Sheng and Wu Guang who staged the first peasant revolt there. That would have been more in keeping with a revolution against oppression and exploitation. For recalling the past and thinking of the present are not two separate things. Mao, on the other hand, thinks first of heroes and of Qin Shi Huangdi and Han Wudi, and not of their crimes but of their achievements. He compares them, unfavourably, with himself, as 'lacking in literary grace'. In the same poem, he says of three dynasty-founding emperors, Tang Taizong, Song Taizu and Genghis Khan, that the first two 'had little poetry in their souls' and the latter 'knew only about shooting eagles'. So for 'truly great men, who wield pen and sword with equal skill and are both intelligent and brave – and who, in one case, start a reign – one must "look to this age alone"'.

Some of Mao's poems are modelled on those by outstanding rebel leaders and emperors, and are correspondingly characterised by aggressivity, hubris and self-aggrandisement. In life, Mao behaved with brutal savagery. Some of his poems are swollen with arrogance and wilfulness, replete with grandiose references to the universe, the sky and the earth and contrastingly raucous, sometimes scatological political slogans that express his determination to 'smash the bureaucratic machine', displaying himself as he wished to be seen – peerless and eternally enduring.

1.

Changsha

To the tune of 'Garden in Spring'   *1925*

This poem about youthful ambition is among the finest published under Mao's name. It is dated 1925, when Mao was a ranking cadre in both the CCP and the Guomindang. Its youthful tone does not seem to match Mao's age and status in 1925, nor does it reflect the fierce political and military events of the time, in which Mao was a central actor. The poem is believed by some to have been collectively written by Mao and fellow-students and teachers at the First Normal School during an excursion in 1920 or 1921, and then claimed by Mao after some revisions.

    Alone I stand in the autumn chill.
    At the cape of Orange Isle
    the Xiang flows north;
    I see ten thousand hills
5   reddened by the thronging woods,
    a hundred barges jostling
    across the jade-green waters.
    Eagles strike the sky,
    fish glide through the shallows;
10   high in the frosty air ten thousand creatures vie for freedom.
    Dejected by the vast expanse of sky
    I ask the boundless land,
    who masters the ups and downs of life?

    I came here with one hundred friends,
15   and vividly recall the fullness of those months and years.
    We were young and still at school,

Title: Changsha is the capital of Hunan Province, where Mao attended high school and worked as a primary-school teacher.
Line 3: The Xiang River is to the west of Changsha.

in the full flower of our lives,
scholars in spirit
and free of all restraint.
Gesturing at China's hills and rivers,   20
our utterances caught fire –
we deemed the high and mighty less than muck.
Do you still recall
how, as we struck out to the middle of the stream,
the waves held back our fleeting boat?   25

沁园春·长沙

独立寒秋,
湘江北去,
橘子洲头。
看万山红遍,
层林尽染;
漫江碧透,
百舸争流。
鹰击长空,
鱼翔浅底,
万类霜天竞自由。
怅寥廓,
问苍茫大地,
谁主沉浮?

携来百侣曾游,
忆往昔峥嵘岁月稠。
恰同学少年,
风华正茂;
书生意气,
挥斥方遒。
指点江山,
激扬文字,
粪土当年万户侯。
曾记否,
到中流击水,
浪遏飞舟?

Qìnyuán chūn: Chángshā

Dúlì hánqiū,
Xiāngjiāng běiqù,
Júzǐzhōu tóu.
Kàn wànshān hóngbiàn,
cénglín jìnrǎn;
mànjiāng bìtòu,
bǎigě zhēngliú.
Yīngjī chángkōng,
yúxiáng qiǎndǐ,
wànlèi shuāngtiān jìng zìyóu.
Chàng liáokuò,
wèn cāngmáng dàdì,
shéi zhǔ chénfú?

Xiélái bǎilǚ céng yóu,
yì wǎngxī zhēngróng-suìyuè chóu.
Qià tóngxué shàonián,
fēnghuá-zhèngmào;
shūshēng yìqì,
huīchì fāng qiú.
Zhǐdiǎn jiāngshān,
jīyáng wénzì,
fèntǔ dāngnián wànhùhóu.
Céng jìfǒu,
dào zhōngliú jī shuǐ,
làng è fēizhōu?

2.

The Long March

A *qilü*   October 1935

The Long March was a major military retreat by the Red Army, staged in October 1934 from its base in Jiangxi and other provinces to escape the pursuing Nationalists. The Communists fought their way through ten provinces, frequently doubling back on their tracks and travelling by night to avoid attack. They traversed much of China, passing through hard terrain in the west right up to the borders of Tibet. They then went north and finally settled in northern Shaanxi in October 1935, by which time just a few thousand of the original 100,000 marchers were left. The Long March was vital in establishing Mao's pre-eminence in the Party and building its reputation as a determined, dedicated fighting force.

> The Red Army does not fear the trials of the march,
> taking the many peaks and rivers in its stride.
> Five Ridges ripple past like gentle waves,
> the majestic Wumeng Mountains roll like balls of clay.
> The Jinsha River thaws the cloud-tipped cliffs,
> and the glacial chains of the iron bridge that spans the Dadu.
> Cheerfully we stamp across the Min Shan's thousand *li* of snow.
> After vanquishing the pass, Three Armies beam with joy.

Line 3: The Five Ridges are Dayu, Qitian, Dupang, Mengzhu and Yuecheng, in Guangdong, Guangxi, Hunan and Jiangxi.
Line 4: A range between Guizhou and Yunnan.
Line 5: A river on the upper stretches of the Yangtze.
Line 6: The Dadu is a tributary of the Yangtze at the border between Sichuan and Tibet. The Luding Bridge comprised thirteen iron chains covered by loose planks of wood.
Line 7: A snow-covered mountain range between Sichuan and Gansu.
Line 8: The Three Armies were the First, Second, and Fourth Front Red Armies.

The Long March

七律•长征

红军不怕远征难，
万水千山只等闲。
五岭逶迤腾细浪，
乌蒙磅礴走泥丸。
金沙水拍云崖暖，
大渡桥横铁索寒。
更喜岷山千里雪，
三军过后尽开颜。

Chángzhēng

Hóngjūn bù pà yuǎnzhēng nán,
wànshuǐ-qiānshān zhǐ děngxián.
Wǔlǐng wēiyí téng xìlàng,
Wūméng pángbó zǒu níwán.
Jīnshā shuǐ pāi yúnyá nuǎn,
Dàdù qiáo héng tiěsuǒ hán.
Gèngxǐ Mín Shān qiānlǐ xuě,
sānjūn guòhòu jǐn kāiyán.

3.

Snow[1]

To the tune of 'Garden in Spring'

August 1945

Mao's best-known poem, officially dated February 1936. However, Mao told the American journalist Robert Payne that he composed the poem on his way from Yan'an to Chongqing in August 1945: 'I wrote it in the airplane. It was the first time I had ever been in an airplane. I was astonished by the beauty of my country from the air.'[2] The notes to the first official English translation say the poem was written in 1945.[3] The poem captures Mao's mood at the start of his battle with Chiang Kai-shek for national power in August 1945 – unlike in February 1936, when the Party and the Red Army had been reduced to a few thousand and were under siege in a region of deserts and loess hills.

---

1 Mao gave this poem to his poet friend Liu Yazi at Chongqing Airport on 28 August 1945. Liu sent it to a newspaper in Chongqing without formally seeking Mao's agreement. The poem elicited praise for Mao as a poet but criticism for his imperial mentality. Mao was in Chongqing, China's wartime capital, to negotiate a peaceful settlement with Chiang Kai-shek at the end of the Sino-Japanese War.
2 Robert Payne, *Portrait of a Revolutionary: Mao Tse-tung*, New York: Abelard Schuman, 1961, p. 225.
3 Mao Tse-tung, *Nineteen Poems*, Beijing: Foreign Languages Press, 1958.

Snow

A northland sight:
one hundred *li* sealed off by ice,
a thousand *li* of swirling snow.
Both sides of the Great Wall,
a vast expanse of white.   5
The great river's rushing waves
are stilled upstream and down.
The mountains dance like silver snakes
and charge like waxen elephants,
in an attempt to reach the sky.   10
On a clear day, the land,
dressed up in red and white,
is fairer still.

Mountains and rivers of such beauty
made countless heroes bow in homage.   15
Alas, Qin Shi Huangdi and Han Wudi
lacked literary finesse.
Tang Taizhong and Song Taizu
were not accomplished writers,
and Genghis Khan,   20
favoured by Heaven for a generation,
knew only how to bend the bow at eagles.
Now these people represent the past.
For true talent
look to today.   25

Line 6: The Yellow River.
Line 16, 'Huangdi': Qin Shi Huangdi united China.
Line 16, 'Wudi': Han Wudi rejuvenated the Han Dynasty.
Line 18, 'Taizong': Emperor Taizong, the second emperor of the Tang Dynasty, who laid the foundations for Tang prosperity.
Line 18, 'Taizu': Emperor Taizu, the founding emperor of the Song Dynasty.
Line 20: Genghis Khan, the Mongol leader who rose from humble beginnings to establish the largest land empire in history by uniting the nomadic tribes of the Mongolian plateau and central Asia with China.
Line 25: These three lines are modelled on Su Shi.

沁园春•雪   Qìnyuán chūn: Xuě

北国风光,   Běiguó fēngguāng,
千里冰封,   qiān lǐ bīngfēng,
万里雪飘。   wàn lǐ xuěpiāo.
望长城内外,   Wàng Chángchéng nèiwài,
惟馀莽莽;   wéi yú mǎngmǎng;
大河上下,   dàhé shàngxià,
顿失滔滔。   dùn shī tāotāo.
山舞银蛇,   Shān wǔ yínshé,
原驰蜡象,   yuán chí làxiàng,
欲与天公试比高。   yù yǔ tiāngōng shì bǐgāo.
须晴日,   Xū qíngrì,
看红妆素裹,   kàn hóngzhuāng sùguǒ,
分外妖娆。   fènwài yāoráo.

江山如此多娇,   Jiāngshān rúcǐ duōjiāo,
引无数英雄竞折腰。   yǐn wúshù yīngxióng jìng zhéyāo.
惜秦皇汉武,   Xī Qínhuáng Hànwǔ,
略输文采;   lüè shū wéncǎi;
唐宗宋祖,   Tángzōng Sòngzǔ,
稍逊风骚。   shāo xùn fēngsāo.
一代天骄,   Yī dài tiānjiāo,
成吉思汉,   Chéngjísīhàn,
只识弯弓射大雕。   zhǐshì wāngōng shè dàdiāo.
俱往矣,   Jù wǎng yǐ,
数风流人物,   shù fēngliú-rénwù,
还看今朝。   hái kàn jīnzhāo.

4.

The People's Liberation Army Captures Nanjing

A *qilü*   *April 1949*

In early 1949, peace talks envisaged a division of China along the Yangtze River, into Communist and Nationalist spheres. This initiative was supported by the Americans and Russians. But the CCP had the upper hand in the civil war, and Mao aimed to eliminate the Guomindang entirely. The poem shows Mao's strength of character and determination.

Storms sweep and lour on Mount Zhong,
as our mighty million-strong army crosses the great stream.
Tiger crouching, dragon coiling, the strategic point outshines its past,
while we heroically turn earth to sky and sky to earth.
Boldly we chase our worn-out foe,
rather than ape Xiang Yu the Conqueror, who preferred to fish for compliments and fame.
If sentient, the skies in growing old
will find that in the human world seas become mulberry fields.

Title: Nanjing was the Nationalists' capital.
Line 1: Mount Zhong lies east of Nanjing.
Line 2: The Yangtze River.
Line 3: A reference to Nanjing, which had been the national capital several times in the past.
Line 5: A modified quote from Sunzi's *Art of War*, a military classic.
Line 6: Xiang Yu (232–202 BCE) was originally the strongest rebel against the Qin Dynasty. After the fall of the Qin, he had both the capacity and opportunity to eliminate his main rival for power, Liu Bang. However, wishing to appear magnanimous, he allowed Liu Bang to live. In the end Liu defeated Xiang, who committed suicide.
Line 8: Copied from a line by Li He.

The People's Liberation Army Captures Nanjing

人民解放军占领南京

钟山风雨起苍黄,
百万雄师过大江。
虎踞龙盘今胜昔,
天翻地覆慨而慷。
宜将剩勇追穷寇,
不可沽名学霸王。
天若有情天亦老,
人间正道是沧桑。

Rénmín jiěfàngjūn zhànlǐng Nánjīng

Zhōngshān fēngyǔ qǐ cānghuáng,
bǎiwàn-xióngshī guo dàjiāng.
Hǔjù-lóngpán jīn shèng xī,
Tiānfān-dìfù kǎi ér kāng.
Yí jiāng shèngyǒng zhuī qióngkòu,
bù kě gūmíng xué Bàwáng.
Tiān ruò yǒuqíng tiān yìlǎo,
rénjiān zhèngdào shì cāngsāng

5.

Reply to Mr Liu Yazi

A *qilü*   *April 1949*

After capturing the capital and eliminating the main force of the Guomindang, victory is in sight. Mao's poem to his friend calls on men and women with education to serve the new regime.

I can't forget our drinking tea in Guangzhou,
and, while the leaves turned yellow, your requesting verses in Chongqing.
Returning to the old capital thirty-one years on,
at the time of falling flowers I read your polished lines.
Do not let grievance overfill and break your heart,
but let your eye range over wider things.
Do not say that the waters of the Kunming Lake lack depth –
for watching fish they far surpass the Fuchun River.

和柳亚子先生   Hè Liǔ Yàzǐ xiānshēng

饮茶粤海未能忘，   Yǐnchá Yuèhǎi wèinéng wàng,
索句渝州叶正黄。   suǒjù Yúzhōu yè zhèng huáng.
三十一年还旧国，   sānshíyī nián huán jiùguó,
落花时节读华章。   luòhuā shíjié dú huázhāng.
牢骚太盛防肠断，   láosāo tàishèng fáng chángduàn,
风物长宜放眼量。   fēngwù cháng yí fàngyǎn liàng.
莫道昆明池水浅，   mòdào Kūnmíng chíshuǐ qiǎn,
观鱼胜过富春江。   guānyú shèngguò Fùchūnjiāng.

Title: Liu Yazi was a poet, left-wing member of the Guomindang, and fellow-traveller of the CCP.
Line 1:   Mao and Liu were colleagues in the Guomindang in Guangzhou in 1925–26.
Line 2:   Mao and Liu exchanged poems in Chongqing in August 1945.
Line 3:   The old capital is Beijing, which Mao left in 1918 as an unemployed young man and to which he returned in 1949 as ruler.
Line 4:   A reworking of a line by Du Fu.
Line 7:   The lake at the Summer Palace in Beijing.
Line 8:   A river in Zhejiang.

6.

Reply to Mr Liu Yazi

To the tune of 'Sand of the Silk-Washing Brook'

October 1950

In imperial China, the emperor and his courtiers exchanged poems to celebrate their accomplishments at the beginning of a new dynasty. Courtiers eulogised the virtues and achievements of the emperor, who would reply modestly and courteously. After the establishment of the PRC in 1949, Mao and his poet friends seemed to revive this tradition. Mao wrote: 'At a song-and-dance performance during the National Day celebrations in 1950, Mr Liu Yazi wrote an impromptu poem to the tune of "Sand of the Silk-Washing Brook", to which I replied, using the same rhyme sequence.'

> The night is long, the sky dawns slowly on Red County.
> For a century, demons jigged their wild and lively dance,
> and the five hundred million were unable to unite.
>
> The cock now crows, and under heaven everything turns bright.
> Those playing music include our people from Yutian –
> never before were poets so inspired.

浣溪沙•和柳亚子先生   Huàn xī shā: Hè Liǔ Yàzi xiānshēng

长夜难明赤县天，   Chángyè nánmíng Chìxiàn tiān,
百年魔怪舞翩跹。   bǎi nián móguài wǔ piānxiān.
人民五亿不团圆。   Rénmín wǔyì bù tuányuán.

一唱雄鸡天下白，   Yīchàng-xióngjī tiānxià bái,
万方乐奏有于阗，   wànfāng yuè zòu yǒu Yútián,
诗人兴会更无前。   shīrén xìnghuì gèng wúqián.

Line 1:   Another name for China.
Line 4:   Echoing a line by Li He.
Line 5:   Yutian was an ancient kingdom in what is now Xinjiang.

Reply to Mr Liu Yazi

Liu Yazi's Poem

To the tune of 'Sand of the Silk-Washing Brook'

On 3 October, I attended a soirée in Huairentang. Performances were given by ensembles from the various nationalities in the Southwest, Xinjiang, Yanbian in Jilin Province, and Inner Mongolia. At Chairman Mao's request, I composed the following poem to celebrate the great unity of the nationalities.

> Flaming trees, silver flowers, sleepless and forever bright.
> Brothers and sisters dance with quick light steps,
> lifting their voices to celebrate Full Moon.
>
> But for the leadership of one man,
> how could the hundred nationalities unite?
> This joyful soirée surpasses everything that went before!

柳亚子原词: 浣溪沙   Liǔ Yàzi yuán cí: Huàn xī shā

火树银花不夜天,   Huǒshù yínhuā buyè tiān,
弟兄姐妹舞翩跹,   dìxiōng jiěmèi wǔ piānxiān,
歌声唱彻月儿圆。   gēshēng chàngchè yuè'er yuán.

不是一人能领导,   Bù shì yī rén néng lǐngdǎo,
那容百族共骈阗?   nàróng bǎi zú gòng piántián?
良宵盛会喜空前!   Liángxiāo shènghuì xǐ kōngqián!

Line 3:   The name of a Kazakh folk song.

7.

Beidaihe

To the tune of 'Waves Washing Sands'

Summer 1954

Proud of his success in the early 1950s, Mao compares his own achievements to those of the Han Dynasty warlord Cao Cao.

> Rainstorms sweep this ancient land,
> white breakers leap up to the sky.
> Off Qinhuangdao, no fishing boats appear
> on the boundless sea.
> Where have they all gone?
>
> More than one thousand years ago,
> cracking his whip the Emperor Wu of Wei
> marched eastwards towards Jieshi – his poem still survives.
> Today, the autumn wind still soughs,
> but the human world has changed.

Title: Beidaihe is a summer resort in Hebei on the Yellow Sea, used by top officials for conferences and holidays.
Line 1:   Youyan, comprising parts of modern Hebei and Liaoning.
Line 3:   Qinhuangdao is a port in Hebei named after Emperor Qin, who went there in search of the elixir of life.
Line 7:   Cao Cao founded the Kingdom of Wei in the Three Kingdoms period (220–80). He was known posthumously as Emperor Wu of Wei. Like Qin Shi Huangdi, he is usually portrayed as cruel and merciless. However, Mao appreciated both men as brilliant rulers.
Line 8:   By the sea in Hebei. Cao Cao wrote a poem that began: 'Marching eastwards towards Jieshi'.

Beidaihe

浪淘沙•北戴河

大雨落幽燕,
白浪滔天,
秦皇岛外打鱼船,
一片汪洋都不见,
知向谁边?

往时越千年,
魏武挥鞭,
东临碣石有遗篇。
萧瑟秋风今又是,
换了人间。

Làng táo shā: Běidàihé

Dàyǔ luò yōuyàn,
báilàng tāotiān,
Qínhuángdǎo wài dǎyú chuán,
yī piàn wāngyáng dōu bù jiàn,
zhī xiàng shéi biān?

Wǎngshí yuè qiān nián,
Wèi Wǔ huī biān,
dōnglín Jiéshí yǒu yípiān.
Xiāosè qiūfēng jīn yòu shì,
huànle rénjiān.

8.

Swimming

To the tune of the 'Water Song'

June 1956

In 1956, Khrushchev gave his 'secret speech' denouncing Stalin's personality cult and dictatorship, to the shock of Mao and other CCP leaders. Mao feared that the speech might have a negative impact on the Eighth Congress of the CCP, scheduled for the autumn. To assert his continuing vitality and buttress his power, Mao, aged sixty-three, decided to swim across the Yangtze. The event was highly celebrated in the media. Mao repeated the swim in July 1966, two months after launching the Cultural Revolution.

       Having drunk the waters of Changsha
       and eaten the Wuchang fish,
       now I swim across the thousand-mile-long Yangtze,
       gazing at the open skies of Chu.
5   Let the winds blow, the waves roll,
       better than idling in the yard.
       Today I am at ease.
       The Master said while standing by a running stream:
       'Thus does time flow!'

10   Masts are set quivering by the wind.
       The tortoise and the snake lie still.
       Great plans are hatched:
       a bridge will rise to join up north and south,
       a thoroughfare will span this natural trench;

Line 3   An allusion to a folk song from the Three Kingdoms.
Line 4:   The Hubei-Hunan region formed the Chu Kingdom in antiquity. Echoing a line by You Qing.
Line 8:   Confucius.

Swimming

walls of stone will stand amid the water to the west
to dam the rainstorms of Mount Wu,
filling the narrow gorges with a placid lake.
Were the mountain goddess still about,
how she would marvel at a world so changed.

水调歌头•游泳

才饮长沙水，
又食武昌鱼。
万里长江横渡，
极目楚天舒。
不管风吹浪打，
胜似闲庭信步。
今日得宽馀，
子在川上曰：
逝者如斯夫！

风樯动，
龟蛇静，
起宏图。
一桥飞架南北，
天堑变通途。
更立西江石壁，
截断巫山云雨，
高峡出平湖。
神女应无恙，
当惊世界殊。

Shuǐdiào gētóu: Yóuyǒng

Cái yǐn Chángshā shuǐ,
yòu shí Wǔchāng yú.
Wàn lǐ Chángjiāng héngdù,
jímù Chǔtiān shū.
Bùguǎn fēngchuī-làngdǎ,
shèngsì xiántíng xìnbù.
Jīnrì dé kuānyú,
Zǐ zài chuānshàng yuē:
Shì zhě rú sī fū!

Fēngqiáng dòng,
guīshé jìng,
qǐ hóngtú.
Yīqiáo fēijià nánběi,
tiānqiàn biàn tōngtú.
Gèng lì xījiāng shíbì,
jiéduàn Wū Shān yúnyǔ,
gāoxiá chū pínghú.
Shénnǚ yīng wúyàng,
dāng jīng shìjiè shū.

Line 16:   Mount Wu is on the Yangtze by the Three Gorges Dam, completed in 2012.

9.

Reply to Li Shuyi

To the tune of 'Butterflies Lingering over Flowers'

May 1957

After reading Mao's poems published in early 1957, Li Shuyi sent Mao an earlier poem in which she had mourned her husband Liu Zhixun, who had been Mao's comrade-in-arms. Mao wrote this poem in reply.

> I lost my proud Poplar, you your Willow,
> Poplar and Willow soar to the Ninth Heaven.
> Asked what he has to serve them,
> Wu Gang offers *guihua* wine.
>
> Lonely Chang E spreads her ample sleeves
> to dance for these loyal spirits in unbounded space.
> On earth the taming of the tiger is announced,
> and tears gush from an upset bowl of rain.

Title   Li Shuyi (1901–1997) was a school friend of Yang Kaihui, Mao's first wife.
Line 1, 'Poplar':   Yang means poplar. Yang Kaihui was arrested and executed by a warlord in Changsha in 1930 when the Red Army's attempt to hold the city was defeated.
Line 1, 'Willow':   Liu Zhixun (1898–1932) was Li Shuyi's husband. Liu means willow. Liu was a middle-ranking Communist leader and Red Army officer wrongly executed by his own comrades in a purge in 1932.
Line 4:   Wu Gang offended the gods by seeking immortality and was sent by them to the moon to perform the impossible task of chopping down a self-healing osmanthus tree.
Line 4, 'guihua'.   Wine fermented with osmanthus flowers.
Line 5:   Chang E is the Moon Goddess.

Reply to Li Shuyi

蝶恋花•答李淑一

我失骄杨君失柳,
杨柳轻飏直上重霄九。
问讯吴刚何所有,
吴刚捧出桂花酒。

寂寞嫦娥舒广袖,
万里长空且为忠魂舞。
忽报人间曾伏虎,
泪飞顿作倾盆雨。

Dié liàn huā: Dá Lǐ Shūyī

Wǒ shī JiāoYáng jūn shī Liǔ,
Yáng Liǔ qīngyáng zhíshàng chóng xiāojiǔ.
Wènxùn Wú Gāng hé suǒyǒu,
Wú Gāng pěngchū guìhuā jiǔ.

Jìmò Cháng'é shū guǎngxiù,
wànlǐ chángkōng qiě wèi zhōnghún wǔ.
Hū bào rénjiān céng fúhǔ,
lèifēi dùnzuò qīngpén yǔ.

10.

Farewell to the God of Plague (I)

A *qilü* July 1958

When I read in *People's Daily* on 30 June 1958 that schistosomiasis had been wiped out in Yujiang County, thoughts crowded my mind and I could not sleep. In the warm morning breeze next day, as sunlight fell on my window, I looked towards the distant southern sky and, in my joy, wrote the following lines.[1]

> Green streams, blue hills, but all in vain,
> for even Hua Tuo can't defeat the tiny grub!
> A thousand villages are choked with weeds and in the grip of dysentery;
> ten thousand empty houses in which only ghosts still sing.
> But in my seat I travel eighty thousand *li* in just one day,
> and in the skies survey a thousand Milky Ways.
> Should the Cowherd ask news of the God of Plague,
> tell him that grief and joy both fade as time wears on.

---

1 Note by Mao.
Line 1: Borrowed from a line by the Tang Dynasty poet Du Fu.
Line 2: Hua Tuo (145–208), a physician of the Three Kingdoms period (220–280), is regarded as the best doctor in Chinese history.
Line 4: Borrowed from a line by Li He.
Line 5: Borrowed from a line by Li Shangyin.
Line 7: The Cowherd and the Weaving Girl fell in love. The Weaving Girl's grandmother, the Heavenly Empress, disapproved and took her back to heaven. The Cowherd Star and the Weaving Girl Star were thenceforth separated by the Milky Way. Once a year, magpies form a bridge that allows them to reunite.

Farewell to the God of Plague (I)

送瘟神

其一

绿水青山枉自多,
华佗无奈小虫何!
千村薜荔人遗矢,
万户萧疏鬼唱歌。
坐地日行八万里,
巡天遥看一千河。
牛郎欲问瘟神事,
一样悲欢逐逝波。

Sòng wēnshén

(1)

Lǜshuǐ qīngshān wǎngzì duō,
Huá Tuó wúnài xiǎochóng hé!
Qiān cūn bìlì rén yí shǐ,
wàn hù xiāoshū guǐ chànggē.
Zuò dì rìxíng bāwàn lǐ,
xúntiān yáokàn yīqiān hé.
Niú Láng yùwèn wēnshén shì,
yīyàng bēihuān zhú shì bō.

11.

Farewell to the God of Plague (II)

A *qilü*   *July 1958*

During the Great Leap Forward, private ownership and family farming were abolished and rural households were organised into people's communes, as a short cut to communism and a realisation of the principle 'from each according to their ability, to each according to their needs'. Mao's radical aim was not shared by his more pragmatic colleagues and was scorned by the Russians. The regime's unexpected success in eliminating schistosomiasis from Yujiang in Jiangxi was welcome news for Mao, who was eager to mobilise the population and to convince his colleagues of the soundness of his plans.

> The spring wind stirs the branches of the willow tree,
> six hundred million are equal to the Emperors Yao and Shun.
> Red rain forms waves that act according to our will,
> green mountains turn to bridges on command.
> Silver mattocks hack the Five Ridges in the sky;
> iron arms rock the earth and the three rivers.
> We ask the God of Plague, 'Where are you bound?'
> Candles on flaming paper barges light the sky.

Line 1: Echoing a line by Bai Juyi.
Line 2: Yao and Shun were emperors at the start of Chinese civilisation, prized for their virtue.
Line 3: A borrowing from a line by Li He.
Line 5: The Five Ridges are either Dayu, Qitian, Dupang, Mengzhu and Yuecheng, or Mount Tai in Shandong, Mount Hua in Shaanxi, Mount Heng in Shanxi, Mount Song in Henan and Mount Heng in Hunan.
Line 6: The three rivers may be the Yellow River, the Yangtze River and the Pearl River, or a representation of Chinese rivers in general.
Line 8: Chinese peasants dispel evil spirits by burning paper barges.

Farewell to the God of Plague (II)

送瘟神

其二

春风杨柳万千条,
六亿神州尽舜尧。
红雨随心翻作浪,
青山着意化为桥。
天连五岭银锄落,
地动三河铁臂摇。
借问瘟君欲何往,
纸船明烛照天烧。

Sòng wēnshén

(2)

Chūnfēng yángliǔ wànqiān tiáo,
liùyì Shénzhōu jǐn Shùn Yáo.
Hóngyǔ suíxīn fān zuò làng,
qīngshān zhuóyì huà wéi qiáo.
Tiān lián Wǔ Lǐng yínchú luò,
dì dòng sān hé tiěbì yáo.
Jièwèn wēnjūn yù hé wǎng,
zhǐchuán míngzhú zhào tiān shāo.

12.

Shaoshan Revisited

A *qilü*   *June 1959*

Mao paid a visit to his native village in June 1959 amid growing controversy over the Great Leap Forward, which had started to go terribly wrong. Food shortages were becoming increasingly severe and turning into famine. However, Mao remained confident of having found a new path to communism. He wrote this poem to silence his critics and boost the revolutionary enthusiasm of the masses.

I visited Shaoshan on 25 June 1959, after an absence of thirty-two years.[1]

> Vague dreams of parting – how I regret the passage of the days,
> after thirty-two years of absence from my native place.
> Red flags have roused the serfs to rise, halberd in hand,
> against the despot's black fist and lashing whip.
> Sacrifices stiffen their resolve,
> as they command the transposition of the sun and moon.
> I rejoice to see the paddy and the thriving rows of beans,
> and the home-bound heroes in the evening smoke.

---

[1] Shaoshan is the village where Mao spent his first sixteen years.
Line 2: Mao had last visited Shaoshan in 1927, when he wrote his famous *Report on the Peasant Movement in Hunan*.

到韶山

别梦依稀咒逝川，
故园三十二年前。
红旗卷起农奴戟，
黑手高悬霸主鞭。
为有牺牲多壮志，
敢叫日月换新天。
喜看稻菽千重浪，
遍地英雄下夕烟。

Dào Sháoshān

Biémèng yīxī zhòu shì chuān,
gùyuán sānshí'èr nián qián.
Hóngqí juǎnqǐ nóngnú jǐ,
hēishǒu gāoxuán bàzhǔ biān.
Wèi yǒu xīshēng duō zhuàngzhì,
gǎnjiào rìyuè huàn xīntiān.
Xǐkàn dàoshū qiān chóng làng,
biàndì yīngxióng xià xìyān.

13.

Climbing Lushan

A *qilü*   *July 1959*

The CCP's Central Committee met in plenary session in July 1959 to assess the progress of the Great Leap Forward. Expecting criticism, Mao wrote this poem to express his complicated feelings.

> The mountain towers over the great stream, perching as if after flight;
> the road to its verdant crest bends four hundred times.
> Cold-eyed I scan the world beyond the sea;
> hot gusts blow rain onto the river.
> The yellow crane appears to float above the nine beclouded streams,
> while foam-specked billows batter the eastern coast of Wu.
> Who knows where Tao Yuanming has gone,
> now that he can plough fields in the Peach Flower Garden?

登庐山   Dēng Lúshān

一山飞峙大江边，   Yī shān fēizhì dàjiāng biān,
跃上葱茏四百旋。   yuèshàng cōnglóng sìbǎi xuán.
冷眼向洋看世界，   Lěngyǎn xiàngyáng kàn shìjiè,
热风吹雨洒江天。   rèfēng chuī yǔ sǎ jiāngtiān.
云横九派浮黄鹤，   Yún héng jiǔpài fú huánghè,
浪下三吴起白烟。   làng xià Sān Wú qǐ báiyān.
陶令不知何处去，   Táo Lìng bù zhī héchù qù,
桃花园里可耕田？   Táohuāyuán lǐ kě gēngtián?

Title: A mountain in Jiangxi.
Line 1:   The Yangtze River.
Line 5:   The Tower of the Yellow Crane on a cliff west of Wuchang in Hubei.
Line 5, 'streams':   The nine streams stand for the many tributaries of the Yangtze River.
Line 6:   Jiangxi was part of the Wu Kingdom during the Three Kingdoms.
Line 7:   Tao Yuanming was a poet of the Eastern Jin (317–420) and Liu Song (420–479) dynasties. He briefly served as a magistrate in Jiangxi, before resigning to live as a hermit.
Line 8:   A hidden utopia described by Tao, which had no wars and where people lived in harmony and prosperity.

14.

Trotsky Visits the Far East
(Reflections on Reading the Press)

A *qilü*   26 December 1959

The Sino–Soviet split of the late 1950s and 1960s followed Khrushchev's attack on Stalin. Seeing Khrushchev's policies as revisionist, Mao sought to replace him as leader of the world Communist movement. In 1957, he launched an anti-rightist campaign to prevent political liberalisation, and voiced his opposition to the Russian policy of 'peaceful coexistence' with the West. In late 1959, Khrushchev started cancelling aid agreements and withdrew the promise to deliver nuclear weapons to the PRC. Mao's poem is a denunciation of Khrushchev's 'capitulationism' to the West.

> Trotsky came to the Far East,
> hero of neither war nor peace.
> Even Lenin's teachings have been dropped
> but Governor Ye deserved detention in the Dajiu Peak.
> Though in himself he's just a crazy wasp,
> he acts towards his neighbour as a mantis out to block a chariot.
> Everybody speaks well of the West,
> whereas in the Divine Land only idiots emerge.

Title: Mao likens Khrushchev to Trotsky to make him an easy target for attack in circles committed to Stalinist orthodoxy.
Line 4, 'Governor': Ye Mingchen (1807–1859), the governor of Guangdong, was captured by Anglo–French troops during the the Second Opium War (1856–60). In dealing with the Western powers, Ye was well-known for his 'six nots': 'He would not fight, nor would he make peace; he would not defend himself, nor would he die; he would not surrender, nor would he flee.'
Line 4, 'Dajiu Peak': Ye was held prisoner in Calcutta in British India.
Line 8: The Divine Land is China. Mao mocks China's critics.

托洛茨基到远东(读报有感)

托洛茨基到远东,
不战不和逞英雄。
列宁竟抛头颅后,
叶督该拘大鹫峰。
敢向邻居试螳臂,
只怨自己是狂蜂。
人人尽说西方好,
独惜神州出蠢虫。

Tuōluòcíjī dào yuǎndōng (dú bào yǒu gǎn)

Tuōluòcíjī dào yuǎndōng,
bù zhàn bù hé chěng yīngxióng.
Lièníng jìng pāo tóulú hòu,
Yè Dū gāi jū Dà Jiù fēng.
Gǎnxiàng línjū shì tángbì,
zhǐyuàn zìjǐ shì kuángfēng.
Rénrén jìnshuō Xīfāng hǎo,
dú xī Shénzhōu chū chǔnchóng.

15.

An Inscription on a Photograph of Militia Women

A *qijue* February 1961

Mao was proud of the contribution made by Chinese women to the cause.
He wrote this poem to encourage the militancy of militia women.

> Bravely they pose, shouldering their five-foot rifles
> on drill grounds lit by the early morning sun.
> China's daughters are likelier to opt
> for battle outfits than for satin skirts.

为女民兵题照

飒爽英姿五尺枪,
曙光初照演兵场。
中华儿女多奇志,
不爱红装爱武装。

Wèi nǚ mínbīng tí zhào

Sàshuǎng-yīngzī wǔ chǐ qiāng,
shǔguāng chūzhào yǎnbīng chǎng.
Zhōnghuá érnǚ duō qízhì,
bù ài hóngzhuāng ài wǔzhuāng

16.

Reply to a Friend

A *qilü*   1961

At the Lushan meeting in 1959, criticism of the Great Leap Forward was silenced and Peng Dehuai, Mao's chief critic, was denounced and sacked from all his posts. However, Mao was forced to yield economic management to Liu Shaoqi, who effected a retreat from the Great Leap. Mao's prestige was diminished by his failure. He knew that his leadership was under threat, and hints in this poem at his mixed feelings.

White clouds fly over Mount Jiuyi;
catching the wind, the Emperor's daughters ride down to the blue-green hills.
Previously they wet the mottled bamboo with a thousand tears,
but now the red-tinged clouds adorn them in a hundred folds of cloth.
On Dongting Lake, the snow-flecked waves surge skyward,
and people on Long Island sing earth-shaking songs.
I wish to dream boundlessly
of the land of the hibiscus, bathed in the morning sun.

Line 1: In Ningyuan, Hunan.
Line 3: A borrowing of a line by Hong Sheng.
Line 5: In the north of Hunan.
Line 6: Also known as Orange Isle, in the Xiangjiang River west of Changsha. See Poem 1, 'Changsha'.
Line 8: Another name for Hunan, Mao's native province.

Reply to a Friend

答友人

九嶷山上白云飞,
帝子乘风下翠微。
斑竹一支千滴泪,
红霞万朵百重衣。
洞庭波涌连天雪,
长岛人歌动地诗。
我欲因之梦寥廓,
芙蓉国里尽朝晖。

Dá yǒurén

Jiǔyí Shān shàng báiyún fēi,
dìzǐ chéngfēng xià cuìwēi.
Bānzhú yī zhī qiān dī lèi,
hóngxiá wàn duǒ bǎi chóng yī.
Dòngtíng bō yǒng liántiān xuě,
Chángdǎo rén gē dòngdì shī.
Wǒ yù yīn zhī mèng liáokuò,
fúróng guó lǐ jìn zhāohuī.

17.

An Inscription on a Picture Taken by Comrade Li Jin of the Fairy Cave on Lushan

A *qijue*   *September 1961*

Mao wrote this poem for his wife Jiang Qing, to comfort and encourage her in the aftermath of the disaster of the Great Leap.

> In the growing dusk stand sturdy pines,
> tranquil amid the chaos of the clouds.
> The Fairy Cave is Heaven-made,
> incomparably grand among the perilous and lofty peaks.

为李进同志题所摄庐山仙人洞照

暮色苍茫看劲松，
乱云飞渡仍从容。
天生一个仙人洞，
无限风光在险峰。

Wèi Lǐ Jìn tóngzhì tí suǒ shè Lúshān Xiānréndòng zhào

Mùsè cāngmáng kàn jìnsōng,
luànyún fēidù réng cóngróng.
Tiānshēng yī gè Xiānréndòng,
wúxiàn-fēngguāng zài xiǎnfēng.

Title, 'Li Jin':   Li Jin is another name for Jiang Qing.
Title, 'Fairy Cave':   A famous scenic spot.
Line 4:   Borrowing two lines from an erotic work by Linshuan Shanren, an obscure Qing writer.

18.

Reply to Comrade Guo Moruo

A *qilü*   *November 1961*

The deepening of the Sino–Soviet split hardened Mao's belief that the USSR had turned 'revisionist' and was colluding with the West to sabotage the Communist cause. Mao thought China under his leadership was the only hope for Communism, although China had become increasingly isolated internationally and in Eastern Europe. Mao saw himself as a new Monkey King charged with eliminating devils, turning the heavenly palace upside down and bringing justice to the world.

> A clap of thunder bursts above the Earth,
> and devils spring up from a heap of whitened bones.
> The monk can be forgiven for his foolishness,
> but the evil demon will wreak havoc and destruction.
> Furiously the Golden Monkey swings his giant club
> and clears the jade-like firmament of dust.
> Today, we hail the wonder-working Monkey King
> as evil spirits once again release miasmal mists.

Title: Guo Moruo was a writer, historian and political activist, and Mao's friend in poetry.
Line 2:   The ruthless White Bone Demon, a character in the classical novel *Journey to the West*, is adept at disguise.
Line 3:   Tang Sanzang, a character in *Journey to the West*.
Line 7:   The hero of *Journey to the West*.

Reply to Comrade Guo Moruo

和郭沫若同志 — Hè Guō Mòruò tóngzhì

一从大地起风雷, — Yī cóng dàdì qǐ fēngléi,
便有精生白骨堆。 — biàn yǒu jīng shēng báigǔ duī.
僧是愚氓犹可恕, — Sēng shì yúmáng yóu kěshù,
妖为鬼蜮必成灾。 — yāo wéi guǐyù bì chéngzāi.
金猴奋起千钧棒, — Jīnhóu fènqǐ qiānjūnbàng,
玉宇澄清万里埃。 — yùyǔ chéngqīng wàn lǐ āi.
今日欢呼孙大圣, — Jīnrì huānhū Sūndàshèng,
只缘妖雾又重来。 — zhǐyuán yāowù yòu chónglái.

Guo Moruo's Original Poem:

On Seeing *Sun Wukong Subdues the Demons*

Confusing men and demons, right and wrong, the monk
shows mercy to his enemies and malice to his friends.
Endlessly he chants the Incantation of the Golden Hoop,
and three times lets the White Bone Demon go.
The monk deserves a thousand cuts;
the plucking of a single Monkey hair is no great loss.
This timely teaching merits praise –
even the Pig is wiser than the fool.

看孙悟空三打白骨精 — Kàn Sūn Wùkōng sān dǎ báigǔjīng

人妖颠倒是非淆, — Rényāo-diāndǎo shìfēi xiáo,
对敌慈悲对友刁。 — duìdí cíbēi duìyǒu diāo.
咒念金箍闻万遍, — Zhòu niàn jīngū wén wàn biàn,
精逃白骨累三遭。 — jīng táo báigǔ lèi sān zāo.
千刀当剐唐僧肉, — Qiāndāo dāng guǎ tángsēng ròu,
一拔何亏大圣毛。 — yī bá hé kuī Dàshèng máo.
教育及时堪赞赏, — Jiàoyù jíshí kān zànshǎng,
猪犹智慧胜愚曹。 — zhū yóu zhìhuì shèng yúcáo.

Title: Sun Wukong is the Monkey King. *Sun Wukong Subdues the Demons* is an opera adapted from *Journey to the West*.
Line 3: Given to Tang Sanzang by the Buddha to control Sun Wukong. When Tang Sanzang chants a certain sutra, the band tightens and causes pain.
Line 8: Pigsy, a character in *Journey to the West*.

19.

Ode to the Plum Blossom

To the tune of 'The Divination Song'

December 1961

Isolated due to the devastating consequences of the Great Leap Forward, Mao uses the metaphor of the plum tree flowering in winter to show his unyielding character.

On reading Lu You's 'Ode to Plum Blossom', I countered with the following lines.

> First Spring departs with wind and rain,
> but as snow falls it's back again.
> On the icy cliffs that tower high and sheer
> a pretty flower blooms.
>
> Though sweet and fair, it does not seek to make the Spring its own
> but to be Spring's harbinger.
> When the mountain flowers are in full bloom
> it will smile among the rest.

Line 2: Modification of two lines by Wang Guan.
Line 3: Modification of a line by Cen Shen.

Ode to the Plum Blossom

卜算子•咏梅

风雨送春归,
飞雪迎春到。
已是悬崖百丈冰,
犹有花枝俏。

俏也不争春,
只把春来报。
待到山花烂漫时,
她在丛中笑。

Bǔ suànzǐ: Yǒngméi

Fēngyǔ sòng chūn guī,
fēixuě yíng chūn dào,
yǐshì xuányá bǎi zhàng bīng,
yóuyǒu huāzhī qiào.

Qiào yě bù zhēng chūn,
zhǐbǎ chūn lái bào.
Dàidào shānhuā lànmàn shí,
tā zài cóngzhōng xiào.

Lu You's Original Poem: Ode to the Plum Blossom

To the tune of 'The Divination Song'

At the broken bridge outside the post-house
blooms a lonely flower, unseen.
Forlorn and saddened in the falling dusk,
it is suddenly assailed by wind and rain.

Let other flowers fight to make the Spring their own –
the lonely blossom lays no claim to it.
Boots crunch its fallen petals in the dirt,
but its scent endures.

卜算子•咏梅

驿外断桥边,
寂寞开无主。
已是黄昏独自愁,
更著风和雨。

无意苦争春,
一任群芳妒。
零落成泥碾作尘,
只有香如故。

Bǔ suànzǐ: Yǒngméi

Yì wài duànqiáo biān,
jìmò kāi wúzhǔ.
yǐshì huánghūn dúzì chóu,
gèngzhe fēng hé yǔ.

Wúyì kǔ zhēng chūn,
yīrèn qúnfāng dù.
língluò chéng ní niǎn zuò chén,
zhǐyǒu xiāng rúgù.

Title: Lu You was a prolific poet of the Southern Song Dynasty.

20.

Winter Clouds

A *qilü*   26 December 1962

Mao wrote this poem on his sixty-ninth birthday, in the wake of the devastation caused by the Great Leap Forward. At a meeting in 1962, Mao made a self-criticism and reaffirmed his commitment to collective leadership, but he continued to fight what he saw as revisionism and the danger of capitalist restoration. This poem expresses his concern and his determination to fight back.

> Snow drives the thickly wadded winter clouds.
> Of the flowers, most are dead.
> Chill waves roll out across the sky,
> faintly the earth breathes traces of new warmth.
> Only heroes can chase the tigers and leopards off
> and face down wild bears.
> Plum flowers delight in whirling snow,
> while flies die in the freezing cold.

冬云　　　　　　　　　　Dōngyún

雪压冬云白絮飞，　　　　Xuě yā dōngyún báixù fēi,
万花纷谢一时稀。　　　　wànhuā fēnxiè yīshí xī.
高天滚滚寒流急，　　　　Gāotiān gǔngǔn hánliú jí,
大地微微暖气吹。　　　　dàdì wéiwéi nuǎnqì chuī.
独有英雄驱虎豹，　　　　Dúyǒu yīngxióng qū hǔbào,
更无豪杰怕熊罴。　　　　gèng wú háojié pà xióngpí.
梅花欢喜漫天雪，　　　　Méihuā huānxǐ màntiān xuě,
冻死苍蝇未足奇。　　　　dòngsǐ cāngyíng wèi zú qí.

21.

Reply to Comrade Guo Moruo

To the tune of 'Red River'

January 1963

In 1962, after the escalation of the Sino–Soviet split, the CCP published a series of commentaries denouncing the Soviet Union and its satellites as 'revisionist pests', 'flies', 'ants' and 'maggots'.

On this small globe
flies bash against the wall,
buzzing and droning,
howling and shrieking,
weeping and sobbing.
Ants climb up the locust tree, with great-power swagger,
and mayflies plot in vain to shake it down.
The west wind scatters leaves across Chang'an
as the flying arrows twang.

So much to do,
so little time to do it;
the Earth turns,
life is short.
Ten thousand years are far too long to wait,
so seize the day, the hour.
The Four Seas churn, the clouds and waters rage,
the Five Continents shake, the wind and thunder roar.
Away with all pests,
we are matchless and unconquerable.

Line 8: Modification of a line by Jia Dao.
Line 18: In the 1950s, the Communists launched a campaign, 'Away with All Pests,' to eliminate the four pests: sparrows, rats, insects and flies, together, in the early 1960s, with their political equivalent.

Reply to Comrade Guo Moruo

满江红·和郭沫若同志　　　　Mǎn jiāng hóng: Hè Guō Mòruò tóngzhì

小小寰球,　　　　　　　　　Xiǎoxiǎo huánqiú,
有几个苍蝇碰壁。　　　　　　yǒu jǐ gè cāngyíng pèngbì.
嗡嗡叫,　　　　　　　　　　Wēngwēng jiào,
几声凄厉,　　　　　　　　　jǐ shēng qīlì,
几声抽泣。　　　　　　　　　jǐ shēng chōuqì.
蚂蚁缘槐夸大国,　　　　　　Mǎyǐ yuán huái kuā dàguó,
蚍蜉撼树谈何易。　　　　　　pífú hànshù tán hé yì.
正西风落叶下长安,　　　　　Zhèng xīfēng luòyè xià Cháng'ān,
飞鸣镝。　　　　　　　　　　fēi míngdī.

多少事,　　　　　　　　　　Duōshǎo shì,
从来急;　　　　　　　　　　cónglái jí;
天地转,　　　　　　　　　　tiāndì zhuǎn,
光阴迫。　　　　　　　　　　guāngyīn pò.
一万年太久,　　　　　　　　Yīwàn nián tàijiǔ,
只争朝夕。　　　　　　　　　zhǐzhēng zhāoxī.
四海翻腾云水怒,　　　　　　Sìhǎi fānténg yúnshuǐ nù,
五洲震荡风雷激。　　　　　　wǔzhōu zhèndàng fēngléi jī.
要扫除一切害人虫,　　　　　Yào sǎochú yīqiè hàirénchóng,
全无敌。　　　　　　　　　　quán wúdí.

Guo Moruo's Original Poem

To the tune of 'Red River'

When the ocean turmoil grows,
the mettle of a hero shows.
Six hundred million people,
strongly united,
firm in principle, 5
can shore up the collapsing sky
and make order out of chaos.
Across the world the cock-crow sounds,
and day breaks in the east.

The sun rises, 10
and the icebergs melt.
True gold
is tested and refined by fire.

Reply to Comrade Guo Moruo

15
Four great books
show us the way.
How laughable that Jie's dog barked at Yao;
clay oxen plunge into the sea and disappear.
On the east wind red flags of revolution fly,
and the universe turns red.

郭沫若原词

沧海横流，
方显出英雄本色。
人六亿，
加强团结，
坚持原则。
天垮下来擎得起，
世披靡矣扶之直。
听雄鸡一唱遍寰中，
东方白。

太阳出，
冰山滴；
真金在，
岂销铄？
有雄文四卷，
为民立极。
桀犬吠尧堪笑止，
泥牛入海无消息。
迎东风革命展红旗，
乾坤赤。

Guō Mòruò yuán cí

Cānghǎi héngliú,
fāng xiǎnchū yīngxióng běnsè.
Rén liùyì,
jiāqiáng tuánjié,
jiānchí yuánzé.
Tiānkuǎ xiàlái qíng dé qǐ,
shì pīmí yǐ fú zhī zhí.
Tīng xióngjī-yīchàng biàn huánzhōng,
dōngfāng bái.

Tàiyáng chū,
bīngshān dī;
zhēnjīn zài,
qǐ xiāoshuò?
Yǒu xióngwén sìjuǎn,
wèimín lìjí.
Jiéquǎn-fèiyáo kān xiàozhǐ,
níniú-rùhǎi wú xiāoxī.
Yíng dōngfēng gémìng zhǎn hóngqí,
qiánkūn chì.

Line 14: The four volumes of Mao's *Selected Works*.
Line 16, 'Jie': King Jie, the last king of the Xia Dynasty (2070–1600 BCE), known for his brutality.
Line 16, 'Yao': Emperor Yao, known for his virtue.

22.

On Reading History

To the tune of 'Congratulating the Bridegroom'

1964

Sidelined by the Party bureaucracy after the failure of the Great Leap Forward, Mao prepares to fight back. In this poem, he praises past rebel leaders and identifies with them.

When apes and humans disengaged
the human world was in its infant stage –
the early stone age.
Then copper ovens started belching fire.
When, may I ask, would that have been?   5
Just a thousand years of heat and cold ago.
It's hard to meet a true friend in this life –
on the battlefield they're likelier to shoot at you.
Blood soaks
the fields around the town.

After finishing a book, my head turns white as snow,   10
and I remember little of it,
apart from a line or two about the past.
The Five Emperors and Three Sovereigns
cheated great numbers with their holy deeds.
How many truly great men would you say have lived?   15
The bandit Zhi and Zhuang Jiao will never fade from mind –
nor will King Chen, bravely brandishing his golden axe.
The song goes on
while dawn breaks in the east.

Line 7: A line from Du Mu.
Line 14, 'Five Emperors': The Yellow Emperor, Zhuanxu, Ku, Yao and Shun.
Line 14, 'Three Sovereigns': Yuren, Fuxi and Shennong.
Line 16, 'Zhi': A bandit in the Spring and Autumn period.
Line 16: Zhuang Jiao (? –256 BCE), a rebel leader in the Warring States period.
Line 17: Chen Sheng (? –208 BCE), a rebel leader during the Qin Dynasty.

贺新郎•读史

人猿相揖别,
只几个石头磨过,
小儿时节。
铜铁炉中翻火焰。
为问何时猜得?
不过几千寒热。
人世难逢开口笑,
上疆场彼此弯弓月。
流遍了,
郊原血。

一篇读罢头飞雪,
但记得斑斑点点,
几行陈迹。
五帝三皇神圣事,
骗了无涯过客。
有多少风流人物?
盗跖庄蹻流誉後,
更陈王奋起挥黄钺。
歌未竟,
东方白。

Hè xīnláng: Dú shǐ

Rén yuán xiāngyī bié,
zhǐ jǐ gè shítou móguò,
xiǎo'ér shíjié.
Tóngtiě lúzhōng fān huǒyàn.
Wèi wèn héshí cāidé?
Bùguò jǐ qiān hánrè.
Rénshì nánféng kāikǒu xiào,
shàng jiāngchǎng bǐcǐ wān gōngyuè.
Liúbiàn le,
jiāoyuán xiě.

Yī piān dúbà tóu fēixuě,
dàn jìdé bānbān diǎndiǎn,
jǐ háng chénjì.
Wǔdì Sānhuáng shénshèng shì,
piàn liǎo wúyá guòkè.
Yǒu duōshǎo fēngliú-rénwù?
Dào Zhí Zhuāng Jiǎo liú yù hòu,
gèng Chén Wáng fènqǐ huī huángyuè.
Gē wèijìng,
dōngfāng bái.

23.

Climbing the Jinggang Mountains Again

To the tune of the 'Water Song'

May 1965

Mao's return to the Jinggang Mountains, where he started his guerrilla activities in 1927, was highly symbolic. Although he had reluctantly accepted the changes brought in by Liu Shaoqi, he still planned to take back authority. In September 1962, he launched the Socialist Education Movement against 'capitalist roaders' in China and revisionists abroad. Khrushchev's downfall in October 1964 encouraged him. In this poem, depression gives way to a new mood of confidence and optimism.

I have long aspired to ride the clouds
and reclimb the Jinggang Mountains.
At the end of my journey of one thousand *li*
I find my old haunt thoroughly transformed.
Orioles call and swallows dart on every side,   5
murmuring streams wind through the hills,
and new roads climb into the clouds.
After passing through the Huangyang gap
no other risks remain along the route.

Flags and banners flap   10
in the thunderous winds
of this human world.
Thirty-eight years have passed
in the twinkling of an eye.
In the Ninth Sphere we can embrace the moon,   15

Title: The mountains between Jiangxi and Hunan where Mao and Zhu De founded the Red Army in September 1927.
Line 15, 'Ninth Sphere': Heaven.
Line 15, 'Moon': Echoing a line by Li Bai.

Climbing the Jinggang Mountains Again

plunge deep into the Five Seas on turtle hunts,
and return laughing and singing of our victory.
Nothing on earth is difficult
if you dare to scale the heights.

水调歌头•重上井冈山

久有凌云志,
重上井冈山。
千里来寻故地,
旧貌变新颜。
到处莺歌燕舞,
更有潺潺流水,
高路入云端。
过了黄洋界,
险处不须看。

风雷动,
旌旗奋,
是人寰。
三十八年过去,
弹指一挥间。
可上九天揽月,
可下五洋捉鳖,
谈笑凯歌还。
世上无难事,
只要肯登攀。

Shuǐdiào gētóu: Chóng shàng Jǐnggāngshān

Jiǔ yǒu língyún zhì,
zhóngshàng Jǐnggāngshān.
Qiān lǐ lái xún gùdì,
jiùmào biàn xīnyán.
Dàochù yīnggē-yànwǔ,
gèngyǒu chánchán liúshuǐ,
gāolù rù yúnduān.
Guò le Huángyángjiè,
xiǎnchǔ bù xū kàn.

Fēngléi dòng,
jīngqí fèn,
shì rénhuán.
Sānshíbā nián guòqù,
tánzhǐ yīhuī jiān.
Kěshàng jiǔtiān lǎnyuè,
kěxià wǔyáng zhuōbiē,
tánxiào kǎigē huán.
Shìshàng wú nánshì,
zhǐyào kěn dēngpān.

Line 16: The ocean.

24.

Two Birds: A Dialogue

To the tune of 'Dear Niannu'

Autumn 1965

Mao uses a story told by the Daoist sage Zhuangzi to ridicule Khrushchev and express his confidence in defeating revisionism.

> The roc unfolds its wings and soars
> for ninety thousand *li*,
> raising a cyclone.
> Bearing the clear sky on its back, it glances down
> at the towns and cities of the human world.　　　　5
> Gunfire rakes the sky,
> shells pit the earth.
> A sparrow in a bush takes fright:
> 'What can I do?
> I need to fly away.'　　　　10
>
> Roc: 'Where will you fly?'
> Sparrow: 'To a fine-jade palace
> in the Fairy Hills.
> Under the autumn moon two years ago
> a pact was signed by three great powers.　　　　15
> There'll be goulash soup galore –
> hot potatoes
> and stewed beef.'
> 'No need to fart!
> You see the world turn upside down.'　　　　20

Line 3: Echoing the Daoist philosopher Zhuangzi.
Line 13: Again, echoing Zhuangzi.
Line 15: The Partial Nuclear Test Ban Treaty signed by the Americans, the British and the Russians in 1963.
Line 18: Quoting Khrushchev in April 1964.
Line 19: Mao jeers at Russian coarseness.

Two Birds: A Dialogue

念奴娇•鸟儿问答

鲲鹏展翅,
九万里,
翻动扶摇羊角。
背负青天朝下看,
都是人间城郭。
炮火连天,
弹痕遍地,
吓倒蓬间雀。
怎么得了,
哎呀我要飞跃。

借问君去何方,
雀儿答道: 有仙山琼阁。
不见前年秋月朗,
订了三家条约。
还有吃的,
土豆烧熟了,
再加牛肉。
不须放屁!
试看天地翻覆。

Niànnú jiāo: Niǎo'er wèndá

Kūnpéng zhǎnchì,
jiǔwàn lǐ,
fāndòng fúyáo yángjiǎo.
Bèifù qīngtiān cháoxià kàn,
dōushì rénjiān chéngguō.
Pàohuǒ liántiān,
dànhén biàndì,
xiàdǎo péngjiān què.
Zěnme déliǎo,
āiyā wǒyào fēiyuè.

Jièwèn jūn qù héfāng,
Què' er dá dào: Yǒu xiānshān qiónggé.
Bù jiàn qiánnián qiūyuè lǎng,
dìngle sān jiā tiáoyuē.
Háiyǒu chīde,
tǔdòu shāo shúle,
zàijiā niúròu.
Bùxū fàng pì!
Shìkàn tiāndì fānfù.

25.

The Desire for Action

A *qilü*

June 1966

In May 1966, Mao launched the Cultural Revolution and started his political comeback against the 'capitalist roaders' in China. A month later, this poem anticipates violent political storms and calls for action in the name of the people.

> At a time when the capital is not at ease
> I come south again in search of inspiration.
> Green pines point fiercely at the clear blue sky,
> dead leaves drift away upon the stream.
> A clap of thunder shakes the world,
> bright banners are paraded through the streets.
> I stand at the railing, to watch the driving rain.
> The nation's people yearns for action.

有所思

正是神都有事时，
又来南国踏芳枝。
青松怒向苍天发，
败叶纷随碧水驰。
一阵风雷惊世界，
满街红绿走旌旗。
凭阑静听潇潇雨，
故国人民有所思。

Yǒusuǒ sī

Zhèngshì Shéndū yǒushì shí,
yòu lái nánguó tà fāngzhī.
Qīngsōng nùxiàng cāngtiān fā,
bàiyè fēnsuí bìshuǐ chí.
Yī zhèn fēngléi jīng shìjiè,
mǎnjiē hónglǜ zǒu jīngqí.
Pínglán jìngtīng xiāoxiāo yǔ,
gùguó rénmín yǒusuǒ sī.

Line 8: Echoing a line by Du Fu.

26.

Inspection

To the tune of the 'Melody of Tranquillity'

August 1971

During the Cultural Revolution, Mao was apotheosised and Mao Zedong Thought was established as the supreme guide in all things. Institutions were smashed by Red Guards and replaced by revolutionary committees. The revolution aimed to 'sweep away all cow ghosts and snake spirits' and all those who pursued revisionism and promoted bourgeois ideas.

> The Southern inspection tour of ten thousand *li*
> leads me to think of emperors in ancient times.
> Their influence lingers in the air around,
> Qin Shi Huangdi, Suiyang, Kangxi.
>
> They performed their exploits on their own behalf,
> while I work for the common good.
> Smash the bureaucracy's machine,
> denounce the bourgeoisie.

Line 4, 'Suiyang': Emperor Yang of the Sui.
Line 4, 'Kangxi': Emperor Kangxi of the Qing.

Inspection

清平乐 · 视察

南巡万里,
不觉忆古帝。
威加海内有余风,
秦皇、隋炀、康熙。

彼辈功业为己,
我今操劳社稷,
踏破官僚机器,
挥斥资产阶级。

Qīng píng yuè: Shìchá

Nánxún wàn lǐ,
bùjué yì gǔdì.
Wēi jiā hǎinèi yǒu yúfēng,
Qín Huáng, Suí Yáng, Kāngxī.

Bǐ bèi gōngyè wéi jǐ,
wǒ jīn cāoláo shèjì,
tàpò guānliáo jīqì,
huīchì zīchǎnjiējí.

27.

Presented to Guo [Moruo] the Elder after Reading *On Feudalism*

A *qilü* August 1973

In 1971, Lin Biao, Mao's designated successor, died in a plane crash, allegedly after trying to kill Mao. In 1973, Mao and his wife Jiang Qing launched a campaign to purge China of Confucian thinking and to denounce Lin Biao as a traitor. The campaign also targeted Zhou Enlai. In this poem, Mao urges Guo Moruo to toe the line and denounce Confucianism. Guo is said to have made an immediate self-criticism, declaring that all his previous works were useless and should be burned.

> Regarding Qin Shi Huangdi, I advise less condemnation,
> for the details of his burning books and burying men alive await our explication.
> The achievements of the Ancestral Dragon remain despite his death,
> and Confucianism is in essence chaff.
> One hundred generations have preserved Qin's institutions,
> and the *Book of Ten Criticisms* is a useless work.
> Peruse *On Feudalism* by an author of the Tang,
> do not regress from Zihou's stand to the position of King Wen.

Title: A work by the Tang thinker Liu Zongyuan (773–819) criticising feudalism and defending the Qin Dynasty.
Line 2: In 213 BCE, Qin Shi Huangdi burned Confucian books and buried Confucian scholars alive.
Line 3: Qin Shi Huangdi.
Line 6: A book by Guo Moruo criticising Qin Shi Huangdi and praising Confucianism.
Line 8, 'Zihou': Meaning Liu Zongyuan.
Line 8, 'King Wen': King Wen (1152–1056 BCE) of the Zhou Dynasty, admired by Confucius as a model of benevolence and wisdom.

Presented to Guo [Morou] the Elder after Reading On Feudalism

读《封建论》呈郭老

劝君少骂秦始皇,
焚坑事件要商量。
祖龙魂死业犹在,
孔学名高实秕糠。
百代多行秦政治,
十批不是好文章。
熟读唐人'封建论',
莫从子厚返文王。

Du 'Fēngjiàn lùn' chéng Guō lǎo

Quàn jūn shǎomà Qínshǐhuáng,
fénkēng shìjiàn yào shāngliáng.
Zǔ Lóng húnsǐ yè yóuzài,
Kǒngxué mínggāo shí bǐkāng.
Bǎi dài duō xíng Qín zhèngzhì,
Shípī bùshì hǎo wénzhāng.
Shúdú Tángrén 'Fēngjiàn lùn',
mò cóng Zǐ Hòu fǎn Wénwáng.